THE
URBAN
DESIGN
PROCESS

THE URBAN DESIGN PROCESS

Hamid Shirvani

 VAN NOSTRAND REINHOLD COMPANY
——————————— New York

Library of Congress Catalog Card Number 84-29938
ISBN 0-442-28033-5 (cl.)
ISBN 0-442-28064-5 (pb.)

Printed in the United States

Designed by Ben D. Kann

Van Nostrand Reinhold Company, Inc.
115 Fifth Avenue
New York, New York 10003

Van Nostrand Reinhold Company Limited
Molly Millars Lane
Wokingham, Berkshire RG11 2PY, England

Van Nostrand Reinhold
480 La Trobe Street
Melbourne, Victoria 3000, Australia

Macmillan of Canada
Division of Canada Publishing Corporation
164 Commander Boulevard
Agincourt, Ontario M1S 3C7, Canada

16 15 14 13 12 11 10 9 8 7 6 5 4 3 2 1

Library of Congress Cataloging in Publication Data
Shirvani, Hamid.
   The urban design process.
   Bibliography: p.
   Includes index.
   1. City planning.   I. Title.
HT166.S463   1985   307.7'6   84-29938
ISBN 0-442-28033-5 (cl.)
ISBN 0-442-28064-5 (pb.)

To the memory of my father
Honorable M. Shirvani

Preface

URBAN DESIGN is a complex interdisciplinary field that encompasses architecture, landscape architecture, urban planning, civil and transportation engineering, psychology, real estate development, law, and other specialties. Due to this complexity, it has been quite difficult to put together an all-inclusive text. The field has been evolving over the past several decades, and yet there are but a few books exclusively on the subject.

My intention has been to produce, for the first time, a state-of-the-art volume on urban design. In attempting to do so, I have drawn on both academic and professional literature and have also included a current survey of urban-design practice in cities throughout the country. I do not claim that the model introduced in this book is the only one for the design of urban areas; rather, the volume serves as a synthesis of existing complex approaches, problems, issues, and prospects. It is hoped that the volume opens a new avenue for debate and dialogue among professionals and scholars.

I would like to express my gratitude to many of my colleagues for helping me with this book. I am indebted to Alan Canter (Denver), Rebecca Cedillo (San Antonio), Ellis Crow (Long Beach, CA), James Ecker (Omaha), Richard Hauersperger (Charlotte-Mecklenburg, NC), John Heath (Atlanta), Mare Herbert (Oakland, CA), Mark Hinshaw (Bellevue, WA), John Hyslop (Milwaukee), Rob Jacobi (Healdsburg, CA), Robert Jones (Honolulu), Warner Leipprandt and Richard Counts (Phoenix), William Wiley Rice, Jr. (Oklahoma City), Tom Niederauer (Dallas), David Preece (Beloit, WI), Ralph Smith (Memphis), Michael Stepner (San Diego), Phyllis Taylor and Cynthia Bruce (Albuquerque), James Tool (Fort Worth), Larry Watts (Birmingham), and the planning departments of Buffalo, El Paso, and Columbus for supplying me with firsthand information about their cities and for responding to my questionnaires. Special thanks go to my friend and colleague, Michael Stepner, for his unfailing support, and to Richard Hedman and Stephen Quick, for providing me with essential information. Andrew Euston, Anne Vernez-Moudon, Ralph Sanders, and many others provided me with data. I am thankful to all of them.

A fellowship from the SUNY Research Foundation helped me to do research for a part of this book. I would like to express my appreciation to the SUNY Research Foundation; Robert G. Reimann and Donald F. Behrend of the State University of New York, College of Environmental Science and Forestry, for their assistance.

I am particularly grateful to Bethel Kogut for reviewing the manuscript and for her perceptive and valuable editorial assistance. I am also grateful to John Stilgoe for reading the manuscript and for his helpful suggestions.

I greatly appreciate the help provided by my research assistants: Rebecca Green, Anne Hutchinson, James Kastner, and Mark Lichtenstein for literature researches; and Jack Dahlinger and Timothy O'Byrne for graphics production. Special thanks go to George Snyder for helping me with the photography and to Sarah Remon for typing the manuscript—and for her endurance.

Finally, I am indebted to Wendy Lochner, Senior Editor, and Cynthia Achar, Associate Editor, of Van Nostrand Reinhold.

Contents

CHAPTER 1   *Introduction*   *1*

CHAPTER 2   *Elements of urban physical form*   *5*

The Domain of Urban Design, *6* / Land Use, *8* / Building Form and
Massing, *11* / Circulation and Parking, *23* / Open Space, *27* /
Pedestrian Ways, *31* / Activity Support, *37* / Signage, *40* /
Preservation, *44*

CHAPTER 3   *The human dimension reexamined*   *49*

Limitations of Planning/Urban Design, *50* / Shortcomings of Citizen
Participation, *51* / Available Social Data and Research, *55* / Nature of
Social Data Relevant to Design, *61* / Current Role and Use of Social Data in
Design, *62* / Translation of Human Dimensions Into Planning/Urban
Design, *63*

CHAPTER 4   *The dimension of natural environment*   *69*

Urban Climate and Air Quality, *73* / Solar Energy and Solar Access, *76* /
Urban Geology and Soils, *83* / Urban Hydrology and Water Quality, *85* /
Urban Vegetation, *90* / Urban Wildlife, *96* / Role of Natural
Processes, *98*

CHAPTER 5 *Design method/process* 105

The Internalized Method of Design, *106* / The Synoptic Method, *110* /
The Incremental Method, *116* / The Fragmental Process, *116* / The
Pluralistic Process, *117* / Radical Process, *118*

CHAPTER 6 *Design criteria* 121

Nonmeasurable Criteria, *122* / A Comparative Analysis of Nonmeasurable
Criteria, *126* / The Continuum and Traditional Approaches to Design
Criteria, *131* / Measurable Criteria, *133*

CHAPTER 7 *Products* 141

Policies, *144* / Plan, *145* / Guidelines, *147* / Programs, *153*

CHAPTER 8 *Implementation: administrative mechanisms* 157

Organization of the Administrative Framework, *158* / Techniques for
Implementing Urban Design, *163*

CHAPTER 9 *Implementation: legal mechanisms* 167

Incentive Zoning, *168* / Performance Zoning, *172* / Special
Districts, *173* / Transfer of Development Rights, *174* / Sign
Ordinance, *176* / Interim Ordinances, *178* / Antidemolition
Ordinances, *179* / Historic Districts, *180* / Mandated Environmental
Impact Report, *181* / Design Review, the Essential Element, *182*

CHAPTER 10 *Implementation: financial mechanisms* 185

Marketing the City, *186* / Basic Financial Mechanisms, *187* / Methods of
Alternative Financing, *194* / Public/Private Partnerships for
Codevelopment, *197*

CHAPTER 11 *Urban design prospects* 203

Index 207

Introduction

CHAPTER 1

THERE ARE numerous ways of defining "urban design." Some definitions are outdated; some are more complete than others; still others reflect specialized orientations. This is not surprising, considering the ever-changing context of the field. It is therefore most realistic to define urban design by briefly discussing its concerns and methods through some examples.

Consider a housing development for the elderly located near a neighborhood shopping center that is physically inaccessible to the aged residents. Or consider a major downtown street lined with exclusive buildings that meet the street at pedestrian level with solid blank walls—a typical inward-looking building found in many American cities.

Sometimes, one has a difficult time walking comfortably along a street because pedestrian areas are too narrow and traffic is heavy. At other times, one finds him- or herself in a pedestrian no-man's-land of overly broad sidewalks. Some urban areas are completely given over to massive boxes made of concrete and glass with no attempt to soften the impact through better architectural design, plantings, and green spaces. Another typical problem is incompatibility between buildings and other uses or activities within the urban setting: here a fifty-story building blocks sunlight to a public park or a church, interfering with effective and enjoyable use of the space. Inconsistencies of context and setting occur where a thirty-story office building with a black glass facade is slotted in beside a three-story brownstone.

Many of these design disasters are found in suburban communities as well. Nowadays one often encounters confusing residential developments where curvilinear street or road configurations lack the hierarchy of size and organization so important for orientation and definition of space. Insensitive densities and open-space provisions also occur in suburban areas. Consider a recent condominium development that is double-loaded, that is, constructed with a corridor in the center and units on either side, with but fifteen feet of area allotted between residences.

Ever more compelling and encompassing urban-design issues center on rapid expansion and growth in areas that have water shortages or where overuse of such high-quality natural resources as waterfront properties or wooded lands is likely. Finally, there is the question of social equity in urban design. Does an urban design serve the public or only a special group?

These and many other concerns form the context of urban design:

Urban design activities seek to develop the policy framework within which physical designs are created. It is that level of design that deals with the relationships between the major elements of the city fabric. It extends in both time and space in that its constituent parts are distributed in space and constructed at different times by different persons. In this sense, urban design is concerned with the management of the physical development of the city. Management is difficult in that the client is multiple, the program indeterminate, control partial, and there is no certain state of completion. Its concern is with both the urban built environment and the natural environment as impinged upon by urban development (*UD Review, 1976: 1*).

Contrary to those that would claim that it is a post-urban-renewal phenomenon urban design is not a new field. That claim is based on trivial issues of terms and title rather than on the substantive issues of professional practice. Urban design has existed as long as man has existed. What has changed over time are the contexts and approaches of urban design. One major benchmark in the field was most certainly the industrial revolution in Europe, which essentially directed the attention of design away from individual service to an autocratic ruler and toward a pluralistic "public" of clients. The discipline has been known at various times by different names—"town planning" in Europe and later "city planning" and "urban planning" in the United States. The field has also been shaped by major professional and theoretical trends, including the "Organism" of Sir Patrick Geddes and his followers as embodied in the Chicago World's Exposition of 1898: the city-beautiful and city-functional era; systems analysis; Structuralism; the semiotic approaches of the 1960s; and most recently, the incrementalism and neorationalism of the 1970s.

Although it is legitimate to characterize these influences as "planning" trends, the argument here is that "urban design" has always been part of the overall framework of planning, whether it has been termed town, urban, or city planning. That is, "design" has been in one way or another the underlying concern of much broader planning decisions. In short, one has to first decide whether to build or not to build; should the decision—the plan—be to build, then a second category of decision must be made concerning what and how to build so that a form, configuration, location, and manner will have the least negative environmental impact. ("Environment" here, of course, encompasses natural/physical and socioeconomic factors.)

While urban design was not an outgrowth of the urban renewal programs that took place during the 1950s and 1960s, urban design did begin to emerge as a distinct subfield of planning during this period. The reason for this is that for the first time in several decades urban renewal created major opportunities for large-scale intervention in the city planning and building process. A negative side effect, of course, is that urban design's close association with urban renewal programs tainted and continues to confuse the thought of many about the methods and potential of the field. One common error is to view urban design as so-called large-scale architecture. One cannot deny that in any city, there may well exist various large-scale public, private, or joint public/private projects that may be referred to as "urban design," but it is important to recognize that major projects are not the only focus of urban design.

To gain insight into the relation of urban design to planning, we must look closely at recent trends within the planning profession and in particular at the failure of physical city or urban planning at the turn of the century. By the 1960s and early 1970s, the consequences of this failure redirected planning practice and theory to the root problems of public policy and political economy. The change of emphasis, together with urban renewal, created a need for a new focus or discipline within the planning field: "urban design." Recent developments in urban design can be seen as attempts to infuse traditional physical or land-use planning with new approaches and context definitions that have evolved within broader urban-policy frameworks. Therefore, throughout this book, the phrase "planning/urban design" has been used in place of *urban design* to reflect this emphasis.

Today, urban design "roughly embraces three different groups" with three different orientations: development, conservation, and community (Appleyard, 1982: 122). Development orientation forms a large part of urban-design practice and is basically a continuation of large-scale private-sector development projects, building complexes, or infrastructural facilities. The conservation orientation focuses on environmental quality and is at the other end of the spectrum, often at odds with the real estate market's attempts to control it; the Urban Design Plan of San Francisco is a prime example of this approach. The third community orientation, has received the least attention; it is based on low-cost neighborhood improvements through citizen participation, community-action groups, and advocacy planning (Appleyard, 1982).

A realistic approach to urban design must incorporate all three orientations. Indeed, urban design should aim for balance among the three. Of course, the key to the urban design process remains the "public". Urban design should serve the public at large, the plural society.

This book is an attempt to bring together the components of urban design into an overall framework. The volume is, in fact, a reader in urban design: it discusses each component, examines the state of the art of each, as well as the problems and opportunities associated with them. It is reasonable to say that *The Urban Design Process* is a micro-synthesis of urban design components.

We will start by defining elements of urban physical form, or the "domain of urban design." Next, in chapter 3, we will turn to an examination of the role of the human dimension in urban design. Chapter 4 focuses on a dimension that has not been given similar attention in the past—the natural environment. Design methods and processes are discussed in chapter 5. Chapter 6 reviews design criteria, including nonmeasurable and measurable qualitative criteria. Design products are discussed in chapter 7. Chapters 8, 9, and 10 cover implementation mechanisms: administrative, legal, and financial. Finally, chapter 11 considers some prospects for the future of urban design.

References

Appleyard, Donald. "Three Kinds of Urban Design Practice." In Ann Ferebee, ed., *Education for Urban Design*. Purchase, NY: Institute for Urban Design, 1982.
UD Review 1, no. 1, 1976.

Elements of urban physical form

CHAPTER 2

AFTER TWO decades of practice, there is still some confusion over what constitutes the elements of urban design, partly because the word *elements* may refer both to components or ingredients. In other instances, it may also connote the physical products, such as buildings and roads, which result from urban design projects. I shall use *elements* to mean physical elements—that is, the more specific definitions and descriptions of the context of urban design.

The contextual framework of urban design is often ignored in planning and design literature. In certain cases, the issue is hardly recognized. Furthermore, there are various opinions concerning the domain of urban design. Some think of urban design primarily as beautification: trees, street furniture, paving, lighting, signs, and the like. Others consider it the center and focus of planning. Of course, there are various groups in between. These ambiguities leave professionals uncertain about the extent and scope of the discipline.

Obviously we should reject emphatically a superficial association of urban design with mere beatification programs. We should view urban design as one of the main tasks of urban planning, but, of course it is not the only function of urban planning. With this basic assumption in mind, various physical elements that should be included under the urban design umbrella will be discussed in this chapter.

The domain of urban design

We can start identifying the elements of urban design by defining the domain of urban design. Urban design is that part of the planning process that deals with the physical quality of the environment. That is to say, it is the physical and spatial design of the environment. However, it should be quite clear to us that in designing the environment, planners and designers cannot design all elements and components; they cannot in every instance design entire buildings. It might be possible to do this in new towns or planned residential communities, but in an existing community, such complete design is quite difficult.

In addition, the domain of urban design extends from the exterior of individual buildings outward, with consideration of positive and negative effects of individual buildings on each other's interiors. Barnett (1974) uses an excellent phrase to define this domain, "designing cities without designing buildings." Let us say that the spaces between the buildings are the domain of urban design. But how do we design these spaces?

Using the nomenclature of the Urban Design Plan of San Francisco (1970), we can distinguish among the purposes of four interrelated groups of spaces: (1) internal pattern and image, (2) external form and image, (3) circulation and parking, and (4) quality of environment (Wilson *et al.*, 1979). Internal pattern and image describe the purpose of spaces between urban structures at the microlevel, that is, key physical features of the city's organization: "focal points, viewpoints, landmarks and movement patterns." External form and image focus on the city's skyline and its overall image and identity. Circulation and parking look at street and road characteristics: "quality of maintenance, spaciousness, order, monotony, clarity of route, orientation to destination, safety and ease of movement," and parking requirements and locations. Finally, quality of environment includes nine factors: compatibility of uses, "presence of natural elements," "distance to open space," "visual interest of the street facade," quality of view, and quality of maintenance, noise, and microclimate (Wilson *et al.*, 1979: 37).

The domain of urban design as just set forth does not pinpoint very specific physical elements (plaza, mall, seating areas, trees, lampposts), but it is a reasonable way of grouping them and gives direction to study and identification of the more specific elements that are unique or important to a community. Since every community has different physical characteristics, the range of specific elements may vary extensively from one community to another, from one downtown to another, from one city to another.

In the past, most planners and designers have emphasized the first two groups of elements—internal pattern and image and external form and image—probably because these two groups are strongly oriented toward the form-making aspects of urban design. Yet when we also consider these elements from the standpoint of function and environmental quality, the spaces created for people (both those who are walking in the streets and those who are living inside the buildings) are potentially more pleasant.

For example, we might observe a beautifully designed plaza that very few people use, simply because it does not have any direct sunlight or it is windswept. On the other hand, there are plazas that have been designed only tolerably well, and crowds of people use them. It is undoubtedly true that there might be a number of factors involved (location, support for activity, and so on), but such environmental considerations as wind, noise, sun, view, and natural elements always contribute significantly to successful urban design.

Having thus identified the framework for analysis of urban design —that is, the domain of urban design—we now shall attempt to identify a method of presenting this information in the form of policies, plans, guidelines, and programs. Variations in analysis of the elements of urban design (or lack of any analysis at all) has created variety in the form and range of policies, plans, guidelines, and programs in different cities. Even close examination of the urban design of various cities does not make one certain that planners have used a framework of analysis or have identified a specific element as the most important one to zero in on. Perhaps a lack of comprehensiveness in their framework has caused concentration on a few physical items.

 However, we can now move from the four groups of analysis just outlined to a third categorization of the elements of urban design:

1. Land use
2. Building form and massing
3. Circulation and parking
4. Open space
5. Pedestrian ways
6. Activity support

7. Signage
8. Preservation

To define these elements, let us now proceed in an organized and detailed manner through the specific elements that urban design must address in developing policies, plans, guidelines, and programs. The categories we are using are of course interrelated. Urban design strategies for specific urban areas or cities will necessarily have to group, or distinguish among, the physical elements identified here according to the problems and opportunities of the area under study.

Land use

Land use has been the focus of traditional physical planning as well as recent general and community development plans. It is quite clear that land use is still one of the key elements of urban design. After all, it determines the basic two-dimensional plans on which three-dimensional spaces are created and functions are performed. Land use decisions establish the relationship between circulation/parking and density of activities/uses within urban areas. There are different areas within an urban setting with different capacities for intensity, access, parking, transportation system availability, and finally, demand for individual uses.

A land use plan developed in conjunction with land use policies determines the relationship between plan and policy and provides a basis for assigning appropriate functions to specific areas. In the past two major problems of land use policies have been (1) lack of diversity of use in an area; in other words, compartmentalization and segregation of land use in urban areas, and (2) failure to consider environmental and natural physical factors. We are, of course, entering a new phase of planning and, thus, a third factor is becoming apparent: infrastructure. Many old industrial cities in the United States, particularly in the north and northeast, are now facing tremendous problems of maintenance and repair of an often obsolete infrastructure.

Thus the key issues for consideration in future land use decisions are mixing uses in urban areas to promote twenty-four-hour vitality by improving circulation via pedestrian facilities and better use of infrastructure systems; natural environment base analysis; and improvement of infrastructure systems with necessary maintenance plans and operations.

In addition, there are a number of secondary factors that should be considered along with the key issues. Residential use, for example, plays a critical role in generating the desired mixed use in urban areas. It is also equally important to introduce and stimulate some nonresidential activities into purely residential areas; for it is ultimately residential use that ensures twenty-four-hour activity in a neighborhood and true mixed use development.

Preservation of the natural environment and basing the land use plan on natural factors and ecological data additionally influence location and density of uses. The natural environment issue should provide the framework within which building form and massing can be created. These issues, will be discussed in detail in chapter 4.

Modifications of existing land use patterns constitute an additional factor in improving an existing urban or built environment. By adjusting the permitted use and density of developments, a different character and function can occur. Many old industrial cities of the northeast are now experiencing such change and have made a great deal of progress (figs. 2-1, 2-2). In the long run, these minor changes over time can be linked and thereby generate yet more significant changes.

Land uses and associated pedestrian activities represent still another key issue for urban design. It is fair to say that the functions of different streets have a major influence on establishing the street's character and the activities it will support. Street-level pedestrian activity creates a more humane, pleasant, and safe environment; therefore, it is necessary for land use to be considered from two perspectives: (1) in general and (2) at street level. Issues associated with street-level activities are discussed in the following section on Activity Support.

Seattle, Washington, has used an interesting technique that responds to many of the issues just discussed by developing "floor area districts" (fig. 2-3). Floor area districts are "based on the special land use and transportation conditions of different areas within downtown so that land use provisions can be tailored to more directly address concerns related to how individual areas should develop"(Seattle, 1982: 25).

Floor area districts cover the following land use concerns in a systematic way:

- The types of uses to be permitted within an area.
- The functional relationships that should exist between different downtown areas.
- The maximum amount of floor area that can be occupied by each permitted use.
- The scale of new development.
- The types of development incentives that are appropriate and the extent to which they can be used in specified downtown areas.

The city has identified twelve floor area districts to adjust the existing floor area allowances and address the special land use and transportation conditions associated with each. Figure 2-4 presents an exam-

2-1: Charlestown Mall, Utica, NY: an old garment factory that has been converted into a shopping mall with minimal conversion costs. The mall is quite successful at present.

2-2: Madison High School, Syracuse, NY: an old high school building that has been converted into residential condominiums.

ple of one of these twelve floor area districts, the retail core. It is still too early to judge Seattle's urban design program, the effects and outcomes of the plan are as yet unclear. Their approach, however, underscores the central role and importance of land use decisions in urban design.

Building form and massing

Traditional zoning ordinances deal with this aspect of physical form by setting specifics of height, setbacks, and coverage. There are also more elaborate and involved regulations concerning form and massing that the Urban Design Plan of San Francisco (1970) refers to as "height" and "bulk," and the Long Beach, California, Design Guidelines (1980) refers to as "building appearance and configuration."

This last description brings a new issue into play: appearance. Are we not concerned about what the buildings look like as well as their height and bulk? Their colors, materials, textures, and the facade

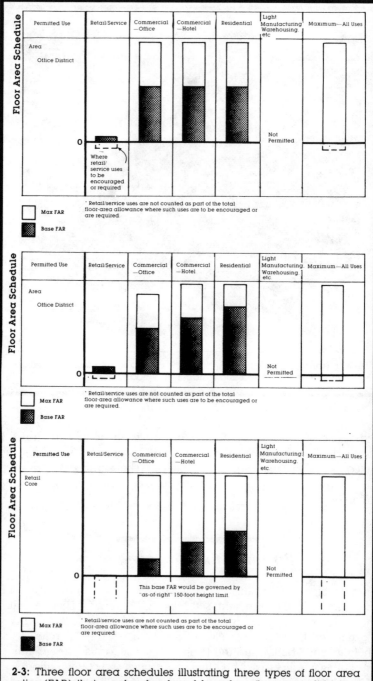

2-3: Three floor area schedules illustrating three types of floor area ratios (FAR) that can be developed based on floor area districts of Seattle, Washington (Source: City of Seattle, WA).

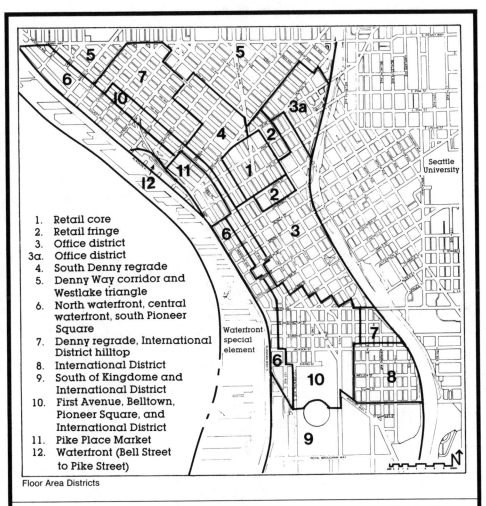

1. Retail core
2. Retail fringe
3. Office district
3a. Office district
4. South Denny regrade
5. Denny Way corridor and
   Westlake triangle
6. North waterfront, central
   waterfront, south Pioneer
   Square
7. Denny regrade, International
   District hilltop
8. International District
9. South of Kingdome and
   International District
10. First Avenue, Belltown,
    Pioneer Square, and
    International District
11. Pike Place Market
12. Waterfront (Bell Street
    to Pike Street)

Floor Area Districts

2-4: Map of downtown Seattle, Washington, illustrating twelve floor area districts (Source: City of Seattle, WA).

forms? Traditionally, these issues have been left in the hands of the individual architect and his client. Today, we must acknowledge that there are as many opportunities for adverse effects as there are for the positive qualities associated with the appearance of a building.

An example of the problems that can be associated with appearance is the amount of glare caused by glass-boxed office towers. On the positive side, we might find the facade of a building designed to relate harmoniously and compatibly with the surrounding historic buildings so as to enhance the entire area. Building form and massing, therefore, encompasses height, bulk, floor area ratio (FAR), coverage, street-line setbacks, style, scale, material, texture and color.

Building height guidelines are used in the Urban Design Plan of San Francisco (1970: 9) to "indicate where low buildings should remain to enhance the hill forms of the city or to provide views [and] where taller buildings could be located and enhance the city's present patterns of development." Similarly, with regard to bulk, buildings are to "reflect the design framework by proposing ways that new buildings can complement existing patterns of development." (1970: 9) (figs. 2-5, 2-6).

According to the Long Beach Design Guidelines, "Building Configuration and Appearance" includes: "height, massing, scope, scale, proportion, materials and finishes, color, lighting, and storefront design. The intent of these guidelines is to assure harmonious relationships between buildings, the immediate visual environments and the overall downtown design framework" (1980: 13) (fig. 2-7).

Figure 2-8 depicts the interesting guidelines used in Jacksonville, Florida, to express clearly the differences between two distinct appearances for one building (Jacksonville II, 1972) (fig. 2-8).

These examples illustrate various ways different cities have defined the elements of building form and massing. However, one cannot adequately define or encompass the qualities associated with this element simply by summing up guidelines. This is a very critical issue, one which has long been the focus of debate and discussion between architects and planners.

The main issue is how much control "urban design" should establish and how much flexibility and freedom should be left in the hands of the architect or the individual building designer. But while we can endlessly debate who should do what, we might do better by returning to a so-called traditional definition (which, by the way, still holds true), namely that buildings and open space together constitute the domain of urban design. As distinguished urban designer, Paul Spreiregen (1965: 66) noted, we should develop a "vocabulary for discussing [the city's] form and appearance" in order to see "the effects of various actions and policies that affect the city in terms of its buildings, parks, streets and places." The nature of planning/urban design at the local government level at least dictates a sort of concrete and/or "rational" method of analysis, one that minimizes subjectivity and puts a premium on objectivity. This fact, however, has often been accepted at face value by various cities. Some have just modified their existing land use controls and added floor area ratio (FAR) together with other design guidelines—examples are many. On the other hand, some cities have made a comprehensive physical data analysis and then developed building form and massing criteria based on such study and analysis. Examples in this group are San Francisco and Seattle. There are, of course, many cities in between these single-strategy and relatively rationalized, comprehensive approaches.

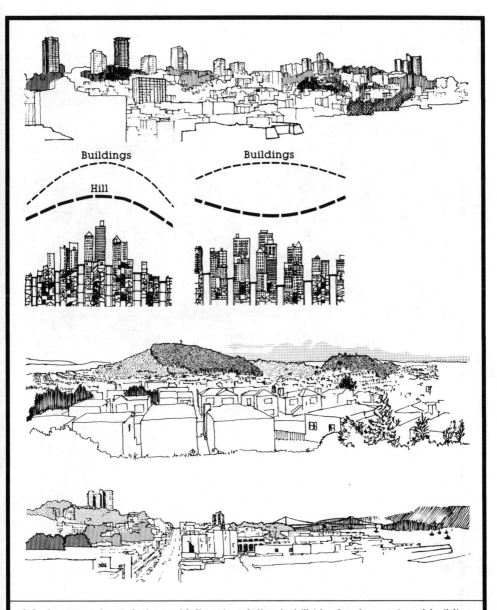

Buildings

Buildings

Hill

2-5: An example of design guidelines in relation to hillside development and building height as a part of the San Francisco Urban Design Plan (Source: City of San Francisco, CA).

2-6: Another example of San Francisco urban design plan design guidelines identifying building height in relation to the existing built environment, as well as a poor example illustrating a totally incompatible building (Source: City of San Francisco, CA).

Building Massing

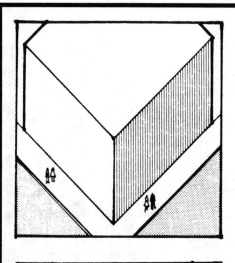

Large unbroken expanses of wall area make a building appear bulky and overly imposing to the street-level pedestrian.

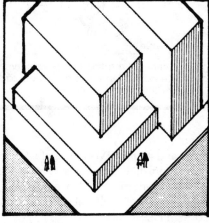

Varying building height and setback and establishing lower scale adjacent to pedestrian areas reduce the appearance of bulk.

2-7: City of Long Beach design guidelines in regard to building configuration and appearance (Source: City of Long Beach, CA).

There is no doubt that a realistic and comprehensive study of the existing built form and physical fabric of a community is a prerequisite for developing building form and massing (Spreiregen, 1965). However, such a study should not merely focus on height, bulk, setbacks, and soon, which are the substance of urban design and not methods of analysis of urban physical form. A good example of physical analysis is represented in *Residential Design Guidelines,* (1979) prepared by the San Francisco Planning Department (fig. 2-9). Another good example is The Third Street Mall Design in Santa Monica,

Elements of urban physical form **17**

2-8: City of Jacksonville design guidelines illustrating two possible variations of building facade design, a poor office-boxed type and a different facade with some variation and contrast (Source: City of Jacksonville, FL).

California, by the Arroyo Group and Studio Works (Santa Monica, 1980) (fig. 2-10). These studies are on different scales, but both are in-depth analyses of urban physical pattern that also consider elements as well as *entity*—that is, the social, political, and economic frameworks within which the design takes place.

Recommended building form and massing result from such studies to establish a contextual framework within which new physical forms can be generated in harmony with existing forms. Therefore, as an essential element of urban design, building form and massing require in-depth analysis of urban architecture as well as public health and safety requirements (Spreiregen, 1965) (fig. 2-11).

The critical distinction between design guidelines as implementation techniques and the role of planning and urban design theory as the conceptual basis or frame of reference for these techniques is exemplified by building form and massing concepts. Bacon's (1974) explication of the "design structure" underlying Philadelphia's plan for the redevelopment of its downtown and the design and implementation guidelines that emerged from that plan illustrate this issue very well.

Although Bacon is chiefly concerned with the interrelationships of

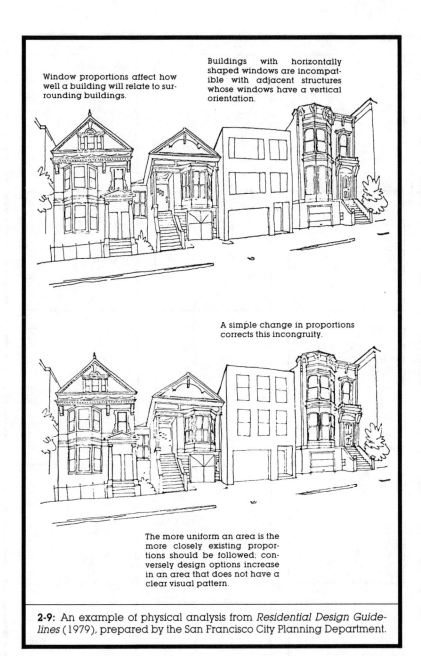

Window proportions affect how well a building will relate to surrounding buildings.

Buildings with horizontally shaped windows are incompatible with adjacent structures whose windows have a vertical orientation.

A simple change in proportions corrects this incongruity.

The more uniform an area is the more closely existing proportions should be followed; conversely design options increase in an area that does not have a clear visual pattern.

2-9: An example of physical analysis from *Residential Design Guidelines* (1979), prepared by the San Francisco City Planning Department.

architecture and planning, his discussion of design structure, which he terms "the binding together of perception sequences shared by large numbers of people," has a more far-reaching application: it establishes the role of a referential context, a comprehensive, func-

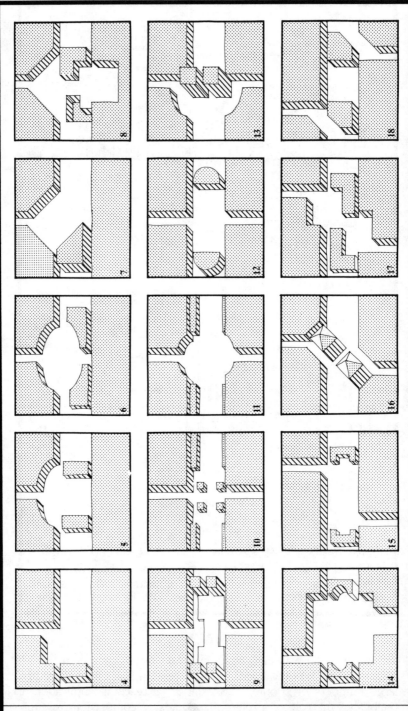

2-10: Another example of physical analysis presenting eighteen alternative solutions for the Third Street Mall Design in Santa Monica, CA, by Arroyo Group and Studio Works (Source: City of Santa Monica, CA).

Far and near scale in a building group.

A building
projecting
into a space.

A building on a space.

The surface of Saint Peter's Square is
bowl shaped.

A building in a space.

The surface of Red Square is humped.

2-11: Spreiregen's analysis of urban architecture: relationships between buildings and open space (Source: Paul D. Spreiregen. *Urban Design: The Architecture of Towns and Cities.* New York: McGraw-Hill Inc., 1965).

tional, areal plan that integrates design and planning goals so as to provide the raison d'être for architectural expression and all other form-giving statements—for example, guidelines and ordering principles (Bacon, 1974: 264).

Even among thorough and well-organized design guideline documents it is rare, that this larger design reference is discussed or that the rationale behind the guidelines is documented. Visual and pedestrian arguments are sometimes used (as in USR&E, 1977 study; see also Cullen, 1979), but the rationales behind guidelines are more frequently implicit rather than explicit—and the whole approach becomes little more than an encyclopedic checklist inventory that could be applied to any urban community. Therefore, such design guidelines as those pertaining to building mass and form are principally effective where they incorporate or refer to a design structure—as in a plan that demonstrates a clear areal focus, such as Philadelphia's Market East developments. (SFUDP, 1970, with its topographic references that apply to the city as a whole, in large part meets this criterion.)

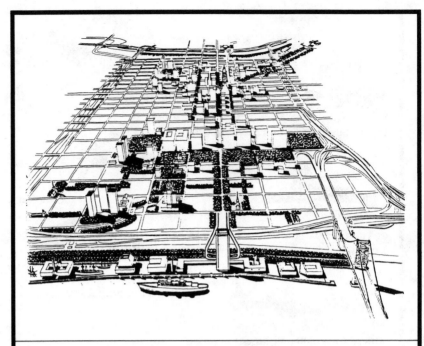

2-12: Bacon's analysis of Philadelphia's design structure (Source: Edmond Bacon. *Design of Cities.* London: Thames and Hudson, 1974).

Philadelphia's redevelopment plan, which evolved over some twenty years (1947–1960), involved such an expanding "design structure," a pedestrian-oriented plan that began in the city's Society Hill district and that eventually incorporated the entire Center City (Bacon, 1974). The two primary elements of the design structure that emerged by 1960 included the paths of movement and massing of huge towers in Society Hill and Washington Square (fig. 2-12): "It is the combination of the mass of the towers and the space of the movement that constitutes the essential design structure. When this is once established, the architect, working within the remaining area, is freed of rigid controls except where they are demanded to maintain the integrity of the design structure" (Bacon, 1974: 264).

The critical guideline emerging from this design structure stipulates that "the architecture may not penetrate the upper air, which must be preserved for the five points [of the towers] to retain their essential order" (Bacon, 1974: 264). Within Center City, the design structure incorporates subareal or district principles that provide additional guides or references for architectural expression as well, such as the eighteenth-century buildings surrounding Pei's towers. In this instance, the context was evoked with muntined windows (Bacon, 1974).

Thus far we have discussed only briefly an intervening level of design principles that link the plan or design structure for a particular area with the implementation mechanisms found in design guidelines. Yet such principles abound in design literature. Greenbie (1981), for example, has approached the general problem of building form and massing from the standpoint of building and land relationships. He has identified "two basic relationships of buildings to land which have to do with whether the structures or the landscape is visibly dominant" (1981: 49). "Where the landscape is visible, interesting and varied . . . structural uniformity" of built form is recommended; where the landscape is not dominant, diversity in structures can be tolerated (1981: 49). Numerous writers have explored building and street alignment (Greenbie, 1981; Tunnard and Pushkarev, 1963; Cullen, 1979), how the sections of buildings shape urban space (Krier, 1979), the effects of built form, urban spaces, and climate (Whyte, 1980), and the importance of integrating activity supports (restaurants, shops, and so on) into building and mass relationships (Whyte, 1980).

The basic urban design principles and techniques presented by Spreiregen (1965) synthesize many of the critical issues relating to building form and massing. These include (1) "scale" as it relates to human vision, circulation, neighboring buildings, and neighborhood size (Spreiregen, 1965: 70–74); (2) "urban space" as a primary element of urban design and the importance of the articulation by urban forms, scale and the sense of enclosure, and the types of urban space (1965: 74–75); (3) "urban mass," which includes buildings, the ground surface, and objects in space that may be arranged "to form urban space and to shape activity patterns, on both large and small scales" (1965: 76).

The essential step in defining building form and massing is, therefore, identification of principles and rationales behind the urban physical form. It is then that one can begin structuring design guidelines and/or implementation mechanisms. Without such analysis and studies, the design guidelines are nothing more than three-dimensional depictions of traditional development controls.

━━━━━━━

Circulation and parking

It is realistic to assume that the automobile has become an essential part of American life and that the trend will probably continue in the future. However, serveral factors will contribute to its continuance. First, increases in efficiency of the automobile to a large extent counteract increases in the cost of gasoline. Second, the relative unavailability of public transportation in this country is matched by a seeming unwillingness (with some notable exceptions) to invest in it—as evidenced by current policies of the present administration. No matter what lies ahead for the automobile, the fact remains that present American downtowns and suburban areas must include parking. Indeed, a large part of most downtown areas is already covered by ugly surface parking lots and some parking structures, both often inappropriately located and poorly maintained (fig. 2-13).

The parking element has two direct effects on quality of the environment: (1) survival of downtown commercial activity (to which parking is essential) and (2) severe visual impact on the physical form and fabric of the city. Failure to recognize the importance of regulating automobile usage and of providing adequate and attractive parking areas has made quite a number of American downtowns look half-developed and generally abominable. Therefore, two of the main items that should be included in any urban design agenda are access to individual properties and parking. The provision of adequate park-

2-13: An example of downtown surface parking in vacant lots, Syracuse, NY.

ing with least visual impact is essential to the success of urban design. There are various ways of handling parking that permit virtual elimination of surface parking.

First, of course, is the construction of parking garages in those parts of the city where structures have been built without provision for parking. Preferably such construction should be accompanied by regulations mandating establishment of parking as a part of plans for any new structures. The ground level of a parking garage can be set aside for retailing in order to continue activity at street level and provide visual quality there (fig. 2-14).

A second approach is the "multiple use program," which maximizes use of existing parking by means of a program that shares

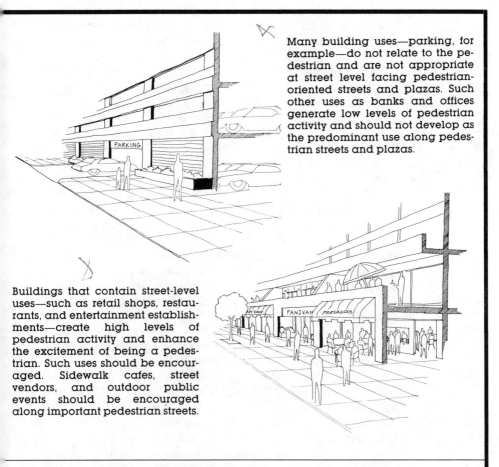

Many building uses—parking, for example—do not relate to the pedestrian and are not appropriate at street level facing pedestrian-oriented streets and plazas. Such other uses as banks and offices generate low levels of pedestrian activity and should not develop as the predominant use along pedestrian streets and plazas.

Buildings that contain street-level uses—such as retail shops, restaurants, and entertainment establishments—create high levels of pedestrian activity and enhance the excitement of being a pedestrian. Such uses should be encouraged. Sidewalk cafes, street vendors, and outdoor public events should be encouraged along important pedestrian streets.

2-14: City of San Diego guidelines illustrating two examples of integrating parking structures at street level (Source: City of San Diego, CA).

different uses and attracts different people at different times. For example, office and retailing can share parking spaces with theaters and nightclubs since these facilities are used at different times.

Third, is "package-plan parking." A business with a large number of employees (or several businesses together) may form a parking district or provide a few blocks of all-day remote parking.

Finally, the fourth program is urban-edge parking. Here, a city or a private developer can with the aid of the city develop parking areas or structures on the periphery of congested urban areas.

The circulation element of urban design offers one of the most powerful tools for structuring an urban environment. It can shape, direct, and control activity patterns (and therefore development) in a city, as when a transportation system of public roads, pedestrian ways, and transit systems links and focuses movement. It can also be a structuring principle itself, defining and characterizing such urban forms as distinct districts, activity areas, and so on. The Irvine Company's (n.d.) "Streetscape Concept," an urban design component of its General Plan Program (the city's comprehensive master plan), illustrates this point very well by suggesting that people mentally organize the environment "spatially" (that is statically, as an arrangement of objects) and "temporally" (that is, experientially) so as to differentiate the larger environment into districts, subdistricts (villages), and the like. The Irvine plan uses the road system along with "meaningful visual sequences—orchestrated views from roads" (a "streetscape program") as an instrument for organizing Irvine, California, into a "city of villages."

The techniques used are organized around three major principles. First: roads should be "positive visual open space elements" in themselves. Design guidelines proposed to promote this quality include (1) screening and landscape treatment of undesirable visual elements, (2) height and setback requirements for development adjacent to the road, (3) right-of-way parkway and median plantings, and (4) enhancing the natural environment as viewed from the road. Second: the road is to give orientation to the driver and to make the environment legible. Specific techniques for this include (1) providing "landscape palettes" to enhance environmental districts and villages along roads, (2) establishing a streetscape palette of street furnishings and lighting to ensure that the streets are as well lit in the night as in the day, (3) including in the general roadway plan a system of vistas of and visual references to adjacent land uses and landmarks, and (4) differentiating the order and importance of roads with streetscaping, right-of-ways, setback, adjacent land use, and so on. Third: public and private sectors should combine in partnership to achieve these goals.

Another set of traffic management strategies for bringing environmental and transportation objectives together is exemplified in the Central Washington Civic Design and Transportation Study (Washington, D.C., Office of Planning and Management, 1974). This proposal separates streets of central Washington into two systems: a "private system" of grid streets for pedestrians, autos, and trucks, and a "public system" of diagonal, north-south, and east-west boulevards intersecting the circles and squares so characteristic of Washington. This public system would serve pedestrians, buses, bicycles, as well as other transit systems. The plan is designed to create transportation alternatives for commuters while reducing travel time so as to make the city center function as a single district or neighborhood (see also Washington, D.C., Office of Planning and Management, *Proposed Comprehensive Plan for National Capital,* 1967).

In recent years, Toronto has taken a different approach by striving to decentralize and limit growth by encouraging nodal growth or a "system of centers" (Toronto, 1976). The support for decentralization emerged out of debates surrounding a major transit issue: expressway expansion that encouraged office workers to bring their cars downtown. The challenge to redirect growth away from a downtown that was seen as "big enough" was met by such strategies as (1) abandoning expressway structures and (2) encouraging new centers of growth. Transportation was seen as the critical link in these strategies since ties between the nodes and downtown had to be assured, at least in the early stages (Toronto, 1976: 191). Bus transit was seen as the primary means of transporting employees.

As they impinge on urban design considerations, the general goals of many current trends in transportation planning include (1) improving mobility in central business districts, (2) discouraging the use of private vehicles, (3) encouraging the use of public transportation, and (4) improving access to the central business district (Brambilla and Cianni, 1977). The degree of success each city has had varies. Moreover, the issue that most cities have neglected is how to deal with ugly highways, which have chopped up the center city. How to incorporate highway structures aesthetically and functionally and how to reduce such adverse impacts as noise, dust, and so on are all questions within the domain of urban design. Here and there, some work is being done in response to these issues, but a great deal of analysis and planning remains to be done, preferably in conjunction with consideration of other design elements.

Open space

Open space holds different meanings for different professionals. Here it is defined as all landscape, hardscape (roads, sidewalks, and the like), parks, and recreational space in urban areas. Empty parcels of land in urban areas such as "super holes" from the urban renewal era are not considered as open space. There is no claim that this is the best way of grouping open spaces, but this is a useful way of referring to them. Open-space elements include parks and squares, urban green spaces, as well as the trees, benches, planters, water, lighting, paving, kiosks, trash receptacles, drinking fountains, sculptures, clocks, and so on that are found within them. Pedestrian ways, signs, and amenities that also may be considered as open space elements are discussed separately in what follows.

Open space has always been an essential element of urban design and is, indeed, a crucial area of consideration. However, in the past, open space usually has been considered secondary to building form and massing or architecture. In other words, open spaces have been designed mostly after architectural decisions have been made. The design of open spaces has been, therefore, an addendum to the design process rather than an integral part of it. The key issue, then, is that open spaces should be considered an integral part of urban design.

Open space has been little valued in American cities. In particular, its downtown role has not been well realized. One reason may be overreliance on European open-space models that have not fit well into the fabric of American cities, which seem to demand both functional and symbolic dimensions in its open spaces. As Heckscher (1977: 6) states: "People overlook the fact that many American downtowns are loosely knit, with as much as half their total area awaiting development or used for parking. In such circumstances, it is enclosure that is principally required, not openness."

The spatial organization of American cities is one of the key issues that must be dealt with in open space planning or replanning of urban environments. As Heckscher (1977) has pointed out, models for successful open-space planning drawn from Europe and elsewhere are not always adaptable in an American context of loosely knit downtowns and where the traditional park, often oversized or (now) disadvantageously located, must be supplanted by newer forms of open space that support a variety of activities. Such forms include pedestrian and bicycle routes, historic area walks, waterfront areas, and structured linkages of open spaces that coordinate cultural, commercial, and governmental complexes.

However, quite beyond such "redevelopment" opportunities, it is essential to recognize that open space, like building massing and form, is a unique structuring element in urban design, that the framework and sequence of open spaces differ from city to city and must be grasped in each particular instance before an urban design program or plan can be created.

Dallas is a case in point. Its "Natural Open Space Plan" (1978) incorporates open space into urban design and land use planning programs by considering ecological and development issues simultaneously. The plan focuses on such key natural areas in the region as escarpments, prairies, and bluffs and includes acquisition, regulation, and management clearly motivated by protectionist and conservation themes:

> This plan concentrates on lands which should generally remain open and not be altered or developed for active uses, because of their special natural *resource* and/or *hazard* characteristics. Lands in the city considered to have resource characteristics include areas of ecological, aesthetic, or cultural significance. Lands which provide potential hazards to development include those subject to flooding and prone to erosion and slope instability. To a large extent, the resource and hazard characteristics are found on the same lands, which strengthens the justification for their preservation (Dallas, 1978:1).

Some particularly interesting aspects of the approach taken in Dallas are identification of potential incentives for financing and administering the open-space plan and the recommendations for linking ecological and development issues. "Although the City does not as yet have an overall plan to strike the appropriate balance between competing goals, such as economic development and environmental protection, the Open Space Plan recognizes the inevitable conflicts" (Dallas, 1978: 3). The starting point for the Dallas plan is a critique of "the inadequacies of the city's existing framework for regulation of development in fragile areas" (1978: 33). This involved a review of existing zoning practices pertaining to floodplain, escarpment, altered drainage system, and creek areas as well as several recommendations for environmental review, zoning ordinance revisions, overlay designations, and grading-management controls. In particular, the Dallas study recommended an amendment to the zoning ordinance that would "provide variable credit for open space set aside to reduce lot or site sizes by a formula which considers the relative usability and accessibility of open space" (1978: 43) (fig. 2-15).

The classic study undertaken by Lynch and Appleyard (1974) for the city of San Diego also emphasized development, environmental quality, and public accessibility issues in its recommendations for open-space planning. Like the Dallas study (which also included a study of the predevelopment, "natural base" resources of the city), the proposals for San Diego emphasized the need to address growth, especially suburban development issues. Specific recommendations were that inland suburban growth be slowed, "smaller, less homogeneous development" be encouraged, and climatically "more appropriate" settlement forms (that is, site planning with appropriate densities, and so on) be adopted (Lynch and Appleyard, 1974: 28, 29).

The special character of San Diego's physical setting, its coastal areas, arroyos, canyons, and the like, which have been threatened by

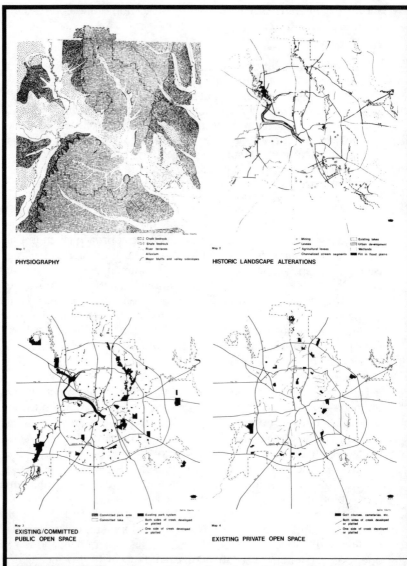

2-15: City of Dallas open space plan based on physiography, historic landscape alterations, existing public open space, and private open space (Source: City of Dallas, TX).

urban growth, provide the critical focus for San Diego's open-space policies.

San Diego will grow and change, but the city is already here and what is here will continue to be a major determinant of quality. A careful look at what should be saved and repaired in the existing city is our first task. Conservation of the natural setting is surely an urgent priority, and the finer parts of the city can also be preserved. But much of San Diego needs repair and restoration. As in any city that has grown fast, mistakes have been made. Public use and public access have been preempted. The public environment is all too often simply the left-over space in between. (Lynch and Appleyard, 1974: 9)

Key open-space planning tasks identified in the San Diego study were (1) a survey of urban and rural districts throughout the San Diego region "to judge their ability to absorb further growth"; (2) long-term plans for "the recapture of San Diego Bay for public use"; (3) a conservation and public-use plan for San Diego's special landscapes —its valley and canyon network—which incorporates various implementation strategies such as transfer of development rights, water and landscaping management as well as provisions for biking and bike trails; and (4) an open-space circulation study of commercial arterials "leading to proposals for the public action needed to convert these strips into humane landscapes" (Appleyard and Lynch, 1974: 47).

The efforts in these cities illustrate one of the principles of open-space planning for urban design that Tankel (1963: 69) succinctly states: "the significance of open space is not its quantity but how it is arranged in relation to development."

Pedestrian ways

For a long time, planning for pedestrians in the design of urban areas was neglected. When suburban shopping malls did consider the welfare of pedestrians *and* vehicles, their advantage over downtown shopping areas was increased. Pedestrian ways are an essential element of urban design, and they are not just part of a beautification program. Rather, they are a comfort system as well as a support element for retailing and for the vitality of urban spaces.

A good pedestrian system reduces dependency on automobiles in a downtown area, increases trips downtown, enhances the environment by promoting a human-scale system, creates more retailing activity, and, finally, helps to improve air quality. Downtown Minneapolis is presently one of the most successful American downtowns. The contribution of a pedestrian element, the Skyway System, is quite obvious (see fig. 2-16).

The pedestrian element should aid in the interaction of basic urban design elements, should relate strongly to the existing built environment and activity pattern, and should fit in effectively with future physical change in the city. The key issue in pedestrian planning is

2-16: An example of one skyway in the Minneapolis skyway system.

balance, "how much to give pedestrians and how much to [give] vehicles" (PAS 368, 1982: 3). That is to say, we have to balance the use of pedestrian elements to support livable, attractive public spaces while at the same time allowing for such related activities as delivery services, access, and individual property requirements.

This balancing also has to deal with interaction between pedestrians and vehicles and not simply with pedestrians alone. Safety plays an important role in pedestrian design. Equally important is the provision of space adequate to the number of people who walk there. When urban spaces are larger than required for the number of people who may use them, barren, open spaces and underuse of amenities result. When spaces are too narrow or too small, congestion, as well as underuse and underappreciation of amenities similarly result. Congestion, of course, is not always a negative feature in an urban setting, particularly in plazas, as Whyte (1980) has shown. "Self-congestion," as he terms it, the tendency for "people to attract people," appears to be an important characteristic of actively used urban plazas. Programming and design that include such activity supports as entertainment, food service, and well-located rendezvous points can enhance this tendency and enliven pedestrian areas (Whyte, 1980). What Whyte's research does is remind us that there are few hard and fast rules for designing pedestrian systems.

Next, consider the amenities along the pedestrian system. If there is nothing along the pedestrian way but banks or corporate headquarters, fewer people need to walk nearby. In fact, few are attracted to the area except by necessity. However, if there are small and active retailing establishments or department stores, the number of people attracted will be several times larger. Lastly, we must consider the public amenities offered within the pedestrian element: benches, planters, lighting, and the like. Too little attention has been directed toward these items.

The Uptown Pedestrian, an urban design study prepared by the City of Charlotte, North Carolina, is an outstanding example of careful attention to pedestrian design and programming. The study has divided the pedestrian issues into three groups: functions and needs, psychological comfort, and physical comfort. Guidelines deal with each of these issues (Charlotte, 1978) (fig. 2-17). *The New Orleans*

2-17: An example of City of Charlotte design guidelines for providing public service facilities—such as information and rest rooms—in pedestrian centers (Source: City of Charlotte, NC).

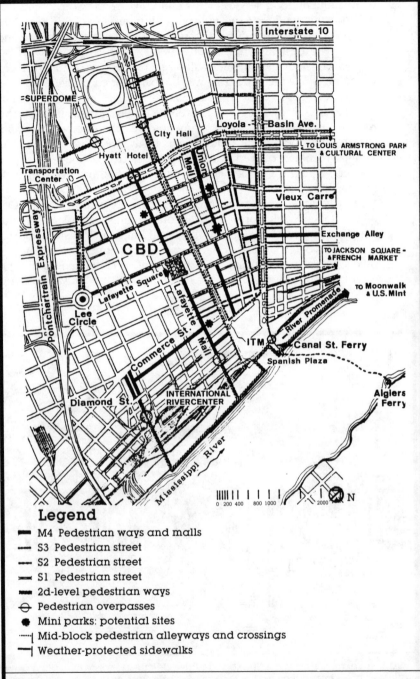

Legend

— M4 Pedestrian ways and malls
–– S3 Pedestrian street
-–- S2 Pedestrian street
⇒ S1 Pedestrian street
⚏ 2d-level pedestrian ways
⊖ Pedestrian overpasses
● Mini parks: potential sites
····| Mid-block pedestrian alleyways and crossings
—| Weather-protected sidewalks

2-18: City of New Orleans urban amenities plan (Source: City of New Orleans, LA).

Urban Amenities Plan ranks streets "according to [their] importance to pedestrian traffic" and then suggests what type of amenities should be incorporated on these streets. The plan's four groups of streets include: typical street, major pedestrian street, pedestrian boulevard, and pedestrian mall or auto-restricted zones (New Orleans, n.d.: 1) (fig. 2-18).

A "balancing strategy" in pedestrian planning does not strive for equity between vehicles and pedestrians (PAS 368, 1982: 3). Nor is pedestrian planning necessarily done primarily by design:

> Balancing street space is both a design problem and a management problem, because it can be achieved by making physical changes in a street (as by creating a traffic-free mall or by widening sidewalks) and by changing regulations which control street functions (PAS 368, 1982: 3–4).

Another very important concept in pedestrian planning is that such pedestrianization schemes as malls and crossing or amenity areas have to be carefully tailored to meet specific problems. No solution will be universally successful. Context (for example, the residential, commercial, or functional nature of the route) as well as coordination with other functional and vehicular systems are two key ingredients in the design and redesign of pedestrian ways. Changes in the balance of a given street to improve pedestrian flow, for example, can be a surprisingly complex issue depending upon (1) the activity supports along the street—is there a lane needed for window shopping?—and (2) street furniture—does the location of trees, signposts, lights, and so on, which are managed by district agencies, allow for the 1½-foot aisle most pedestrians seem to require between their path and these objects? (PAS 368, 1982; Wood 1979). Still, there seems to be no rule of thumb for determining either the maximum or minimum width of walking space (PAS 368, 1982).

Hartford, Connecticut, for example, found that by linking a street-widening and amenities program to a new parking and traffic management plan, including a bus transit plan, they were able to increase pedestrian flow—and, most important, window shopping and rest stop opportunities—and reduce conflicts between buses and other vehicles. One of the strengths of Hartford's plan was its inherent flexibility: the solution was partially physical—sidewalks along Main Street were widened to accommodate pedestrian flow and amenity zones (for bus shelters, seating, and so on)—and partly functional—vehicular access was restricted to buses only from 7 A.M. to 6 P.M., thereby reducing pedestrian-vehicle conflicts and promoting safety and commercial activity along the street (PAS 368, 1982).

A similar scheduling and traffic restriction solution was used in New York City to promote shopping along Pell and Doyers streets in Chinatown. There, vehicular access (except by delivery vehicles issued special permits) was prohibited during peak-use periods. The narrow streets in this historic shopping district were repaved with a continuous surface (with bollards providing pedestrian-vehicle separation during shared use hours) to expand pedestrian area to the entire street and to facilitate simultaneous use of both sides of the street by shoppers (PAS 368, 1982).

The advantages of the recommendations discussed above stem from their flexibility. No single solution is used; instead, in each instance a combined physical design and traffic, parking, and circulation management strategy was adopted that addressed existing problems but that also anticipated change. Pedestrian street amenities are, of course, essential physical components of a design solution. Decisions need to be made about the kinds of amenities needed and their location. Maintenance and user needs also have to be assessed and incorporated into the planning design process. These include consideration of visibility to oncoming traffic, accessibility (to buses, for example), information (such as transit information, directions to local services, and so on), and comfort (scaled and conveniently located setting, and so on) (PAS 368, 1982). However, once a decision has been made and the amenity has been sited and set firmly in place, we often lose sight of the fact that amenity planning and design must also be flexible.

A final and critical consideration is the coordination of amenities—that is, in what ways they ought to relate to one another and to their environment. Functional ties among amenities, for example, involve considerations of coordinated or at least linked patterns of use. For example, shoppers' rest areas may be located at bus stops. "A designer should not only be able to identify the kind of use a single amenity will receive, but also be able to anticipate uses *between* amenities" (PAS 368, 1982: 37).

Coordination and suitability context involves largely aesthetic concerns, but these also have functional facets. Wood (1979) identifies five criteria to be considered when selecting amenities: suitability, scale, materials, fixings (installation mountings), and numbers. Suitability addresses the primary function of the street furniture—illumination levels, seating comfort, and the like. Size and scale, particularly when the field of selection offers different materials (such as wood, steel, cement, and so on) are considerations that involve aesthetic issues in addition to function since concrete will have different dimensions and a different visual impact from timber when used for the same purpose. Maintenance requirements, durability, and flexibility, along with the number and variety of facilities provided are additional criteria for street furniture (Wood, 1979).

Activity support

Activity support includes all the uses and activities that help strengthen urban public spaces, for activities and physical spaces have always been complementary to each other. The form, location, and characteristics of a specific area will attract specific functions, uses, and activities. In turn, an activity tends to become located in a place that best fits the requirements of that activity. Therefore, how we design an urban environment may or may not attract a large number of uses and activities. The interdependency of space and use is a crucial element of urban design.

New York City's urban designers were most aware of this relationship when they directed the Fifth Avenue Special Zoning District toward saving street-level retailing; the gradual demise of such retailing was changing the character of the area. Yet some recent projects in other downtown areas pay no attention to this principle and thus have had a negative impact on their urban environments. For example, large-scale, mixed-use development projects usually do not have much street-level connection with the rest of the urban environment. Such developments may be termed "inward looking" projects. A prime example is the Bonaventure Hotel in Los Angeles (fig. 2-19). Making a cold and useless pedestrian plaza without retailing, or constructing a long corporate building without shops are additional examples of inefficient urban design that does not consider activity support in and near a building.

Activity support does not include only the provision of pedestrian ways or plazas, but also consideration of the major functional and use elements of the city that generate activities. These may include department stores, recreational parks, a civic center, a public library, and others. In many instances, these activity supports are designed and located in the urban areas without much attention to their implications and workability. For example, a mall may be less than successful because it does not connect two activity centers. Closing a street to traffic and making it a mall is not enough to ensure that people will come in droves. The resulting mall must link A and B activity nodes, or it must include several activity nodes such as department stores. Crowds of people justify the use of space.

> Shopping, eating, watching, resting, going to and from work are the vital signs of a healthy downtown. (Long Beach, 1980: 5)

> The goal should be the allocation of major activity hubs to the most functionally desirable places, intermixing them with complementary uses, then linking them to each other with a pedestrian movement system that is safe, diverse, exciting

2-19: Bonaventure Hotel, Los Angeles, CA: an example of an "inward looking" building in downtown Los Angeles.

and designed to pedestrian needs and functions. (Charlotte, 1978: 19)

The integration and coordination of activity patterns is perhaps the single most important facet of activity support programming. As Spreiregen (1965: 79) has commented, activity patterns of larger cities exist "as a series of hubs, many of them determined in their geographical extent by our ability to walk from one part to another." One criterion for the effective functioning of such hubs is that different areas of a city—both old and new—provide "varying degrees of intermixture with complementary facilities" (Spreiregen, 1965: 80). This type of "mixed use" promotes "diviersity and intensity of use" as well as vitality of other urban design elements within the design structure (for example, the open-space system) (Spreiregen, 1965: 80).

Whyte (1980: 50–53, 94–101) has also explored the role of activity support in enhancing other physical design elements, especially open spaces. In particular, he has endorsed the importance of food services, entertainment, and such stimuli as sights and physical objects (fig. 2-20).

The manner in which activity supports and opportunities are developed, coordinated with, and integrated into the existing urban physical fabric appears to be the critical issue. Ramati's (1981) discussion of the revitalization of Beach Twentieth Street in Queens, New York, illustrates this point very well. Her case study traces the decline of this once prosperous retailing and recreational center as private cars and new bridges bypassed the area that had been linked to nearby towns on the railroad. While the street retained its importance as a community shopping area, noise, declining image, and inconvenience arising from lack of parking, poor street lighting, and inadequate amenities (no benches and so on) detracted from its value to the community. In the 1970s, the Queen's Borough Planning Office commissioned a study to identify major problems in the area. The recommendations included basic highway improvements and repair, as well as modification of road widths around Beach Twentieth to facilitate parking and traffic movement (Ramati, 1981).

A central part of the revitalization plan that developed out of the study included the goal of creating a new street image for Beach Twentieth. Critical issues that were identified included (1) the substantial congestion of the thoroughfare—delivery traffic, and parking maneuvers that disrupted the street's retail activities, (2) narrow sidewalks, bus stop crowding, and dangerous pedestrian crossings, and finally, (3) visual clutter and deterioration of the physical fabric of the street's shops (Ramati, 1981).

The park and shop problem, which had been successfully addressed elsewhere (in Nicollett Mall, Minneapolis; in Kalamazoo, Michigan; and in Fulton Mall, Fresno, California), was used to convince merchants that reduced shop-front parking need not result in reduced business. Off-street parking on an adjacent block with direct access to Beach Twentieth Street was used to reduce parking-traffic conflicts and to expand parking facilities. This solution permitted sidewalk widening to accommodate greater pedestrian flow. A restoration program was developed that emphasized the existing physical and spatial continuity of the street, with particular attention to storefront activities. Widening of sidewalks, a canopy proposal, new paving, landscaping, and pedestrian amenities located to support retailing and entertainment activities were among the techniques used (Ramati, 1981).

The integration of indoor with outdoor activities is also an important dimension of activity support planning. Coordination with the built environment entails, for example, pedestrian-level access and attractions. In terms of physical design, this goal dictates windows, clearly designated entryways, and such specific land uses as retailing and food service. The outdoor cafe is an example of a design and marketing technique that combines some of these features by bring-

2-20: Plazas for People: New York City's design guidelines for design of urban plazas (Source: New York City Planning Department).

ing together street and building. This technique can work on a small scale, as in a community shopping district (Ramati, 1981) or on a large scale, as in Manhattan's massive plaza settings (Whyte, 1980).

Signage

Advertising signs have become increasingly important visual elements in American towns and cities, particularly since World War II, and their increase has not been without controversy. With interstate highway systems came large and small traffic signs in addition to the billboards of ubiquitous chain restaurants. Other billboards and signs direct the traveler to off-the-highway attractions, which present their own array of signs. In cities, the number of billboards and signs has also increased.

From the urban design standpoint, the size and design quality of private advertising signs must be regulated in order to establish compatibility, lessen negative visual impact, and at the same time reduce confusion and competition with necessary public and traffic signs.

While we should not denigrate the importance of signs for the businesses in an area, we do have to be concerned with the quality of the physical environment. "Well-designed signs contribute to the character of a building's facade while enlivening the streetscape, in addition to communicating information about goods and services of individual businesses" (Long Beach, 1980: 25).

Long Beach, Design Guidelines separate sign communication into

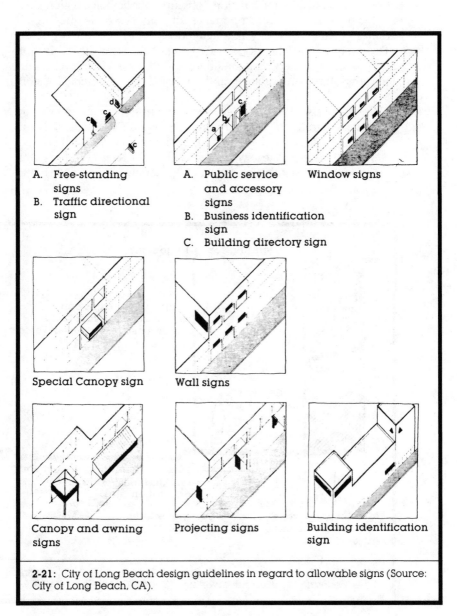

A. Free-standing signs
B. Traffic directional sign

A. Public service and accessory signs
B. Business identification sign
C. Building directory sign

Window signs

Special Canopy sign

Wall signs

Canopy and awning signs

Projecting signs

Building identification sign

2-21: City of Long Beach design guidelines in regard to allowable signs (Source: City of Long Beach, CA).

two levels, direct and indirect. Specifying business identity, location, and the goods and services provided is the "direct" purpose of signs. Image, character, and the form of the sign create the "indirect" level of communication (1980: 25) (fig. 2-21). The guidelines specify requirements for each level.

The Charlotte Uptown Pedestrian Study, on the other hand, presents sign shortcomings as conflicting information, confusing information, unavailable information, obscure public information, and similarity—stressing the importance of sign design in the overall aesthetic quality of the city although it does not identify the two levels of communication (Charlotte, 1978) (fig. 2-22). The City of Boston Sign Code has placed sign guidelines within a legal framework, thus indicating their importance and ensuring enforcement (Boston, 1975).

Minneapolis's (1969) design recommendations for street-name signs demonstrate how even the most common functional signs can incorporate "direct and indirect" communication. While their recommendations stipulate city-wide standards for sign visibility (location, mounting standards, reflective materials, and so on) and

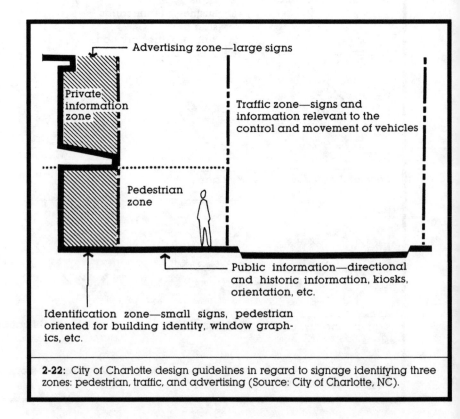

2-22: City of Charlotte design guidelines in regard to signage identifying three zones: pedestrian, traffic, and advertising (Source: City of Charlotte, NC).

legibility (typeface, spacing, location, and so on), the option for distinctive neighborhood treatments is provided through alternatives in background colors (Minneapolis, 1969a). An updated version of this report (Minneapolis, 1969b) expands the recommendations to include strict guidelines and standards for all public signage. Specific recommendations are made with regard to semantic aspects of sign communication, including the use of graphics and letter designations (as in "P" for parking) to replace wordy messages (Minneapolis, 1969b: 5–6).

Halprin (1980: 68) discusses the balance that must be struck in private signage between controlling chaos and creating interest while also transmitting information:

> In addition, there are vast areas of advertising signs which transform our city streets into a chaotic, endless, linear ugliness. The typical example is seen everywhere, a kind of urban nightmare not good enough to be surrealistically exciting, a folk art gone haywire, a hodgepodge of bad lettering, confused gigantism, disjointed agglomerates.

> The opposite of this, of course, is the overpolite uniformity of signs in some of the newer, more elegant shopping centers, where everything is carefully controlled, in good taste, and completely uninteresting. There is a point where good taste can become ineffably dull.

One approach to establishing functional criteria for signage is to regulate the size of signs in order to assure their legibility when seen from moving vehicles. Considerations include traffic speed and reaction distance, number of words required in the message, and the size of letters (Claus, 1976). Another approach, geared both to direct and indirect communication, attempts to suit signs to the functional and physical context in which they are found. Specific guidelines being developed for Cincinnati include (1) the use of signs that reflect "the special character of an area," (2) adequate spacing of signs from one another to ensure visibility and to avoid overcrowding and chaos (that is, to provide a basis for regulating projecting and oversized signs), (3) the use of signs "harmonious with the architecture of the buildings on which they are located," (4) restrictions on flashing signs except for such special uses as theaters and other places of entertainment, and (5) prohibition of large signs located to dominate vistas from such major pedestrian congregation areas as squares and parks (Richardson, 1976: 207–216).

Guidelines developed for the Chestnut Street-Walnut Street commercial area of Philadelphia include standard proposals for sign style and placement, as well as color and lighting (Philadelphia, 1982). In addition, the guidelines incorporate aesthetic or visual considerations by emphasizing the importance of simplicity: messages should contain the name and nature of the business only. Dimensions are also provided for typeface. Related criteria for temporary signs (for example, those announcing sales), accessory (advertising) and nonaccessory (billboard) signs as well as display windows have also been developed for the Chestnut Street area. Scale, duration of display, and maintenance standards are included.

Dallas uses comprehensive citywide guidelines common to all zoning districts as well as special guidelines for business, nonbusiness, and special-provision zoning districts (such as historic or special-character areas) to administer its sign-control plan (Dallas, 1983).

Preservation

Preservation does not refer solely to a concern for historic structures and places. In a broader view, it has also come to mean consideration for all existing structures and places, temporary or permanent. That is not to say that all of these should be preserved, but rather that attempts should be made to preserve them as long as they are economically vital and culturally significant. Structures and places of historical significance must have a longer life.

In urban design, preservation must address protection of existing neighborhoods and urban places (squares, plazas, shopping areas, and the like) as well as historical buildings and places. It must also focus on preservation of activities: unless we can maintain the activities that take place in an historic structure or find a better but still compatible use for the structure, we have accomplished only part of our mandate. Preservation has become an acceptable focus for urban design, and its emphasis has increased as developers have learned that preservation and redevelopment of historic places attract people. Well-known examples include the Vieux Carré in New Orleans, Georgetown, D.C., and Ghiradelli Square in San Francisco.

Some cities have successfully initiated an urban design program by capitalizing on interest in historic preservation. Regulation of other elements follows once preservation has paved the way. Emphasis on historic preservation brings a variety of benefits to a community—cultural, economic, social, and planning (California, 1976). Cultural benefits include historic resources that offer educational and/or aesthetic enrichment as well as the more elusive "sense of attachment" that is often associated with places and structures long after their original use has disappeared. Economic benefits, of course, provide an important stimulus for preservation planning. Four basic types can be identified: (1) increase in property value, (2) increase in retail sales and commercial rents, (3) avoidance of replacement costs (a resource/conservation argument), and (4) increased tax revenues. Social and planning benefits derived from preservation activities are less tangible but not in any respect less important than these benefits. Historic preservation efforts can be a significant force in restoring community confidence in the social as well as economic value and future of neighborhoods, districts, downtowns, and, indeed the community as a whole (California, 1976).

In recent years, preservation policies have moved away from "restrictive" measures toward protective techniques. In the process, a range of design and development tools has emerged, including survey methods, guidelines, controls or ordinances, review policies, and incentives (Roddewig, 1981). A central feature of this emerging preservation strategy is a dual emphasis on the protection of historic elements and the role they can play in fostering and encouraging economic growth and development (Roddewig, 1981). New Orleans, Louisiana; Lexington, Virginia; and Savannah, Georgia, have realized the economic benefits of preservation through tourism. San Francisco's Ghiradelli Square and Seattle's Pike Place Market are examples of major commercial centers created or given a new life through preservation efforts. Instances of neighborhood and residential revitalization spurred by preservation programs are found all over the country (Munsell, 1982; Roddewig, 1981).

Preservation ordinances vary from locale to locale, but typically they have emerged through one of three sources: a state enabling legislation, a municipality's "home-rule" initiatives, or as a result of powers available in a city's charter (Roddewig, 1981: 7). Despite these variations, the following features are generally common to all ordinances: (1) standards for historic designation, (2) provision for some kind of architectural review by a board or preservation commission, (3) review standards for preservation, demolition, and alteration, and (4) a formal set of procedures for landmark protection.

The Secretary of the Interior's Standards for Rehabilitation (n.d.) is the standard reference or model for preservation efforts in numerous communities. Many areas, however, have had to develop their efforts individually to meet the specific preservation task at hand. Some, for example, focus on key architectural elements. Lincoln, Nebraska, developed comprehensive guidelines to address building materials, roof profiles, and so on. Rochester's approach is also architecturally based, but somewhat more generic as it emphasizes visual compatibility through height and spacing considerations, roof shape, and the relationships among various materials (Roddewig, 1981). Murtaugh (1982) has drafted guidelines for districts as well as for buildings within districts. District criteria include (1) "location," which considers the association of "buildings, sites, objects and spaces" in traditionally accepted arrangements, (2) "design," which pertains to such aesthetic components of architectural detail as scale, ornament, proportion, height, texture, materials, and rhythm, (3) "setting," which captures the sense of a district through boundaries or focal points within them, (4) "materials," the features of materials (color, type, and so on) associated with a locality, (5) "workmanship," the "aesthetic efforts" characteristic of the area, and (6) "feeling" as well as (7) "association," which consider historic events, personages, and aesthetic qualities embodied in the historic district (Murtaugh, 1982: 388–389).

Criteria for district features include scale, proportion, rhythm, silhouette, height, materials, colors, textures, and design. The urban design problems and needs of historic districts, however, may be due to their new character as developments as much as to their intrinsic historic qualities. Development may introduce problems in such areas as signage, paving, landscaping, lighting, street furniture, and sidewalks (Roddewig, 1981).

References

Bacon, Edmond. *Design of Cities.* London: Thames and Hudson, 1974.

Barnett, Jonathan. *Urban Design As Public Policy.* New York: Architectural Record Book, 1974.

Boston, City of. *The Boston Sign Code.* 1975.

Brambilla, Roberto, and Cianni, Longo. *For Pedestrians Only: Planning, Design and Management of Traffic-Free Zones.* New York: Whitney Library of Design, 1977.

California, State of. *Historic Preservation Element Guidelines.* Sacramento, CA: Office of Planning and Research, 1976.

Charlotte, City of. *The Uptown Pedestrian.* Charlotte, NC, 1978.

Claus, Karen E. "Some Procedural Suggestions for Design Review." In *Proceedings of the Urban Signage Forum:* 406–416. Washington, D.C.: U.S. Department of Housing and Urban Development, 1976.

Cullen, Gordon. *The Concise Townscape.* New York: Van Nostrand Reinhold Company Inc., 1979.

Dallas, City of. *Natural Open Space Plan.* Dallas, TX: Department of Urban Planning, 1978.

Dallas, City of. *Sign Manual, Interpretive Materials for Sign Regulations.* Dallas, TX: Department of Planning and Development, 1983.

Design Council and the Royal Town Planning Institute. *Street Ahead.* New York: Whitney Library of Design, 1979.

Greenbie, Barrie B. *Spaces.* New Haven, CT: Yale University Press, 1981.

Halprin, Laurence. *Cities.* Cambridge, MA: The MIT Press, 1980.

Heckscher, August. *Open Spaces, The Life of American Cities.* New York: Harper and Row, 1977.

The Irvine Company. *General Plan Program Urban Design Element.* Newport Beach, CA: The Irvine Company, n.d.

Jacksonville, City of. *Jacksonville Form and Appearance.* Vol. I. Jacksonville, FL: Planning Department, 1971.

Jacksonville, City of. *Jacksonville Form and Appearance.* Vol. II. Jacksonville, FL: Planning Department, 1972.

Krier, Rob. *Urban Space.* New York: Rizzoli, 1979.

Long Beach Redevelopment Agency. *Design Guidelines for Downtown Long Beach*. Long Beach, CA: The Arroyo Group, 1980.

Lynch, Kevin, and Appleyard, Donald. *Temporary Paradise? A Look at the Special Landscape of the San Diego Region*. San Diego, CA: San Diego Department of City Planning, 1974.

Minneapolis, City of. *Signs on the Streets*. Minneapolis, MN: Metro Center 85, 1968.

Minneapolis, City of. *Street Name Signs*. Minneapolis, MN: Metro Center 85, 1969a.

Minneapolis, City of. *Signs on the Streets*. Minneapolis, MN: Metro Center 85, 1969b.

Munsell, Ken. "Rehabilitation Derelict Houses in Peekskill New York." *Small Town* 13, 3 November (1982): 32–36.

Murtaugh, William J. Commentary in *Preservation and Conservation Principles and Practices*. Proceedings of the North America International Regional Conference. Washington, D.C.: The Preservation Press, 1982.

New Orleans, City of. *Urban Amenities Plan*. New Orleans, LA, n.d.

Philadelphia, City of. *Facade and Sign Guidelines—Chestnut Street—Walnut Street Commercial Area*. Philadelphia, PA, 1982.

Planning Advisory Service (PAS) No. 368 (Project for Public Spaces, Inc. and Davis, Stephen C.). *Designing Effective Pedestrian Improvements in Business Districts*. Chicago, IL: APA Publications, 1982.

Ramati, Raquel. *How to Save Your Own Street*. New York: Dolphin Books, 1981.

Richardson, Robert. "Guidelines for Signs in Business Districts." In *Proceedings of the Urban Signage Forum*. Washington, D.C.: U.S. Department of Housing and Urban Development, 1976.

Roddewig, Richard J. *Preservation Ordinances and Financial Incentives: How They Guide Design*. Washington, D.C.: National League of Cities, 1981.

San Francisco, City of. *San Francisco Urban Design Plan*. San Francisco, CA, 1970.

San Francisco, City of. *Residential Design Guidelines*. San Francisco, CA: Department of City Planning.

Santa Monica, City of. *Third Street Mall*. Santa Monica, CA: The Arroyo Group and Studio Works, 1980.

Seattle, City of. *1982 Downtown Alternative Plan*. Seattle, WA: Executive Department, 1982.

Spreiregen, Paul D. *Urban Design: The Architecture of Towns and Cities*. New York: McGraw Hill Book Company, 1965.

Tankel, Stanley B. "The Importance of Open Space in the Urban Pattern." In Lowdon Wingo, Jr., ed., *Cities and Space, The Future Use of Urban Land*. Baltimore, MD: Johns Hopkins University Press, 1963.

Toronto, City of. *Master Planning Toronto*. Toronto, Canada: City of Toronto Planning Board, 1976.

Tunnard, Christopher, and Pushkaren, Boris. *Man-Made America:·Chaos or Control?* New Haven, CT: Yale University Press, 1963.

U.S. Department of Interior. *The Secretary of Interior's Standards for Rehabilitation and Guidelines for Rehabilitating Historic Buildings*. Washington, D.C., n.d.

Urban Systems Research and Engineering (USR&E). *Environmental Assessment of Visual Quality—Draft*. Cambridge, MA: USR&E, Inc., 1977.

Washington, D.C. Office of Planning and Management. *Proposed Comprehensive Plan for the National Capitol.* 1967.

Washington, D.C. Office of Planning and Management. *Central Washington Civic Design and Transportation Study—Draft of Work Program.* 1974.

Whyte, William H. *The Social Life of Small Urban Spaces.* Washington, D.C.: The Conservation Foundation, 1980.

Wilson, John S.; Tabas, Philip; and Henneman, Marian. *Comprehensive Planning and the Environment* Cambridge, MA: Abt Books, 1979.

Wood, Alfred A. "Selecting and Siting Street Furniture." In Design Council, *Streets Ahead.* New York: Whitney Library, 1979.

Urban design: the human dimension reexamined

CHAPTER 3

FOR MORE than two decades environmental planners and designers have researched the human dimension of urban planning and design. The term *human dimension* is used here to avoid excessive use of the jargon transferred from psychology and the social sciences into the planning and design field. In simplest terms and remembering that urban design is itself a field with many dimensions, the human dimension is the most important. After all, urban design attempts to serve people.

Research into the human dimension started in architecture and then expanded slowly and tentatively into planning and urban design. Most of the early literature focused on neighborhood livability, on the quality of life in urban areas, and on criticism of existing practice as it addressed these issues inadequately.

As a result of this research, many planners and designers came to understand that we cannot separate people from their environment. More to the point, we cannot analyze and interpret relationships between man and environment until we are able to pose the proper questions about such relationships. Robert Gutman made this point in a paper titled "Site Planning and Social Behavior" (1966) in which he identified the fundamental problem as one of translating "architectural theories into terms which can be tested with empirical techniques" (Gutman, 1966: 113). Now, almost two decades later, we are still grappling with the same basic issues. This chapter focuses on the nature of the translation problem, the various ways in which planners, designers, and design theorists have come to grips with it, and a detailed examination of the key issues and problems as well as the theoretical and practical perspectives on the human dimension of urban design. The intention is to determine the status of the field with regard to the human dimension. Elaboration on the following crucial aspects of the issue is the basis for thorough analysis:

1. Limitations of planning/urban design
2. Shortcomings of public participation
3. Available social data and research
4. Nature of social data relevant to design
5. Current role and use of social data in design
6. Translation of the human dimension into planning/urban design

Limitations of planning/urban design

The scope of planning/urban design is unclear even to practicing professionals. In the traditional sense, *design* means an "art" of personal expression and creation employed in service to an individual. Most of the early city plans and architectural design of great past cultures were based on one client's desire, usually a monarch or other ruler. Later, design was made more generally available to the wealthy classes, but the one-to-one interaction between designer and client was still the norm. This pattern persisted into the late nineteenth and early twentieth centuries, when industrialism became dominant and brought with it a pluralistic society. Indeed, one of the main causes of the failure of design in the twentieth century is inability to deal with pluralism.

While design by designer continues to be a luxury service, people all over the world have designed and built their own communities without the assistance of professionals. Although few planners and designers acknowledge it, most of the great city designs are products of generations of nondesigners who have built their communities for their own use based on their cultural needs (see Rapoport, 1977, 1982).

Since the advent of industrialism, planning has taken place in a context of pluralistic decision making. The present-day meaning and function of planning/urban design in a given country is subject to the institutional framework and the political economy of that country. In capitalist countries, where planning can control the market only to a limited extent, urban design as a subfield of planning is subject to certain constraints. Therefore, from the beginning, we have to make it clear that the scope of planning/urban design is limited.

Urban design as the creation of spatial environments for a pluralistic society based on its collective norms and in response to human behavior is an idea no more than two decades old. Problems associated with the human dimension are not the only ones urban design faces, but they are strongly interrelated with its other problems and ultimately interdependent with them. Without considering all the interrelated and interdependent problems, we cannot achieve an environment of high quality, a livable city neighborhood. As Gans (1976: 565) points out, the main questions are

- Do planners have "the power to influence patterns of social life"?
- Should they use this power?
- Do ideal patterns exist that should be advocated as planning goals?

Gans also reminds us:

> The planner has only limited influence over social relationships. Although the site planner can create propinquity, he can only determine which houses are to be adjacent. He can thus affect visual contact and vital social contacts among their occupants, but he cannot determine the intensity or quality of the relationships. This depends on the characteristics of the people involved (Gans, 1976: 571).

Shortcomings of citizen participation

Generally speaking, planning is never value-free. Both normative literature, which develops a theory and then applies it to the real world and positive literature, which attempts to improve or enhance the existing situation, tend to support this statement, as does the profession's origin and historical development:

> In certain kinds of planning—urban and regional planning are especially susceptible—there is confusion between the general goals of society, which is in the last analysis a question of how society defines the good life, and the more specific

goals which form in detail the aims of a particular plan (Dakin, 1963: 23).

Since the late 1950s, planners have tried to incorporate the human dimension into the activity of practical planning via various public participation processes. At least two basic trends can be identified: facilitation approaches (Sanoff, 1980; Cutler and Cutler, 1976) and political activist roles, often termed "advocacy planning" (Davidoff, 1965; Peattie, 1968).

FACILITATION APPROACHES

Facilitation approaches use participatory methods for defining as well as solving problems of planning and urban design. Facilitation methods incorporate informed citizen involvement into critical phases of the design process. As Sanoff points out:

> Interest in user needs or user participation is not rooted in romanticism about human involvement but rather in the recognition that users have a particular expertise different than, but equally important to, that of the designer. This expertise then needs to be integrated into the process that concerns itself with environmental change. Although designers and planners have gracefully embraced this aspect of human involvement in decision-making, the question of the designer's accessibility to many community groups is still left unanswered. (Sanoff, 1980: 1)

According to Sanoff, design-assistance techniques take different forms. There are educational approaches, as exemplified by Cutler and Cutler (1976), where the designer's role is to enhance the "user groups' ability to reach decisions pertinent through ... a communicable procedure" such as one that makes the group aware of critical environmental alternatives (Sanoff, 1980: 1). Particularly important techniques of this kind are questionnaire and rating mechanisms, training and use of graphic communication, and the use of various simulation techniques (Cutler and Cutler, 1976). But how precisely is information gleaned from these procedures to be used? According to Cutler and Cutler, citizens' preferences are to serve as a guide to the issues, not as a blueprint for design (1976). Sanoff is easily as equivocal on this point when he cautions that public participation may actually suggest or require a "greater reliance on professional acumen" (1980: 1).

ADVOCACY APPROACHES

Activist or advocacy models for public participation take a different approach to promoting public involvement in planning. Information and education are important to advocate planners who view their technical skills as political resources for the groups they serve, but their primary efforts are directed at helping the disenfranchised and unorganized to unite for planned actions and to jockey for political position in the planning process. As Arnstein points out, informed decision-making is of little value without the power to enforce the decisions (1969).

There seem to be three key characteristics of advocacy planning that distinguish it from traditional, politically neutral, practice. First, there is the recognition of conflicting interests surrounding plan-making—a view that argues that it is unrealistic for planners to state objectives in terms of equality for all or the community interest (Reiner *et al.*, 1963). According to this planning view, both "best" and "general welfare" solutions must be rejected (Peattie, 1968: 81). It is interesting to note that this perspective need not entail actual public involvement in the planning process. Reiner *et al* (1963: 270–271), for example, propose a methodology, a specific sequence of analytical operations that need not be informed at all by public participation in order to make values explicit.

Second, advocacy models also establish general criteria for the kind of information necessary in planning processes and for how the information should be used. Arguing that the data planners rely on can be too technical for the average citizen to understand, Forester (1980: 3) establishes four other philosophical conditions for communication with the public. He asserts that information must be "comprehensible," "sincere and trustworthy," "appropriate and legitimate," "accurate and true." Forester argues that participants in the planning process are misinformed to the extent that these conditions are not met. Bureaucratic language, confused attribution of responsibility, false reassurance by agencies, "neutral" techniques, misrepresentation of facts relating to costs and benefits are some of the "structural" sources of misinformation that the advocate planning strategies attempt to counter (Forester, 1980: 3–6).

Finally, one of the major obstacles encountered by advocacy planners is that the groups they serve, typically underrepresented in the planning process, are also the most difficult to bring into active participation roles. Planning for the poor is particularly hard to define in terms of "community" for purposes of identifying a consultant-client relationship (Peattie, 1968). Moreover, lower- and lower-middle-class people, the typical clients of the advocate planner, are not only difficult to organize but are likely to think in terms of short-term costs and specific threats rather than the neighborhood or community's long-term interests (Peattie, 1968). These limitations mean that an advocate planner usually assumes the traditional planning role of advisor rather than decision-maker. That is, an advocate planner always faces the dilemma of whether to adopt a political or an apolitical stance—and usually chooses the latter to avoid problems of advocacy planning that are rooted in a broader political decision-making framework.

Yet, as planners/designers, it is essential that we do somehow come to terms with the tasks, issues, and problems of citizen participation. The reasons for this, of course, are not entirely professional or ethical; rather, citizen participation in one form or another has been mandated by federal legislation since 1946, when the Administrative Procedures Act set minimum standards for openness in decision-making processes in federal agencies. The Freedom of Information Act of 1966 and the National Environmental Policy Act of 1970 that followed expanded this trend toward administrative accountability (Gil and Lucchesi, 1979).

Certainly there are numerous stories that could be cited of successful experiments with citizen participation, but there are probably as many unproductive cases that could be cited as lessons on how and when planners should strive for active public participation—and when they should not. But the issue of concern here is how effectively any of the approaches just discussed incorporate the human dimension into planning problems, especially those that are conceived of as urban design problems. For although there is an array of techniques available to planners to sensitize and inform the public about particular planning/design strategies, it might well be asked whether such strategies, are reducible to simple vocabulary or priority-determination techniques, particularly in their early conceptual phases. Putting it another way, planners have to ask themselves if the very nature of relevant planning/design information often prevents the "informed" user from meaningfully playing a role in the planning process. It is clear that we need to examine critically an assumption that underlies public participation methods: whether a user's knowledge of judgment is necessarily more enlightened or informed than that of a conscientious planner/designer. Under many circumstances, the user's input can be widely accepted, but whether or not user information provides an unassailable "authoritative text" on the human dimension of a particular planning question is another issue entirely. To elevate participation strategies to a methodology that can be packaged and applied to a variety of planning/design tasks is, therefore, an essential human planning problem.

Available social data and research

Identification of the kinds of social data and research relevant to planning/urban design forms another major issue of the human dimension. It is important to recognize that there is a range of approaches to research into the human aspects of design, each using different kinds of data. Three frequently used approaches are cultural (Rapoport, 1977, 1982; Porter, 1980), cognitive (Proshansky, 1974; Kaplan and Kaplan, 1982), and behavioral (Zeisel, 1974; Perin, 1970; Porteous, 1977). In the following discussion, an attempt has been made briefly to discuss these evaluation methods and the problems associated with each.

CULTURALLY RELATED SOCIAL DATA

Cultural approaches stress that human beings impart meaning to the environment, design it, modify it, and control it. Essentially, such approaches have been confined to nonapplied social-science research questions. Only to a lesser degree have they been brought to bear on planning and design. In some respects, the various cultural approaches to environmental questions seems to be the most removed from practical application to the planning/design fields. Much of the research into the semiotic or cultural significance of environments, while informative, is addressed to scholarly questions: planning/design principles can rarely be extracted directly from this work, which uses environmental studies to explore such theoretical questions as the nature of cultural systems (Rapoport, 1977, 1982; Gottdiener, 1983).

Interestingly enough, however, it is the cultural approach that provides us with a starting point from which we can begin to understand the appropriate role and limits of design in relation to the human dimension. In his most recent work, Rapoport (1982) distinguishes direct from indirect effects to explain the way in which environments can influence behavior. In short, it is social situations and the cultural systems to which they refer that shape behavior. People act in accordance with their reading of environmental cues, but:

> The critical point is that the effects are *social,* but the cues on which the social situations are judged are *environmental*—the size of the room, its location, its furnishings, the clothing and other characteristics of the experimenter (which are, of course, a part of the environment). They all communicate identity, status, and the like and through this, they establish a context and define a situation. The subjects read the cues, identify the situation and the context and act accordingly. The process is

rather analogous to certain definitions of culture that stress its role in enabling people to co-act through sharing notions of appropriate behavior. The question then becomes one of how the environment helps people behave in a manner acceptable to members of a group in the roles that the particular group accepts as appropriate for the context and the situation defined. (Rapoport, 1982: 56)

Cues, then, let people know what kind of setting they are in: "public/ private," "men's/women's," and so on— *who does what, where, when, how, and including or excluding whom"* (Rapoport, 1982: 56, 59). According to Rapoport, the designer's job is to make these cues comprehensible (Rapoport, 1982). His research in urban settings has begun to isolate a number of "physical surrogates" that serve as indicators of the socioeconomic conditions of a given area and population, including such features as land crowding, nonresidential land uses and activities, litter, condition of private free space, and architectural styling (Rapoport, 1982).

The issue of comprehensibility, of course, has been taken up by many nonanthropological writers and provides the focus of cognitive studies. David Crane's (1960) ideas on regional organizations, as exemplified in his influential paper, "The City Symbolic," is a case in point. But as for the human dimension, the issue is not whether or how cultural data can be used to define and solve urban design problems, but rather whether relevant cultural data can, or ought to be used in a culturally pluralistic planning context. Once again, what may be a perfectly legitimate academic pursuit appears to be inappropriate to the practicing planner. Rapoport (1977) has attempted—with little success—to extract from his work a number of methods compatible with urban diversity and cultural pluralism in the city. Key elements are design/planning strategies that permit personalization, uniqueness, and variability at the local scale (the neighborhood, for example) but that at the larger urban scale are integrative:

These general systems need a high degree of redundancy-eikonic, symbolic, physical and social cues should all be congruent and consistent and reinforce each other. They should also overlap, so that different people, using different routes and having different activity systems and home ranges should all know what the city has to offer. These important overall elements which help orientation and cognitive structuring, should be physically accessible to most people (i.e., related to major movement systems) and related to the most widely shared images and symbols (i.e., symbolically and associationally accessible). (Rapoport, 1977: 363)

It can be suggested that once these behavioral and cultural systems achieve a level of generality, we are no longer dealing with cultural concepts per se, but instead cognitive predictions themselves may be culturally shaped to reiterate. It is evident that these concepts, however valid or valuable, are so abstract that as planning-design considerations, they prescribe neither a method nor a solution.

COGNITIVE APPROACHES TO SOCIAL DATA

Cognitive or environment-based approaches view cities as geographical and physical systems as well as social, political, cultural, and economic ones. The particular concern is "the study of human behavior and experience in relation to the urban setting" (Proshansky, Ittelson, and Rivilin, 1976: 491). However, it is to the physical environment and its design characteristics that environmental psychology directs its attention rather than to social and cultural variables played out against an environmental setting.

One key issue, then, is the physical quality of the environment found in cities, including work settings, recreation, transportation, public eating facilities, residential dwellings, and so on.

> The essential point is that the "city dweller" is socialized not just by people, personalities, and social groups, but by spaces and places; by physical systems that are internalized as conceptions of time, movement, distance, familiarity, safety, beauty, and purpose that provide structure for that individual (and his existence) we call the "urban dweller." (Proshansky, Ittelson, and Rivilin, 1976: 493)

Another issue concerns the role of "identity" in the city, especially "place identity"—namely, those qualities or properties of an urban physical setting that provide the individual with a sense of who and what he is, how to behave in particular settings, and so on (Proshansky, Ittelson, and Rivilin, 1976: 493–494).

One major theme of the research and writing that addresses these issues is that the kinds of behavior characteristic of urban environments are "functional" in the context of the environment. Even behavior that tends to amplify classic urban anonymity, behavior we tend to view negatively, serves a functional purpose. Milgram (1976), for example, attributes the often aggravated, but apparently quite generalized lack of social responsibility among urban dwellers (failure to assist strangers in crises, failure to be civil or polite, and so on) to the anonymous character of the densely populated environment in which he lives:

> In discussing the effects of overload, I do not imply that at every instant the city dweller is bombarded with an unmanageable number of inputs, and that his responses are determined by the

excess of input of any instant. Rather, adaption occurs in the form of gradual evolution of norms of behavior. Norms are evolved in response to frequent discrete experiences of overload; they persist and become generalized modes of responding. (Milgram, 1976: 499)

Similarly, Lofland (1976) suggests that anonymity in the city is tempered or overcome by a cognitive and physical process he terms "spatial ordering." His argument starts from the spatial characteristics of modern cities, notably the specialized uses of public spaces (for example, the designation of certain spaces as appropriate for certain kinds of activities but not for others), the spatial segregation of activities, and ultimately the spatial segregation of persons. Location, according to Lofland, is a key perceptual or ordering principle for urbanites, particularly in understanding social environments:

The modern city dweller's penchant for linking "who" to "where" turned up again and again in my interviews with various residents of San Francisco and its surrounding suburbs. Ask them if they're ever afraid in the city, and they will tell you that it depends on where in the city they happen to be. Ask them if they ever talk to strangers, and they tell you about a bar they know of where everybody talks to everybody else. Ask them about people, and their responses are brief. Ask them about places, and they cite chapter and verse. (Lofland, 1976: 521)

An important premise of the cognitive approaches is that the urban experience is unique:

The city experience differs fundamentally from the rural. Because of the city's large size, density, and heterogeneity, social organization and interaction are more complex and problematic. The sheer immensity of the modern setting encourages unique experiences (LaGory and Pipkin, 1981: 37).

Influences on urban social life include (1) "complex patterns of interaction," (2) "exposure to strangers," and (3) "exposure to unconventional norms" (due to the social, economic, and cultural diversity of city inhabitants) (LaGory and Pipkin, 1981: 37–78).

A major ordering principle and characteristic of cities is their unique spatial character. Lynch's (1960) work as well as cognitive research approaches (Moore and Golledge, 1976) have addressed structuring elements (such as paths, nodes, sequential experience) as well as the importance of legibility and so on. Along with others, LaGory and Pipkin (1981) have begun to abstract from this research sociospatial principles (not unlike Rapoport's) for urban planning.

Their recommendations take the form of general guidelines or goals rather than prescriptions for design.

1. *Providing for diversity of spatial experience.* LaGory and Pipkin argue that "the impact of space on behavior must be understood mainly in cognitive terms" and that planners/designers can influence urban maps and imagery by designing "legible and functional spaces" and "facilitating more accurate, less constrained cognitive imagery" (LaGory and Pipkin, 1981: 298).

2. *Promoting permissive over coercive design.* Here the emphasis is less on strictly physical features than on the population densities that result from them, and the role of population density in controlling crime, ethnic and racial segregation patterns, accessibility to resources, and so on (LaGory and Pipkin, 1981).

3. *Understanding the cognitive and social functions of boundaries.* The essential point is that territoriality, as expressed through physical boundaries, is a critical element in the management and use of neighborhood, community, and public space. Despite the tentative state of cognitive and social research on the subject, planners/designers must be prepared to consider territoriality at varying levels and contexts of the urban fabric (LaGory and Pipkin, 1981).

4. *Diversity, spatial boundaries, and scale.* These issues are essentially inseparable for purposes of urban design, yet planning scale (neighborhood-shared public spaces, and so on) appears to be the main factor in determining acceptable levels of diversity or use of boundaries (LaGory and Pipkin, 1981).

City structure and its effects on environmental cognition has also occupied the interest of some planning researchers (Appleyard, 1976; Zannaras, 1976; Lynch, 1960). Consideration of street pattern configurations, landmarks (buildings, building locations, and so on), and aspects of remembered settings (cognitive maps) has contributed a great deal to urban design concepts (Appleyard 1969, 1970, 1976, 1979; Appleyard, Lynch, and Myer, 1964). However, here again the translation from research to application is fraught with pitfalls. This is not to say that such findings as Lynch's (1960) hypotheses regarding legibility cannot be successfully applied. Appleyard's (1976) plan for the new city of Ciudad Guyana in Venezuela, which incorporated Lynch's legibility principles, demonstrated that cities could be organized in ways that maximize their appearance through regular city street patterns, clearly defined districts, and readily visible landmarks.

However, whether this research on the human dimension can be implemented through design is not the same question as whether it ought to be. For example. there are potential drawbacks to improving urban legibility. There is "the danger of making environments so routine or boring that prediction and exploration become trivial" (Evans, 1980: 280). Similarly, overemphasizing physical dimensions of settings may neglect the symbolic significance of spaces (Appleyard, 1979; Moore, 1979).

Another issue subject to debate is the assumption that physical environments that facilitate the formation of strong cognitive maps are necessarily always desirable (Appleyard, 1976; Lynch, 1960). However, as Evans (1980) points out, the relationship between environmental legibility and such factors as preference, competence, and feelings of personal satisfaction has not been well researched. Kaplan (1973, 1975), for example, has identified two key concepts—coherence (of theme texture, color, graphic pattern, and so on) and moderate uncertainty (established through variety, complexity, structural irregularities, and so on)—that complement and, to some extent, counterbalance legibility yet contribute to cognitive map formation (cited in Evans, 1980: 280).

Our still limited understanding of cognitive representations (Evans, 1980), coupled with serious questions about their practical applications, place very real limits on the role social research can play in design.

SOCIAL DATA GATHERED FROM BEHAVIORAL RESEARCH

A major difficulty with using social research in design and planning is that even where designers are explicit about behavioral "requirements of their design problem, they have difficulty in determining the information parameters needed to resolve the problem" (Meister and Sullivan, 1967: 24–25). One solution to this dilemma is an "anthropological" approach that uses the concept of "behavior circuits" (Perin, 1970: 70–107). Perin focuses on people *doing things* in environments rather than people simply being in them. Perin's concern is what people do, what they want, and what they expect from environments (Perin, 1970). Chapin and Kaiser (1979), working along somewhat similar lines, have developed a framework for analyzing urban activity systems at various physical (for example, home and neighborhood) as well as temporal scales (frequency of use, and so on). The goal of these studies is quite ambitious: to provide congruent or responsive environments for people. As such, behaviorally oriented planners/designers are interested in human needs, but again as Zeisel (1974) points out, needs cannot be determined solely by listening to what users say they need. Need must also "be defined in terms of the underlying social meaning of behavior and perception to the user group" (Zeisel, 1974: 296). This approach to designing for user needs, therefore, takes on a cultural as well as functional aspect: "Physical design implications usually can be formulated in terms of the relationship between the different spaces . . . [however,] . . . the underlying social impact of behaviors and spaces, their latent functions, are usually not consciously known to the residents of a particular setting" (Zeisel, 1974: 298).

Behavioral approaches appear to be well-suited for studying and designing such proximate or smaller-scale environments as residences, residential complexes, and adjacent facilities (such as recreational, shopping, and services). However, it may well be asked how, other than in the most general functional or cognitive/perceptual terms, these approaches aid urban designers in conceptualizing urban-scale projects beyond the site or neighborhood. There are no clear answers to this question.

Nature of social data relevant to design

In dealing with the human dimensions of urban design, it is clear that we must consider the nature of much behavioral, psychological, perceptual, cultural, and social data. But the potential relevance of such data to a particular design problem may not be adequately obtained from users, the sources of the data. As Sommer (1969: 160) explains, "designers need concepts relevant to both physical form and human behavior."

> Much of architecture affects people from beyond the focus of awareness... They are (un)able to express how they feel in different surroundings... Not only do people have difficulty expressing what they feel about architecture, but most of their reactions (are) on an emotional rather than rational level. (Sommer, 1969: 160)

Sommer further cites as an additional problem the "language differences" between designer and client. For example, as a client, a developer is concerned only about the profitability of a project or about his reputation as a "quality" developer (here *quality* means what his clients want or like). For his part, the designer, while taking into consideration all the functional aspects, attempts to create a new idea, form, or product to bring about a new concept and, in some cases, to satisfy his ego. Another problem situation develops when designers try to explain a project or design issue to nondesigners—as they must at public hearings. Many designers make the mistake of using "technical language."

Sommer (1969) outlines two approaches that bring together these language differences: (1) using the semantic differential technique to study "connotative" meanings and (2) increasing sensitivity and correcting "the visual and emotional blindness of people so that they can present their needs and feelings in a form that others can appreciate" (Sommer, 1969: 161). These two approaches, however, presuppose (1) that the kinds of behavior relevant to planning/urban design are reducible to needs and articulable concepts and (2) that people are unable to express such concepts because of their emotional, nonrational, and connotative nature.

Current role and use of social data in design

Whether or not their assumptions are ever articulated, designers often work with a set of notions about how people do, will, or ought to behave in given environments and circumstances. Perin (1970: 20) points out, for example, that "economic determinism" and political factors are the "usual directive for the larger-scale environmental designer." In other words, political economy forms the institutional decision framework for planning/urban design.

Sommer (1969: 157) suggests that the appropriate role for social scientists in the design process is "design evaluation" rather than involvement "in the actual design of buildings." According to Sommer (1969: 158, 159), there are two major reasons for delay in using social-science data in planning/urban design. First, designers are reluctant to supplant their intuitions, and second, "the coalescing of individuals and professions with diverse training, viewpoints, and conceptual style" is very difficult. He stresses the need for "middlemen" acquainted "with the design field as well as with the social sciences to translate relevant behavioral data into terms meaningful to designers." However, Sommer does not explicitly define such "relevant data" and "meaningful terms" (1969: 158–159). Consider also:

> A broad, general, but crucial function that environmental psychology can and should have for the design professional is to make him aware of the implicit assumptions he makes about human behavior and experience when he does, in fact, create physical settings for specific purposes. In effect—like it or not—all design professionals are behavior oriented, at least on an implicit level, when they design a given space. The assumptions they make are by no means trivial. (Proshansky, 1974: 79)

It should be quite clear now that there are a number of problems surrounding the application and accommodation of social-science data and research in planning/urban design. The key problem centers on the how-to question and on such overriding factors as political economy and designer intuition and orientation. Thus, as Proshansky (1974: 79) states:

> The design profession can only begin to consider the implicit assumptions they make about people as refelected in the

spaces and places they create or design for them if it is realized that an inherent part of their task is to evaluate their design efforts.

Translation of human dimensions into planning/urban design

How we translate the human dimension into behavioral criteria for planning and design is the central practical issue. The problem of translation has been dealt with in a variety of ways. Some, such as Perin (1970) and Gutman (1972), have suggested that academic social research is as yet too far removed from the practical and concrete problems planners and designers face, and that, further, the nature of most social research is such that concrete guidelines or immutable criteria cannot readily be extracted and incorporated into planning/design solutions. For example, Sommer (1969) has observed that while performance criteria have been developed for certain design situations, such criteria typically address only a single dimension of a situation, while the issues addressed in practical planning and design require a multigoal approach.

> When a measure fits only a single dimension of a situation, the solution is not to reject all measurements but to develop measures for other aspects. Single item evaluation tends to encourage *criterion-directed performance,* which neglects important but unmeasured aspects of program success (Sommer, 1969: 164).

Sommer (1969) further suggests that planners/designers could avoid many other "translation" problems by extensive evaluation and research of implemented design/planning solutions formulated by social scientists.

Porter (1980) has a somewhat different assessment that provides us with another perspective on the complexity of the translation issue and reminds us of the error of associating "social conditions" too closely with "physical environments."

> Resulting social changes, either gentrification, prettification or abandonment, may seem counter to the original social objectives. Unexpected environmental deterioration downtown may be the result of well-intended commercial developments in the suburbs. As damaging as the unintended side effects may be, the very classification of areas as representing a social condition—shanties as the new poor—when the interaction between people and housing may be better described as systematic in

some other way, as opportunistic, or as random. (Porter, 1980: 47, 54)

It appears, however, that the answer to the proper role of the human dimension in planning and design lies somewhere between explanations that attribute difficulties to the inherent nature of the relation of social science to planning/design problems, and explanations that address the character of the applied research that actually has been conducted, by Zeisel (1981) and others. So-called "translation difficulties" reside in the very way a design problem is defined. Simply stated, different social-science approaches are suited to distinctly different types of problems. There is no overall approach to the human dimension of planning/design issues. Solutions are usually complex and involve social issues in a variety of ways and at many different scales.

It is scale that provides us with one of the keys to understanding the ways in which practitioners (as well as academics) can begin to incorporate social research into urban design practice. The concept of scale, as it is used here, allows us simultaneously to reference and coordinate the relevant physical and social contexts of design in even the most complex and "multiscaled" planning projects. Of course, there is really very little that is revolutionary about this use of the concept. It is derived from simple observation of the different design contexts addressed by existing social research. It should be noted that the bulk of such research focuses on the residence and neighborhood levels. Whyte's (1980) work on public urban spaces is, of course, an important exception, but the scale and context of the physical environments he studies still places his research at the relatively familiar and "contained" (small scale urban spaces, such as plazas) end of the urban-environment continuum. By comparison, the spatial arrangement and patterns of the city as a whole—that is, land use and district organizations, structural networks, and so on—are much larger and more complex (see, for example, Zannaras, 1976). Therefore, the question remains of how to incorporate human dimensions into the urban design and planning processes.

In Gutman's seminal paper, "Site Planning and Social Behavior" (1966), he emphasizes the critical distinction between the spatial quality of a site ("the site plan as a physical variable," a "non-social ... aspect") and "the activities, or social and psychological variables, which represent the complex human responses to the spatial features of a site" (Gutman, 1966: 104–105). The relation between the physical characteristics of a site and the kinds of behavior it influences must, Gutman asserts, be expressed in a series of statements that presupposes a "typology which classifies those features of the site which are especially relevant for discovering the impact of the plan or record of action" (1966: 105). However, no typology has emerged in the years since Gutman's paper was published. This is due to many reasons Gutman identified: "the question to be attended to . . . is not the importance of the existence of spatial environment, but rather whether differences in site plan features result in corresponding differences in behavior" (1966: 112). As a result, concepts and observations drawn from social-science research are often used indiscriminately to rationalize planning/design decisions, regardless of their scale and/or their role in the larger planning context. While we now know a great deal more about all aspects of the human dimension, we are not yet able to translate these findings into planning/urban design.

References

Appleyard, Donald; Lynch, Kevin; and Myer, J. Richard. *The View from the Road*. Cambridge, MA: The MIT Press, 1964.

Appleyard, Donald. "Why Buildings Are Known." *Environment and Behavior* 1 (1969): 131–156.

Appleyard, Donald. "Styles and Methods of Structuring a City." *Environment and Behavior* 2 (1970): 100–116.

Appleyard, Donald. *Planning a Pluralistic City*. Cambridge, MA: The MIT Press, 1976.

Appleyard, Donald. "The Environment as a Social Symbol: Within a Theory of Environmental Action and Perception." *Journal of the American Planning Association* 45, no. 2 (1979a): 143–153.

Arnstein, Sherry R. "A Ladder of Citizen Participation." *Journal of the American Institute of Planners*, July (1969): 216–224.

Chapin, F. Stuart, and Kaiser, Edward J. *Urban Land Use Planning*. Urbana, IL: University of Illinois Press, 1979.

Crane, David A. "The City Symbolic." *Journal of the American Institute of Planners* 26, November (1960): 280–292.

Cutler, Laurence S., and Cutler, Sherrie S. *Recycling Cities for People, the Urban Design Process*. New York: Van Nostrand Reinhold Company Inc., 1983.

Dakin, John. "An Evaluation of the Choice Theory of Planning." *Journal of the American Institute of Planners* 29, no. 2 (1963): 19–28.

Davidoff, Paul. "Advocacy and Pluralism in Planning." *Journal of the American Institute of Planners*, November (1965): 331–338.

Evans, Gary W. "Environmental Cognition." *Psychological Bulletin* 88, no. 2 (1980): 259–287.

Forester, John. "What Are Planners Up Against? Planning in the Face of Power." *The Bulletin of the Association of Collegiate Schools of Planning* 18, no. 2, Summer (1980): 1–7.

Gans, Herbert J. "Planning and Social Life: Friendship and Neighbor Relations in Suburban Communities." In Harold M. Proshanski, William H. Ihelson, and Leanne G. Rivilin, eds., *Environmental Psychology 2nd Edition*. New York: Holt, Rinehart and Winston, 1976.

Gil, Efraim, and Lucchesi, Enid. "Citizen Participation in Planning." In Frank

S. So, Israel Stollman, Frank Beal, and David S. Arnold, eds., *The Practice of Local Government Planning*. Washington, D.C.: International City Management Association and the American Planning Association, 1979.

Gottdiener, Mark. "Urban Semiotics." In John S. Pipkin, Mark LaGory, and Judith R. Blau, eds., *Remaking the City, Social Science Perspectives on Design*. Albany, NY: State University of New York Press, 1983.

Gutman, Robert. "Site Planning and Social Behavior." *The Journal of Social Issues* 22 (1966): 103–115.

Gutman, Robert. "The Questions Architects Ask." In Robert Gutman, ed., *People and Buildings*. New York: Basic Books, 1972.

Kaplan, Stephen. "Cognitive Maps, Human Needs and Designed Environment." In W. Preiser, ed., *Environmental Design Research*. Vol. 1. Stroudsburg, PA: Hutchinson and Ross, 1973.

Kaplan, Stephen. "An Informal Model for the Prediction of Preference." In Ervin H. Zube, Robert Brush, and Julius Fabos, eds., *Landscape Assessment: Values, Perception and Resources*. Stroudsburg, PA: Hutchinson and Ross, 1975.

Kaplan, Stephen, and Kaplan, Rachel, eds. *Humanscape: Environments For People*. Ann Arbor, MI: Ulrich's Books, Inc., 1982.

LaGory, Mark, and Pipkin, John. *Urban Social Space*. Belmont, CA: Wadsworth Publishing Company, 1981.

Lofland, L.H. "The Modern City: Spatial Ordering." In Harold M. Proshansky, William H. Ittelson, and Leanne G. Rivilin, eds., *Environmental Psychology*. 2nd ed. New York: Holt, Rinehart and Winston, 1976.

Lynch, Kevin. *The Image of the City*. Cambridge, MA: The MIT Press, 1960.

Meister, David, and Sullivan, Dennis. "A Further Study of the Use of Human Factors Information By Designers—Final Report." Canoga Park, CA: The Bunker-Ramo Corporation, 1967.

Milgram, Stanley. "The Experience of Living in Cities." In Harold M. Proshansky, William H. Ittelson, and Leanne G. Rivilin, eds., *Environmental Psychology*. 2nd ed. New York: Holt, Rinehart and Winston, 1976.

Moore, Gary T. "Knowing About Environmental Knowing: The Current State of Theory and Research on Environmental Cognition." *Environment and Behavior* 11 (1979): 33–70.

Moore, Gary T., and Golledge, Reginald, eds. *Environmental Knowing*. Stroudsburg, PA: Hutchinson and Ross, 1976.

Peattie, Lisa R. "Reflections on Advocacy Planning." *Journal of the American Institute of Planners*, March (1968): 80–88.

Perin, Constance. *With Man in Mind*. Cambridge, MA: The MIT Press, 1968.

Porter, William L. "Urban Design: A Gentle Critique."*Urban Design International* l, no. 2, January/February (1980): 47, 54, 56.

Porteous, J. Douglas. *Environment and Behavior*. Reading, MA: Addison-Wesley, 1977.

Proshansky, Harold M. "Environmental Psychology and the Design Profession." In Lang, Jon *et al.*, *Designing for Human Behavior*. Stroudsburg, PA: Hutchinson and Ross, 1974.

Proshansky, Harold M., Ittelson, William, and Rivilin, Leanne G., eds. *Environmental Psychology*. 2nd ed. New York: Holt, Rinehart and Winston, 1976.

Ramati, Raquel. *How To Save Your Own Street*. Garden City, NY: Dolphin Books, 1981.

Rapoport, Amos. *Human Aspects of Urban Form.* New York: Pergamon Press, 1977.

Rapoport, Amos. *The Meaning of the Built Environment.* Beverly Hills, CA: Sage Publications Inc., 1982.

Reiner, Janet S. *et al.* "Client Analysis and the Planning of Public Programs." *Journal of the American Institute of Planners,* November (1963): 270–282.

Sanoff, Henry. *Design with Community Participation.* New York: Van Nostrand Reinhold Company Inc., 1978.

Sommer, Robert. *Personal Space: The Behavioral Basis of Design.* Englewood Cliffs, NJ: Prentice Hall Inc., 1969.

Whyte, William H. *The Social Life of Small Urban Spaces.* Washington, D.C.: The Conservation Foundation, 1980.

Zannaras, Georgia. "The Relation Between Cognitive Structure and Urban Form." In Moore, Gary T., and Colledge, Reginald G., eds., *Environmental Knowing Theories, Research and Methods.* Stroudsburg, PA: Hutchinson and Ross, 1976.

Zeisel, John. "Fundamental Values in Planning with the Non-Paying Client." In Jon T. Lang *et al.,* eds., *Designing for Human Behavior.* Stroudsburg, PA: Hutchinson and Ross, 1974.

Zeisel, John. *Inquiry By Design.* Belmont, CA: Brooks/Cole, 1981.

The dimension of natural environment

CHAPTER 4

UNTIL RECENTLY, planning and urban design practice rarely incorporated environmental concerns into city development efforts. While there are some hopeful signs to indicate that this trend is changing, as in such cities as Medford, Massachusetts; Woodland and Austin, Texas; and Denver, Colorado, on the whole, the lack of environmental focus of city design practice still holds true.

At least three major reasons have been put forth to account for the failure of planners/urban designers to incorporate environmental considerations into their work. The first explanation concerns the essentially nonphysical nature of most plans. A second is that apparently no straightforward methodology exists to enable practitioners to integrate environmental issues into comprehensive and/or master plans. Finally, many critics have noted that planning studies, even when they attempt to incorporate environmental factors, focus inappropriately on the natural environment rather than on the relationship between the built and natural environments. Each of these points will be discussed in turn.

PHYSICAL DEVELOPMENT PLANS

The recent call by Lynch (1980), among others (Raymond 1978), for a return to old-fashioned physical planning has been spurred in large part by a growing dissatisfaction with the two traditional approaches to urban physical planning, the master plan and the comprehensive plan. Another contributing factor has been that community planning in urban areas has been decidedly developer-oriented:

> the entire orientation of community planning is directed towards the developer's attitudes, desires and business interests; in the overall process, the real decision maker is the market analyst. All too often, market analysis is the first and major step of planning in order to ascertain the profit maximizing potential for the developer. The role of planning in this circumstance is to depict the market in three-dimensional form. (Shirvani, 1983: 20)

In the absence of a well-thought-out physical plan, environmental issues, however pressing, are extremely difficult to identify, define, and, where necessary, to ameliorate. "Policy-rich" comprehensive plans simply do not come to terms with specific environmental problems except in reference to specific physical design conditions or proposals. As planner T. J. Kent (1964: 91) has argued, physical plans should focus on physical development and, at the same time, relate major physical design proposals to basic policies of a plan. Likewise, Beal and Hollander (1979: 53–54) see the physical development plan as a "guide to decision-making." But where, exactly, do environmental concerns fit in? A number of planners/urban designers—among them, Burchell and Sternlieb (1978; especially in sections by McHarg, Hoppenfield, Krumbolz, Cogger, Linner)—have stressed the importance of both the physical plan and environmental issues. Elsewhere, I have taken this emphasis a step further and have suggested that physical plans for cities should include a "comprehensive geographic information base" that can form "a framework for other policy elements such as housing, transportation, open space, and urban design.":

> Community goals change over time as they are influenced by different citizen's groups, interest groups and political decision-making processes. But the physical city and land on which it is situated are subject to a variety of natural environmental factors: soil, geology, hydrology, vegetation, climate, energy and many more. Forming a base plan with a comprehensive geo-

graphic information base not only directs planning efforts towards betterment of public health and safety, but it also leads it toward more rational goal-setting. In other words, it is time that emphasis be placed on more comprehensive and realistic environmental impact studies which produce a community physical plan as their product. (Shirvani, 1983: 21)

ENVIRONMENTAL PLANNING IN URBAN DESIGN—PROCESS ISSUES

There is little disagreement about the importance of environmental studies and planning in urban design; problems arise, however, with the manner in which these concerns are integrated into planning systems. There are a number of such systems in use by planning agencies across the country, but very few agencies are capable of monitoring natural factors in the urban environment (Spirn, 1980). For example, in Fairfax County, Virginia, the Urban Development Information System (UDIS) has only recently begun to include environmental factors (Wilson, Tabas, and Henneman, 1979; Hysom *et al.*, 1974).

Two recent exceptions to this trend should, however, be noted. The Houston–Galveston Area Council's Environmental Decision Assistance System (EDAS), for example, uses ecological modeling to monitor growth. Their data base incorporates such socioeconomic factors as population and housing characteristics as well as wage and employment data and new construction activity along with such ecological information as water resource data (quality, supply and consumption, sewage treatment permit records, wastewater, surface and subsurface hydrological and drainage conditions, and so on) and environmental deficiencies:

The system combines an input-output model for the region, a regional land use simulation model; and several interrelated submodels, including ones for water supply, Galveston Bay water quality, drainage and flood control, and solid waste (Wilson, Tabas, and Henneman, 1979: 220).

Other examples of environmental monitoring systems on a regional scale include San Diego County's manual access system and the air and water quality programs run by the Environmental Protection Agency (EPA) and the National Water Quality Surveillance System (Wilson, Tabas, and Henneman, 1979).

In a recent proposal to the EPA, McHarg (in Holden 1977: 56) argued for a "supraregional" comprehensive approach to environmental planning:

a national ecological inventory to collect all the information that describes the natural systems of the United States as well as the interaction of natural and human systems. The country would be divided into 34 natural regions—prairies, coastal plan (*sic*), the Rockies, and so forth—and each would have a regional laboratory. The information would all be centralized and coordinated in a national environmental institute. . . . Any party who wanted to interfere with any system would have to employ the available data to predict the consequences of planned actions. But, says McHarg, EPA "hasn't paid any attention to it. It wasn't even published." (Holden, 1977: 156)

Two continuing problems that prevent the direct integration of environmental data into planning information systems—whether the system is computerized and sophisticated or basic and manual—can be traced to two essential deficiencies in the scientific approach to the study of man's interaction with natural systems. First, as McHarg has often emphasized, this research typically underemphasizes man's alteration of nature as a chief factor in any consideration of natural processes. Secondly, there continues to be an arbitrary division of the environment for purposes of study, with a resulting lack of attention to environmental interrelationships and totality (Detwyler, 1971).

URBAN DESIGN AND RELATIONSHIPS BETWEEN NATURAL AND BUILT ENVIRONMENTS

A third and final explanation of the limited role environmental considerations have played in planning lies as much with the character of the data collected as with the way it has or has not been integrated into the planning processes. The problem seems to be that even where extensive environmental data on resources, conditions, deficiencies, vulnerabilities, and so on has been collected, it exists more or less in a vacuum. With very few exceptions, modeling routines rarely profile relationships between the built and natural environments.

The fragmentation of planning responsibility, which results in ineffective intergovernmental and interagency coordination and the failure to use implementation strategies, has been frequently cited as contributing to this lack of comprehensiveness (Wilson, Tabas, and Henneman, 1979; Shirvani, 1981). Nor can the definitional problem be underestimated; until planners and planning processes incorporate conceptual frameworks for identifying and evaluating environmental issues, the role of natural processes in urban design/planning will continue to be underestimated. In this chapter, various elements of the natural dimension will be examined, and some approaches to and examples of their incorporation into the urban design process will be discussed. The purpose is to acquaint the reader with some basic findings relating to the effect of urban development on natural processes. It is to be hoped that this discussion will promote among planners/urban designers a new devotion to the preservation of the natural environment.

Urban climate and air quality

It seems rather obvious to observe that the characteristics of a climate tend to augment or diminish the natural properties present in an area. However, this penomenon is so vital to comfort conditions in a city—and so often ignored—that it deserves emphasis here.

Chandler (1976) sets the determinants of climate as air flow, water balance, heat balance, and air pollution. Even without further amplification at this point in our discussion, it is easy to see that urbanization, its physical/spatial form and arrangement, would affect all three factors. We can expect to find an increase in airborne suspensions, mean and minimum temperatures, fog, and level of precipitation with a corresponding decrease in intensity of solar radiation, wind velocity, relative humidity, and evaporation (Landsberg, 1969).

Rydell and Schwarz (1968) found that man-made changes in topography may be employed to effect changes in temperature and wind speed; that microclimate is influenced by orientation, building materials, and soil; and that the arrangement of physical form as well as the presence of pollutants are factors in air pollution problems. One always has to be certain of the effects of alteration of the urban environment before changes are made.

Increased application of climatology to urban planning/design will provide information on ambient atmospheric conditions as a basis for building climatology design decisions, data allowing for proper design of urban renewal areas, and input for the design of new cities and optimal land-use zoning (Chandler, 1976).

Stuttgart, West Germany, uses comprehensive urban planning/design to help preserve and promote a healthy climate (Kaufman, 1967); its success has been an inspiration for the "greening of Dayton," Ohio (NLC, 1980). Stuttgart has been involved in this kind of planning since 1932 (Loessner, 1978), and there has been an urban climatologist on the city staff for more than forty years (Bartenstein, 1979). In addition, Stuttgart, taking advantage of the necessity for a massive rebuilding program after World War II, incorporated into the planning process natural conditions

that mesh design with the environment, including sidewalks shaded with awnings and trees; retention of water on building roofs to cool the atmosphere through evaporation; use of increased vegetation to absorb pollutants and cool the atmosphere. Modification of building heights to avoid obstruction of major air corridors is also under study. (NLC, 1980: 1)

The main thrust of the program is prevention of air pollution, but general improvement of the environment from the standpoint of health as well as beautification has also been achieved. A principal effect has been a reduction in the heat island phenomenon (USDI, 1982: 1). Likewise:

- Both micro- and macro-level considerations are involved ...
- A major concern is ... moving more air through the city. ...
- Pedestrian walkway(s) with numerous plantings ... add oxygen and encourage evaporation ...
- Where wind velocity and frequency are insufficient to flush the air, oil and coal burning are not permitted, natural gas is used for cooking, and heat and hot water are provided from water heated by city incinerators and stored in collectors. (Loessner, 1978: 35–36)

All efforts are coordinated by a Chemical Investigation Office, whose official function—limited to "review and comment"—has not restricted the office's actual influence (Loessner, 1978: 35). The office is often consulted early in the project planning process, and recently and industry that would have been a major polluter opted against a Stuttgart location—a further indication of the office's power (Loessner, 1978).

The history of pollution monitoring dates back to the late 1940s, when computer modeling of the atmosphere and distribution of pollutants was pioneered. In the 1960s, pollution meteorology and supporting sciences advanced with a concomitant increase in knowledge about air pollution control techniques and the effects of pollution on man, the biosphere, and materials. There was a parallel increase in public awareness of environmental problems. Major field studies were conducted in the 1970s: METROMEX (Metropolitan Meteorological Experiment), SURE (Sulfate Regional Experiment), MAP 35 (Multistate Atmospheric Power Production Pollution Study), and CAP (Chicago Area Program) (Heidorn, 1978).

Numerous meteorological studies have resulted in the compilation of recommendations for improving city air quality. In some representative air pollution studies, researchers learned the following:

1. A wind tunnel study of gaseous pollutants in city street canyons showed that "isolated structures can cause favorable mixing of pollution downwind"; however, "very high concentrations exist in the immediate leeward vicinity of such a building" (Wedding et al., 1977: 557).

2. "The combination of favorable geometry and higher dilution velocities may bring pollution levels down to existing air quality standards" (Wedding et al., 1977: 557).

3. Air pollution can have detrimental effects on the health of the

general population. "Persons engaging in recreational activities near concentrations of automobile traffic are probably subjecting themselves to particularly high levels of air pollution. The more vigorous the... activity, the more hazardous [is] the effect of the pollution (Everett, 1974: 83)."

4. An analysis of 500 air samples for carbon monoxide present during normal urban life revealed that "local traffic density... accounts for 63% of variance." And "attenuation... from busy streets is rapid" (Godin *et al.*, 1972: 305). They also observed that "smoking can bring indoor concentrations above the 24 hour permitted levels" (Godin *et al.*, 1972: 305).

Clearly, there is a need to integrate city air quality management programs into a regional planning/urban design process and to define working relationships among agencies at the federal, state, and local levels (Roberts *et al.*, 1975). A prime successful example of this integration is the Stuttgart urban design plan, which has developed a system of open space connecting downtown to the outlying forest areas, providing necessary air movement into the city to exchange fresh air with polluted downtown air.

Efforts in Dayton, Ohio, to study and reduce the impact of summer temperatures in its urban center present an interesting example of an American city's attempt to devise a comprehensive plan to deal with an air quality issue. This study, which involved cooperation between the city of Dayton, the United States Forest Service Research Office, several universities, and other public and private agencies, aimed at researching "the nature of the city's urban forest resources, [and] how these resources affect the city's natural environment and quality of life" (Rowntree and Sanders, n.d.). The study included three phases:

(1) Determine the characteristics of the urban forest in terms of its horizontal and vertical distributions and its occurrence within the city's land uses, and evaluate existing knowledge of urban forest influences.
(2) Evaluate the significance of the urban forest as an agent of environmental influence and modification...
(3) Determine the city institutional context within which urban forestry now exists and evaluate how its position might be improved in the city government. (Rowntree and Sanders, n.d.)

As a result of the study, Dayton, Ohio, now has a detailed urban tree program and plan, and is implementing a plan for such open spaces as streets, parks, parking lots, and plazas.

While such examples are quite rare, there is growing interest, and several cities—Milwaukee and Cincinnati among them—have already taken steps toward it.

Solar energy and solar access

Since the 1970s, there has been considerable debate about the nature and extent of our energy problems (Miller, Jr., 1980). There is little disagreement, however, over the economic impact of the crisis. As an energy policy report for Portland, Oregon, points out, "The price of energy is going to go up, whether we have to dig deeper, transport faster, or take elaborate measures to protect ourselves from environmental harm" (Portland, 1978: 2).

Another important realization has been that the energy crisis, although national in scope, is essentially a local problem. Local economies are directly affected by energy costs in the form of jobs, costs and types of services provided by government, and, of course, household expenditures (Portland, 1978). Coupled with this recognition of the local impacts of energy economics has been realization of an increasing need to take conservation measures at the local level. National energy policy is essentially concerned with domestic oil production, nuclear power, mandating energy efficient automobiles, and so on—not with cities, which consume some 60 percent of the energy used in the United States (Ridgeway, 1979; Portland, 1978; San Diego, 1977).

Miller identifies three basic approaches to dealing with the energy crisis: (1) develop new energy sources, (2) waste less energy, and (3) use less energy. Acting on the latter two alternatives, he suggests, is best for the United States and represents the largest potential source of new energy (Miller, Jr., 1980). When we consider available resources, as well as inherent energy potentials and requirements of cities, it is clear that a focus on conservative strategies, particularly passive solar and energy transfer, is an appropriate and feasible focus for planning/urban design.

The role and importance of solar energy in planning/urban design was rediscovered after the so-called energy crisis of the early 1970s. It has been almost a decade now since we began experimenting with efficient use of this important natural resource. As a result, it is now quite apparent that planning/urban design efforts can and should incorporate solar considerations into urban environments.

In general, energy conservation measures can be taken at various levels, starting with federal and state legislation, through city public policy, and finally down to requirements for the design of industrial buildings. In the past decade, federal, state, and local governments have adopted a variety of policies concerning energy conservation. Many cities have incorporated an "energy element" into their master plan or general plan. Examples are Seattle, Washington; Davis, California; Northglenn, Colorado; and Hartford, Connecticut (Ridgeway, 1979). The measures at the city level usually center on conservation choices and implementation strategies within industrial, residential, commercial, and transportation sectors, as well as in government and land use planning (Portland, 1977).

But where solar energy is concerned, few cities have developed extensive control measures that would help them incorporate solar issues into their planning/urban design process. Even where cities have developed general guidelines for the incorporation and use of solar energy, benefits have been unclear. There are a number of reasons that can be cited for these disappointing results. Simplistic guidelines, inconsistencies between solar design guidelines and other existing guidelines, and inappropriate implementation strategies seem to account for many shortcomings in solar planning/urban design. The root problem is that most available solar guidelines and control measures focus on new residential and suburban development; very few focus on existing built environments or infill developments in urban contexts. It is obvious that urban environments are typically much more complex than suburban residential settings and require more study, analysis, and, of course, more sophisticated guidelines.

Not surprisingly, the most promising developments in urban energy planning and design have been concentrated in two major areas: passive solar access, which is concerned with (1) the amount and quality of light available (within buildings, along streets and public spaces, and so on), (2) microclimate as affected by solar radiation available to urban spaces (and in conjunction with such related issues as wind patterns), and (3) reflected light from buildings; the second major emphasis has been energy potential or transfers, which encompass (1) provisions for solar access that ensure or promote energy self-sufficiency through active solar devices (with appropriate modification of building codes), (2) recommendations for conservation measures (for example, insulation), and (3) "heat-transfer" planning that coordinates sharing energy byproducts of urban environments between buildings and public transportation systems, for example.

Energy self-sufficiency through combined programs of energy audits, educational programs, such economic incentives as loans, and building code revisions are currently under way in several cities. Solar access and infill are also important elements in energy-conscious neighborhood revitalization in Knoxville, Tennessee, and Portland, Oregon, where building scale and setback guidelines have been used along with solar and energy conservation retrofitting.

Comprehensive energy planning on a community scale is not widely practiced as yet. Planned communities, naturally, have been better prepared to address energy issues. Davis, California, which moved to curb growth in the late 1960s, has incorporated aggressive energy conservation measures into its building code. A public education program, an extensive system of bicycle paths, and a landscaping program for shading streets has further raised energy-saving consciousness (Ridgeway, 1979; Davis, 1977). *Solar Access, A Guide for California Communities* (1980) is a well-developed guidebook and a model for other communities that wish to study the physical design aspect of solar energy and develop regulatory means for both urban and suburban developments. Guidelines not only help analysis, but rather more specifically provide direction for zoning, subdivision regulations, trees and landscaping, and solar access in environmental impact and solar access covenants and easements (Jaffe, 1980) (fig. 4-1, 4-2, and 4-3).

The tasks and role of energy planning in urban design, however, are perhaps better illustrated by the strategies employed in some urban areas than by the opportunities and potentials that can be found in newer planned communities and suburban areas. The mitigation, or incremental, measures that have to be adopted by these older, more established cities are exemplified in an important study undertaken by Dayton, Ohio (discussed in the section of this chapter on *urban climate and air quality)*. As Greenberg notes, the energy efficiency that can be achieved through urban design will be different for different types of cities:

> Some cities have little developable land, and therefore, energy efficiency achieved only through the "retrofit" of the existing environment. Some developing cities can use regulatory tools to achieve energy-efficient design without eroding their development potential, while other cities, "hungry" for more development, can consider only an incentive approach. Some cities will have a great deal of latitude to use creative tools, while others will be severely circumscribed because of restrictive state-enabling laws. (Greenberg, 1981: 6)

The tools and techniques for energy planning/urban design implementation will vary according to the factors cited above as well as the focus of a city's efforts (for example, on existing versus new development) and their economic resources. Accordingly, Greenberg (1981) has identified four major categories of urban design strategies: regulatory, incentive, information transfer, and active project participation.

1. *Regulatory Strategies.* The regulatory strategies that promote energy-related issues are largely directed to new development and rehabilitation projects and derive their authority from government's responsibility to provide for the public health, safety, and welfare (Greenberg, 1981: 7). Typical instruments, some of which have already been discussed, include provisions within building codes, urban design controls, and zoning ordinances. In some cases, these tools are combined with incentives or development bonuses and may be used singly or in combination with prescriptive or performance standards. Prescriptive standards "establish minimum or maximum

A. Identify major objects that could cast shadows on a site plan.

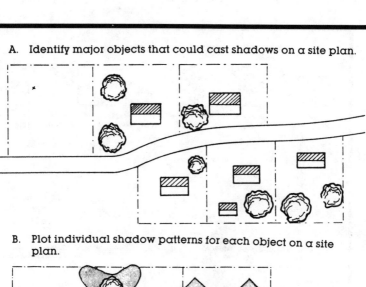

B. Plot individual shadow patterns for each object on a site plan.

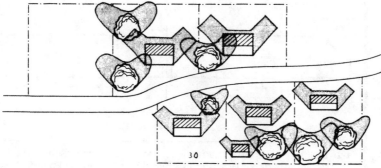

C. Conflicts between areas, or areas where shading is no problem.

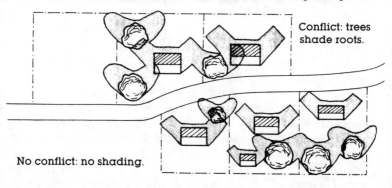

Conflict: trees shade roots.

No conflict: no shading.

4-1: Illustration of solar access analysis by shadow pattern (Source: Solar Access, A Guidebook for California Communities, California Energy Commission).

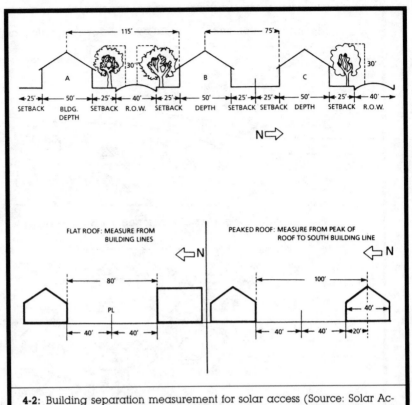

4-2: Building separation measurement for solar access (Source: Solar Access, A Guidebook for California Communities, California Energy Commission).

characteristics of various components of building" (Greenberg, 1981: 7). The *California Solar Access Guidebook* identified five ways in which traditional "euclidian" zoning could be modified to pro-tect solar access: (1) "reduce maximum allowable building heights," (2) reduce frontage requirements for lots along east-west streets to create deeper lots, thereby increasing solar access, (3) "decrease side-yard requirements and increase front- and rear-yard require-ments for lots on east-west streets," (4) increase south lot areas through zero-lot-line zoning, and (5) regulate building height with "bulk plane provi-sions" in place of "straight height provisions" (Jaffe, 1980: 54).

Performance-oriented standards are alternative mechanisms to pre-scriptive codes. With performance-oriented standards, a building's energy budget may be established through computer techniques that take account of the building's projected use along with the number of heating and cooling degree-days. The actual form of the building, however, is not directed by the standard; rather, the acceptability of a

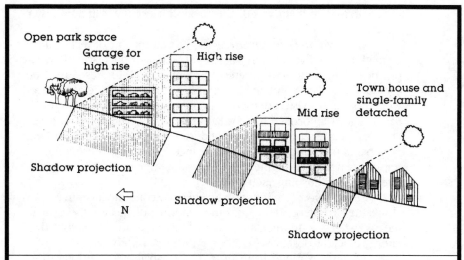

4-3: Solar access analysis for zoning (Source: Solar Access, A Guidebook for California Communities, California Energy Commission).

proposed structure is based on an analysis of its predicted energy budget (Greenberg, 1981).

An example of a performance standard for solar access is provided by California's Solar Shade Control Act, which sets a limit of only 10 percent collector shading allowable from 10 A.M. to 2 P.M. on any day. Once again, the means that may be used to achieve this standard are left open (Jaffe, 1980: 77; California, 1978). As Greenberg (1981) points out, a drawback to performance standard is that local code enforcement agencies rarely have the tools or expertise necessary to understand these solar analyses.

2. *Incentive Strategies* Incentive-based programs aimed at energy efficiency in urban environments can be directed either at new or existing development. One widely used incentive is the development bonus, which rewards energy-efficient components (for example solar hot water systems, extra insulation) that are beyond the requirements of the energy code. The efficiency of such components may be measured either by prescriptive or performance standards (Greenberg, 1981).

Prescriptive components that list bonus items are the easiest energy practices to identify. Boulder, Colorado, also has an incentive policy of issuing building permits on a competitive points system earned through the use of either solar or energy conservation techniques (Greenberg, 1981). Performance approaches are, by comparison, more difficult to identify and have a lower public profile. Sophisticated energy-management systems, for example, may call for design review expertise that exceeds the capabilities of the staff administering incentives.

3. *Information Transfer Strategies.* Dissemination of technical information is one area where most cities can introduce sound energy practices into their communities (Greenberg, 1981). Residential energy audit services and public education programs (neighborhood workshops and so on) are two common means used. Davis, California; San Diego, California; and Portland, Oregon, are among the many cities that have developed public education programs as major components of their energy policies. The incentives in such programs are implicit, whether to augment existing energy measures or to generate interest in establishing such policies.

4. *Active Project Participation Strategies.* Economic incentives used alongside or independently of other energy policies are the primary means whereby municipalities can become directly involved in energy-efficient design (Greenberg, 1981). A variety of tax-incentive tools, which can range from property-tax abatement periods to tax relief, are being used. Even where development pressures are weak and where development bonuses provide no real incentives, tax measures that are, in effect, public subsidies can establish effective public-private partnerships. Loan programs offer another means of providing for enery considerations in design and development. The federal Urban Development Action Grant program's low interest loans to finance projects that might otherwise not be built is perhaps one of the most widely used means (Greenberg, 1981).

Finally, the area of public-private partnerships for promoting energy policies seems to rely on state initiatives. In 1978, for example, a number of bills were passed by the California State Legislature to promote solar commercialization, including measures that would allow banks and savings and loan institutions to make more generous solar loans and increased Cal-Vet loan ceilings to provide for solar equipment installations (California, 1978).

The legal and financial mechanisms discussed above illustrate some of the potentials and problems for cities trying to incoporate solar or other environmental dimensions into their urban design and planning efforts. Comprehensive environmental analysis is still the preliminary step. Moreover, model ordinances, criteria, and techniques can be drawn from the experience of other cities; but in each case, these elements must be tailored to the individual city's environmental conditions, planning framework, economic setting, and resources, including technical expertise.

Urban geology and soils

A city's geological and soil problems are not always as obvious as a house sliding down a hillside on a layer of mud or a homeowner learning that his home is sited on a former hazardous waste dump or a developer discovering that his project cannot be placed in a certain area because of flood-plain regulations. Likewise, the solutions are not as simple as a blanket disapproval of building in "hazardous areas" or bringing in topsoil to improve poor soil. However, these examples do serve to underscore the truism that it is "not only what the surface of the ground looks like but what lies beneath the surface" that is essential knowledge for good planning/urban design (Legget, 1973: 49).

It is difficult to understand why geological considerations have not received proper attention or evoked much interest. Why is not geological information gathering coordinated into a system or format useful to urban designers/planners, as is information on buried utility lines? In Switzerland, central files on subsurface conditions are maintained on all major cities. Similarly, *The Geofond*, a Prague geological index, is constantly improved and expanded. The French Geological Institute also maintains detailed records. Moscow, too, publishes the procedures and results of test drillings (Legget, 1973). Some day, perhaps, gathering this type of information will become as commonplace in the United States as the mandatory boundary survey of property. Indeed, even now, in some cities, no construction may proceed without core samples.

On the whole, incorporation of geological and soil data into planning activities in the United States has been infrequent at best. Two early exceptions are the regional planning efforts in Washington, D.C., and the San Francisco Bay area that took place in the 1950s. Although influential, McHarg's (1969) pioneering efforts to incorporate geological inventorying and analysis into regional planning are not widely emulated, particularly in the practice of urban design.

What are the geological issues that ought to be of concern to urban design? Certainly, soils and geological stability are issues that have enormous impact on urban planning, development, and infrastructure maintenance in many parts of the United States. Landslides, for example, are responsible for greater damage than is generally recognized. In southern California alone, landslides have been found "responsible for the bulk of material moved from valley sides and from sea cliffs" (Leighton, 1976: 209). Consequently, as Fleming (Fleming *et al.*, 1978) has pointed out, reduction of landslides and losses from landslides are both technical and administrative problems. The kinds of geological data needed that could help achieve geologic stability of these slopes involve a systematic planning and reconnaissance program that would include detailed mapping, subsurface explorations, and ingrading inspections (Leighton, 1976).

The next step in controlling losses caused by landslides requires that the data be integrated into a solid, environmentally based land use plan. Such a plan might, for instance, identify areas that have failed, periodically quantify existing (that is, present) conditions, and disseminate this information to the public as well as appropriate agencies that regulate land use (Fleming *et al.*, 1978).

One of the best American examples of a successful landslide reduction program is the one in Los Angeles. Experience there shows that it is possible to reduce damage from landslides and gain community interest in the issues during and immediately after a landslide. The principal elements involved in achieving a successful program to reduce landslides are

- able/concerned local government
- solid base of technical information about hazards and a technical community able to apply and build on the information
- a citizenry that, on the whole, recognizes the need for appropriate regulation
(Fleming *et al.*, 1978: 21)

Seismic and fault hazards represent another important category of geological information relevant to urban design. The March 1964 earthquake in Alaska drew public attention to these geological processes and the devastating effect they can have on entire cities (Dobrovolny and Schmoll, 1975). Yet recent studies have shown that Alaskan geological hazards may still be underestimated. A continuing problem appears to be the gap between inventorying and surveying efforts by geologists and the implementation of those results in establishing land use policies. One estimate suggests that it currently takes as long as two years to gather pertinent earth science information and to formulate suitable land use policies to minimize seismic hazards. Luckily, a number of interim policies can be adopted. For example, tax deduction for property owners whose land is known to be subject to possible ground failure can be considered (Nichols and Buchanan-Banks, 1978). Also, when a planner is supplied with background studies by which to assess fault hazards, easements similar to scenic easements may be a possible solution for reducing losses (Mader and Crowder, 1969). Other possible solutions are density regulation, adoption of building code provisions appropriate to areas with different ground shaking characteristics, and strict enforcement of hazardous building abatement ordinances (Mader and Crowder, 1969).

Flood plain management is another frequently encountered geological issue of concern in urban design. Schneider and Goddard (1978: 38) have noted, for example, that "there is an extremely wide variation in the extent of flood plains in urbanized areas." Even further complicating this and related planning problems is the fact that natural and man-made modifying forces on the land can obscure subsurface conditions that would indicate a flood plain, landslide potential, and so on (Legget, 1973).

Landfills are particularly troublesome. For one thing, soil problems over former landfills may be acute. Not only can there be subsidence and poorly drained areas because of improperly compacted refuse and other fill, but leaching out of chemicals and formation of gases can also occur, causing ground and air pollution. Historically, landfills have destroyed valuable natural areas, have been established with little thought to future use, and have been inadequately restored (Parry and Brummage, 1981). It has been found, for example, that former landfills have a higher temperature than undisturbed earth nearby, that methane and other gases they produce may destroy root systems—resulting in a poor-growth area—and that 1.5 meters of soil is needed to cover the fill properly. Ideally, refuse should not be placed more than two meters deep (Parry and Brummage, 1981). At a minimum, mapping of such features as landfills, faults, and flood plains and the availability of technical experts to interpret the significance of these features are criteria for integrating geological factors into planning/urban design.

Urban hydrology and water quality

"Of all land use changes affecting the hydrology of an area, urbanization is by far the most forceful" (Leopold, 1978: 31). Wolman describes provision of "an adequate water supply and an effective disposal of sewage and the control of air pollution" as "metabolic problems of a city." He also reminds us that "farms, factories and cities frequently draw water from a community supply" (Wolman, 1965: 20–21).

The kinds of hydrological conditions and problems that affect urban areas vary from locale to locale, but, in general, land use affects the hydrology of an area in four ways. First, it affects peak flow characteristics. Second, urban land uses typically increase total runoff. Third, urbanization has profound effects on water quality. Finally, it has impact on hydrological amenities in general (Leopold, 1978).

The increased imperviousness of urban surfaces causes increasing flood peaks during storm periods and decreasing low flows between storms (Leopold, 1978). The storm sewer system itself alters the runoff pattern (Thomas and Schneider, 1978). Further, too many cities do not have separate storm and waste water systems, thereby complicating water disposal. There are also a number of indirect, or secondary, water-related problems in urban areas that Thomas and Schneider (1978: 66) have termed "water nuisances." They are the result of surface revision from (1) excavation—walls of land may slide because certain clays become lubricated by rain; (2) materials that do not reveal their hazardous condition until wet; (3) excavation for construction materials that may penetrate the water table, creating pools that are dangerous play areas; (4) construction that increases sediment yield (Thomas and Schneider, 1978).

In fact, soil erosion and sediment deposition are especially critical problems in urban areas and create as much "environmental blight" as badly paved and littered streets, dilapidated buildings, pollution, and so on. Sediment, also the result of natural conditions, has direct and indirect effects on streams that may be a part of—or remote from —the urban environment. It is especially difficult to recognize and solve sediment-related problems because they may be subject to political and institutional constraints (Guy, 1976). The consequence of this is a lack of computation of the costs of sediment problems; often, estimates are relied upon (Guy, 1976).

Sediment-related problems include:

- public health
- alteration of graded areas of construction sites
- reduced infiltration and groundwater and increased runoff
- reduced flow to or plugging of natural and man-made chemicals
- closed drains
- aesthetically damaged streams
- increased floodwater damage
- increased water treatment costs
- bridge or culvert failure
- increased maintenance costs for streets and other public-use areas
- most importantly, general deterioration of the total environment
  (Guy, 1976)

Because sediment is often a part of a complex environmental problem, many other sediment problems go unnoticed even though they may be environmentally significant (Guy, 1976). Guy suggests that steps to achieve control of urban sediment include public program adjustment (including setting policy toward potential problems), erosion control measures, and education of the public and urban officials.

The Los Angeles area's attempts to control sediment "have involved the construction of numerous 'debris' basins on small streams draining the steep foothill areas" (Guy, 1976: 329). Montgomery County, Maryland, was "the first county to adopt a Sediment Control Program which requires approval of a subdivision development plan by the Department of Public Works which, in turn, is in consultation with the Soil Conservation Service" (Guy, 1976: 330).

Storm-water/sewage-system separation is another important hydrological issue and a pollution problem that many cities face (Environmental Quality, 1977; Environmental Quality, 1979). Urbanization seriously affects groundwater in the East and Midwest. Who can forget the sight of an urban reservoir like that in Greenwich, Connecticut, reduced to a few small pools of water by drought? Another indication of this problem is the ordinances of some Long Island, New York, communities mandating that water drawn from special wells for air-conditioning purposes must be returned to the water table directly rather than through the sewer system. The most pronounced effects of urbanization on groundwater are in the semiarid Rocky Mountain and western states (Hamilton and Owens, 1978).

Through creative land use planning, hydrology problems can be avoided. A new sewage treatment plant can enhance nearby recreational opportunities *and* improve water quality. In Barrington, Rhode Island, a pumping station located next to an outdoor hockey rink was designed to form bleachers at little extra cost. In Monticello, Arkansas, an old water treatment facility is now a city park with a pool and adventure playground (Environmental Quality, 1980).

The "natural drainage system" that has been developed in Woodlands, Texas, protects the community from flooding and provides high-quality water and it costs much less than traditional storm sewers (Spirn, 1980: 102). Woodlands is a new community developed by the Woodlands Development Corporation of Houston, which called on Wallace McHarg Roberts and Todd (WMRT) of Philadelphia to complete the first phase, land planning and design, of the project. The WMRT report for phase one (1973: 3–4) sets as policy:

- [Disturb] the natural hydrologic regimen, both surface and subterranean . . . as little as possible.
- [Maintain] drainage ways and swales in an undisturbed state, [allowing only specified modifications and reducing] peak stream flow during heavy storms [and promoting] percolation of surface runoff during light storms.
- [Develop] a natural drainage system modified to impede water flow over permeable soils [to]

  - promote soil water recharge at the surface
  - reduce runoff
  - control erosion and siltation
  - protect large areas of vegetation in uncleared drainage ways
  - reduce costs over those of a conventional drainage system

Spirn's comments indicate how well this Woodlands' water control system works (figs. 4-4, 4-5).

WMRT (1973: 6) also calls for reuse of waste water, but WMRT also acknowledges the difficulty of balancing in- and outflow in ways that

Normal Solution

Objective is to grade and swale land to facilitate rapid removal of storm water from site.

- Maximizes runoff and erosion problems
- Maximizes vegetation removal and cost of reinstatement
- Minimizes ground-water recharge
- Maximizes cost of drainage system

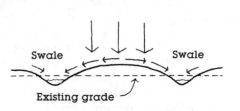

Woodland Proposal

Objective is to impede water flow over permeable soils by minimal impounding.

- Maximizes recharge and minimizes runoff
- Minimizes erosion and siltation problems
- Minimizes vegetation removal
- Minimizes cost of drainage system

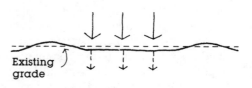

General Drainage Principles

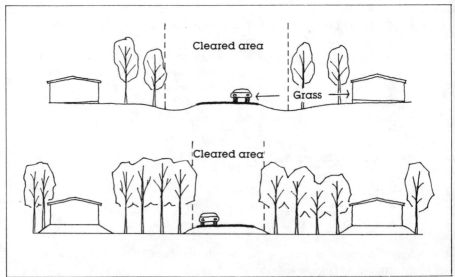

Drainage Solution on Permeable Soils

4-4: Woodland, TX: general drainage principles and drainage solutions for permeable soils (Source: WMRT, Philadelphia, PA).

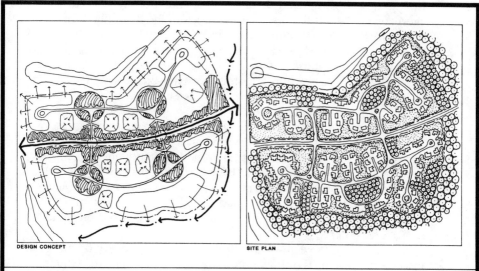

DESIGN CONCEPT

SITE PLAN

4-5: Woodland, TX: example of a design concept and site plan for a cluster residential development (Source: WMRT, Philadelphia, PA).

are "acceptable from either an environmental or a political point of view." The 1983 floods in the Colorado River Basin are proof of this last statement on a much larger scale.

Indeed, planning/urban design for a waterway becomes much more urgent when a flood hazard is already in existence. The Corte Madera Creek area in Marin County, California, had a serious flood for three days in December 1955. This gave the researchers, Royston, Hanamoto, Beck, and Abey (with the assistance of six other architectural and engineering firms), some specific data that they used in a 1977 study. Peak and hundred-year flows could be computed, and methods of controlling these flows determined. Local drainage needed improvement without storm water backup. Special techniques were needed for use during construction and for the long-term. Nine alternative approaches were developed, and a community forum was held to determine resident preferences. The criteria held to be most important were:

- saving vegetation and trees
- providing flood protection from the Creek
- preserving Creek ecology and character
- providing privacy for residents
- protecting area in which flood control channel is completed
- maintaining visual quality for homeowners
  (RHB&A, 1977)

Noting these highest-rated design criteria and applying them to the alternatives enabled the researchers to determine that only three of the alternatives deserved further study (RHB&A, 1977).

"Although the nation's marshes, swamps and bogs are among the most productive landscapes in the world, these liquid assets have suffered greater destruction and abuse than any other natural habitat manipulated by man" (Niering, 1970: 199). Storm-water/sewage systems need to be planned in great detail, and park and vegetative covers can prevent excessive sealing of surface areas by urban materials (Chandler, 1976). As travel becomes more costly, lakes and rivers near population centers will become even more important recreation centers. The quality of lake water is primarily determined by natural processes and human activities in its watershed (Environmental Quality, 1980). A more recently accepted added factor is acid rain. Certainly, waste in or on waterways is a nuisance. Careful planning and design are required.

Too often, city waterways are hidden behind shrubbery or made inaccessible by fences or high walls. This has tended to increase their pollution. Widening and paving of channels does not visually increase their aesthetic appeal (Teagle, 1981). Teagle recommends:

> Treatment of the waterside must vary according to the type and degree of public use ... hard surfacing materials should be confined to areas that receive the heaviest punishment or where the architectural setting dictates a more formal atmosphere. But elsewhere it should be possible to make more use of natural materials and plants, adopting a far more sensitive approach to the problems of flooding, fluvial erosion and general wear and tear than that of the drainage authorities and a more sympathetic attitude to nature conservation than that prevailing in our municipal parks. (1981: 27)

Environmentally sensitive urban planning and design increasingly will require consideration of hydrological resources and effects in all phases of planning for development or redevelopment of infrastructure (for example, drainage, flood and sewage disposal systems, and so on), for protection of water resources (reservoirs and so on), and for recreational planning. The kinds of data-inventorying and analysis techniques available to an urban area will in large part determine the city's long-term success in protecting water quality.

Urban vegetation

Urban vegetation is influenced by—and may in turn modify—soil, water, and climate conditions of the city. We have already spoken of the short life of urban trees because of unfriendly growing conditions.

When funds are limited, designers "must be prepared to adjust plant-ing schemes rather than design with an inadequate growing environ-ment beneath the pavement" (Jewell, 1981: 389).

One answer may be planting above the surface. Saint Paul's 1967 tree planting program used "precast exposed aggregate concrete in-serts" that created a vault "one to three feet above the soil surface" (Jewell, 1981: 388). The entire tree pit for the Denver Transitway Mall cost about $5,500 per tree, including pavement, tree and support systems (Jewell, 1981: 388). Washington, D.C.'s Pennsylvania Avenue required a tree-planting scheme that could withstand heavy pedes-trian traffic. A homogeneous soil and irrigation ring distributes air through the soil. Along less intensely used streets, "a continuous root run of amended soils between the curb and sidewalk" causes tree roots to grow parallel to the curb rather than in the area below adjacent to the paving (Jewell, 1981: 388).

Urban vegetation is subject to at least ten environmental stresses: air pollution, de-icing salt, space, lighting, temperature, waterlogging, dehydration, soil compaction, soil erosion, and physical injury (Mu-drak and Lassoie, 1980: 1–6). While trees are traditionally recognized for their protective but unproductive role, they have been claimed in recent years to contribute to health, particularly by reducing air and noise pollution and in increasing urban comfort (figs. 4-6, 4-7). On the whole, however, their potential role as productive contributors to urban life has been virtually ignored (Appleyard, 1978a). The difficulty is that

> Most of us have no responsiblity for growing or caring for urban trees . . . our relation to them is solely passive and appreciative. . . . (But) they can play many roles. They have multiple func-tions. We will group them under *sensory, instrumental,* and *symbolic* meanings because they are the ways we view environments.
> (Appleyard, 1978a: 3)

The sensory view of trees is the most obvious. We all appreciate the beauty of trees; but they do pollute, providing us with fuzz in the spring, seeds in summer, and leaves in the fall. They do become old and a hazard, threatening to fall in heavy winds or when struck by lightning. Beautiful, mature trees may be destroyed in the process of development, and the urban designer has a role to play in determin-ing their fate.

Trees can be ornamental, too. Consider them lining a drive to an industrial plant, carefully selected to provide fragrant flowers in the spring, lush green foliage in the summer, and many small berries and red leaves in the fall. The role can be more formal. In the Luxembourg Garden of Paris, for example, carefully shaped and sized trees in

In Parking Fields

Along Highways
expressways and parkways

At Shopping Centers
and other commercial
developments

For Reforestation

In City Lots
to transform rubble strewn
areas into useful
community centers

In Playgrounds
parks and city greens

4-6: Benefits from trees in the urban areas (Source: New York State Department of Environmental Conservation).

square planters are placed decoratively (and strategically) in the formal area to provide pockets of shade even in paved areas.

Trees have a useful function, and we have already mentioned one of the most important—shading. But at night, too, the tree crown can moderate energy loss to the sky. Appleyard (1978a: 10), however, reports a disturbing article that claims: "After seasons of heavy rain, trees added substantially to the air pollution levels in the Bay Area, since the hydrocarbons emitted after a chemical reaction produce ozone" (Petit, 1978).

A more usual concern at present is the reverse: the fatal damage to trees from acid rain and other pollutants, a particular problem for the

Summer Shade

Temperature Control
plants cool the air through
evaporation and the
screening of sunlight

Air Cleaning
plants trap the dust particles
borne by the air . . . to be later
washed off onto the ground

Erosion Control
plants and grass protect
the soil and prevent runoff

Shelter

Home for Wildlife

Help in Control of Wind and Noise

4-7: Examples of environmental advantages provided by trees (Source: New York State Department of Environmental Conservation).

northeastern United States. In addition, the "significance to plant health of metals introduced into the air and soil of a city to establish the plant burden," with particular attention to levels of lead in trees, is vital (Smith, 1973: 631).

Petit (1978) saw one possible deficiency in trees as ozone polluters, and the Environmental Protection Agency doubted their value as cleaners of the air. Schmid (1975: 87) reports that in 1973, the EPA considered the role of vegetation as minor in "making a significant contribution to urban air quality." Yet, Schmid continues with evidence (1975: 87) that

- The particulate load in air that went over "heavily vegetated Spring Grove Cemetery in Cincinnati" was reduced by two-thirds (Bach, 1971).
- The concentration of ragweed pollen in a dense stand of hemlock was considerably lower than in the air above the trees (Neuberger *et al.*, 1967).
- There was a reduction in sulphur dioxide near a British hedgerow (Martin and Barber, 1971).

Schmid (1975) recommends evergreens as removers of pollutants, but points out that they may be particularly subject to damage themselves from pollution because their needles are not replaced yearly, as are deciduous leaves.

The evapotranspiration process present in trees and other vegetation puts a great deal of cooling moisture into the atmosphere. In the city setting, the amount of moisture—and the prevention of damage to the tree—may be dependent on adequate watering. Federer (1971) studied a single tree set apart from others and found that it could yield one hundred gallons of water to the atmosphere, if it received enough water itself (Schmid, 1975: 79). Oke's research (1972) discovered that cities in the temperate zone with at least 20 percent plant coverage used more solar energy to evaporate water than to warm the air. "Thirty percent vegetation gives two-thirds of the cooling expected from a complete plant cover" (Schmid, 1975: 81).

Vegetation, soil, atmosphere, and refraction off of objects also offer some noise-muffling properties. "Vegetation and soil provide an excess reduction of sound energy over the decrease attributable to ordinary distance decay" (Schmid, 1975: 91). Vegetation with many stems and leaves appears to absorb high-frequency sound, and tree-covered sites absorb low frequencies well, perhaps because of the presence of permeable soils (Aylor, 1972).

Vegetation and soil along the roadsides reduce wide-band traffic noise, which is certainly of interest to city dwellers. Schmid also describes this use as "practicable within the spatial dimensions of actual residential plots" (1975: 94). Solid walls and embankments do a better job than vegetation and permeable soil, but added vegetation will contribute to the aesthetic quality and further support the sound-deadening effects. Such barriers are best placed nearer to the noise source than to the listener, and they are of little value if the listener is below the noise source. Schmid (1975) observes that most suburbanites apparently do not use vegetation to advantage in reducing street noise, seeming to prefer wide-open expanses of lawn and driveway.

As urban designers, we might prefer to give a good deal of attention to providing the disadvantaged of the inner cities with the trees and vegetation that are so often the province of more well-to-do neighborhoods. An arborist must be consulted in all urban plantings to help choose trees and vegetation that will survive and flourish in the city. Planting a variety of trees along a city block will assure survival of some if disease strikes. Mudrak and Lassoie (1980: 1–10) specify five components of a "successful" community vegetation program:

- a group (task force, commission, or consortium) of community people, including residents, public officials, and public employees committed to managing urban vegetation resources to maximize benefits for people
- ongoing program leadership and broadly based support
- knowledge of the natural resources of the community, particularly the vegetation
- knowledge of social and governmental contexts in which vegetation must survive
- an ongoing process for defining realistic long- and short-range program goals

To discuss the possibility of an urban forest may seem to be a contradiction in terms. Consider, however, Strathclyde Country Park as an example of a multipurpose recreational facility in an "urban multiple deprivation area" near Glasgow, Scotland (Reid, 1981). Policy decisions have been reached to provide management of the woodlands as an amenity while allowing recreational usages in some sectors. We also are speaking of the clustering of trees, carefully planned to avoid the possibility of criminal hideouts. Then there is the random planting of trees along a stream, canal, or street with careful placement to lower maintenance costs. Some cities remove the sod near trees or shrubs, replacing it with sand so that workers on rider-mowers can cut around the trees easily. Larger green-space areas allow the possibility of including a stand of trees.

It may be a long time before there are large urban forests to be managed and the dream of moderating an entire city climate is realized (Herrington, 1978). The role of smaller street-scale vegetation as a modifier of urban microclimate is well established, but more information is needed on specific approaches (Herrington, 1978). In very built-up spaces of the Central Business District we can use vegetation to control the radiant environment. Low vegetation can screen people from infrared radiation from hot surfaces. Recall, too, that grass radiates less energy than blacktop.

The grass "pavement," which Stuttgart used so successfully and

Dayton, Ohio, is currently trying, can also be used in such high-traffic areas as walkways and bikepaths. The openwork concrete grid has proved durable, and the grass grows well among the grids; installations have been in place elsewhere for ten years (USDI, 1982). If traffic is so high that grass might not survive, the use of gravel in between the grids would still provide runoff retention and a measure of the microclimatic effects.

In the *present state of the economy*, we may return some sanity to our urban landscaping along with the achievement of lowered costs. Economy may dictate the retention of indigenous vegetation rather than its wholesale destruction to plant more exotic vegetation (which may not survive) in its place. "The recommendation is that unsown vegetation should not be eliminated too ruthlessly from urban areas" (Gilbert, 1981: 6). To some people, roadsides and vacant land that are covered with a succession of wild flowers as summer becomes fall are weed cover.

Gilbert characterizes natural urban vegetation as "stress-tolerant" and states that it may also have the virtue of maintaining a reasonable year-round appearance (1981: 6). Some planners/urban designers still have a preference for ground cover, pointing out its low maintenance costs, but it is boring to see bank after bank of crown vetch or any of the other groundcovers that tend to overwhelm other established vegetation, natural or planted.

It would give a biased view of the situation, however, were we not to report the findings on public acceptance of returning a bank to its natural state (Gilbert, 1981: 7). The "expectation of the users" proved to be important in a 1971–73 project in Sheffield, England. The planners used such phrases as "cared for," "tended," and "respectable" to reflect their expectations for public landscape. As a result, the Recreation Department resumed mowing the test area in 1974.

The answer may be a combination of cultivated and natural landscapes, but this assumes a large area or at least a number of smaller areas so that a variety of usages may be introduced. What is more immediately and universally important is to realize the value of trees in urban design and the integration of urban forestry in planning and urban design at the levels of both policy and physical design.

Urban wildlife

A basic question that should be addressed before additional wildlife is introduced into a city is this: Why do we want more urban wildlife, for their sake or for our own well-being? (Howard, 1974: 15). Perhaps we can try to benefit both animal and human well-being. Research has shown that: "Serious environmental disruptions usually result from introduction of highly different types of alien plants or animals

...or some other event for which there has not been sufficient time for a new environmental equilibrium to evolve" (Howard, 1974: 17).

To some people, urban wildlife means "pigeons, house sparrows, starlings, bats, rats, and mice" (Howard, 1974: 13). Considering the nature of animals, it is likely that their presence may go undetected by the casual passerby. Benson (1981: 8) states that species that breed on British roadsides include "twenty out of fifty British mammals, all six reptiles, forty out of two hundred birds, twenty-five out of sixty butterflies and eight out of seventeen bumblebees" (Ratcliffe, 1977). Benson (1981) also lists references that indicate the wide variety of urban animal life in Britain. No doubt, a similar list could be compiled for the United States. Actually, birds are the most prevalent American urban vertebrates (Rublowsky, 1967), and the three species mentioned above are those most frequently found.

Are there positive results when animals are attracted to urban open space? Not always: consider a California experience. Flocks of robins seeking pyracantha berries flew against high-speed traffic (Howard, 1974). On the other hand, many ornithologists now believe that the heavy planting of the multiflora roe in the 1950s along highway medians was the most important factor in enabling mockingbirds to increase their range northward (DeGraaf and Witman, 1979). DeGraaf and Witman also have identified the street trees that are valuable for birds and plants and that will withstand city conditions and salt (1979).

Urban animals are subjected to many hazards, probably more than those faced by animals in a rural habitat—but both urban and rural habitats are threatened by development. Traditional urban parks have destroyed natural habitats. There are not many weeds in parks; however, attractive annual plots of millet and sorghum will provide substitute foods for birds (Leedy *et al.*, 1978).

The mere mention of considering the increase of urban wildlife brings forth a list of possible hazards: "structural damage, crop destruction, ornamental plant/landscape damage, aesthetic degradation, human safety, and disease transmission" (Smith, 1974: 113). Smith also reports that there have been occurrences of migrating swallows descending on airport runways to feed on bayberries. Hazard to aircraft resulted. Seagulls living where an airport has been constructed also have been found to interfere with aircraft. The nightly visits of raccoons to garbage cans, the cooing of mourning doves, the chatter —and fouling—of starlings, encounters with skunks—all can be annoying to city dwellers.

The value of "derelict" urban land as a refuge for uncommon rare plants has been shown. Similar findings could well result from a study of urban animals (Benson, 1981). Using a little imagination, we can create urban environments in which animals and humans successfully coexist. For example, a refuge for gray herons was developed in

Regent Park, London, in 1968 by closing off a part of a boating lake (Teagle, 1981).

We need to consider the plight of wildlife before we plant or build. It is also desirable that thought be given to the effects on wildlife before pesticides and other chemicals are introduced. Our track record indicates that sometimes no thought is given to the effects on humans, let alone animals. For example, a commonly used pesticide for eradicating the gypsy moth is suspected of causing birth defects in humans and is known to kill honeybees. The long-term effects of chemicals like dioxin should be a warning to us. Someone on the planning/urban design staff must accept responsibility for urban wildlife management—or perhaps this function might be served by a consultant.

The role of wildlife in the city has not been perceived readily as an urban design concern, but it requires thorough and long-term planning efforts, the participation of urban wildlife specialists, and coordination with such other planning projects as the design and maintenance of public spaces, including parks, cemeteries, and roadways.

Role of natural processes

This chapter has emphasized the role of the natural environment in planning/urban design and has attempted to suggest some ways that natural processes may be incorporated into the urban scene. There are many of us who see this process as an opportunity to enrich our lives by increasing our contact with nature. There is also a message that we should be concerned about destruction of our environment —often by unthinking actions. That protection and enhancement of natural processes will have to compete for a share of urban revenues is obvious. It is hoped that the reader is convinced that such expenditures are worthwhile. The acceptance of this thesis will be measured by its presence in future planning/design reports. An excellent recent example of a work that takes natural processes into account is *Performance Requirements for the Maintenance of Social Values Represented by the Natural Environment of Medford Township, N.J.* (Juneja, 1974).

Many of us believe that we need still more nature in the city, a still wider natural framework. Nature must be all-pervasive, an integral part of the renewal planning of older inner cities. The enormous benefits of these concepts have to be achieved, however, at acceptable cost and through programs of environmental education, which must focus "on reversing the continuing predatory, destructive instincts of our society—even of our established professions—towards the city landscape" (Laurie, 1981: 1). However, urban planners/designers cannot accomplish these goals by themselves. They need access to adequate technical data that emphasizes the significance and impact of such natural factors as geology and hydrology in urban contexts; and they also need technical expertise, or at least access to specialists, in order to incorporate these issues into informed, environmentally sensitive urban planning/design processes. This is an avenue that needs immediate research attention and, we hope, will generate new themes for physical planning and urban design.

References

Appleyard, Donald, and Lynch, Kevin. *Temporary Paradise? A Look at the Special Landscape of the San Diego Region.* San Diego, CA: City of San Diego, 1974.

Appleyard, Donald. *Urban Trees and Forests.* Berkeley, CA: University of California Institute of Urban and Regional Development, Working Paper no. 303, 1978a.

Appleyard, Donald. "Urban Trees, Urban Forests: What Do They Mean?" In proceedings of *National Urban Forestry Conference.* Syracuse, NY: State University of New York, College of Environmental Science and Forestry, 1978b.

Aylor, Donald E. "Noise Reduction By Vegetation and Ground." *Journal of Acoustical Society of America* 51 (1972): 197–205.

Bach, Wilfrid. "Seven Steps to Better Living on the Urban Heat Island." *Landscape Architecture* 41 (1971): 136–141.

Bartenstein, Fred. "Have You Heard of the Dayton Climate Project?" *Urban Innovation Abroad* 3, no. 9, September (1979): 1.

Beal, F., and Hollander, E. "City Development Plans." In So, F. S., *et al.,* eds. *The Practice of Local Government Planning,* Washington, D.C.: International City Manager's Association, 1979.

Benson, J. F. "Animal Communities in an Urban Environment." *Landscape Research* 6, no. 3, Winter (1981): 8–11.

Burchell, Robert W., and Sternlieb, George, eds. *Planning Theory in the 1980's.* New Brunswick, NJ: The Center for Urban Policy Research, Rutgers University, 1978.

California, State of, Office of Appropriate Technology and Office of Planning and Research. *Present Value Constructing a Sustainable Future.* 1979.

California, State of. *Towards a Solar California: The Solar Cal Action Program.* Sacramento, CA: Solar Cal Office, 1978.

Chandler, T. J. *Urban Climatology and Its Relevance to Urban Design.* Geneva, Switzerland: Secretariat of the World Meteorological Organization no. 438, 1976.

Dansereau, Pierre. *Challenge For Survival, Land, Air, and Water for Man in Megalopolis.* New York: Columbia University Press, 1970.

Davis, City of. *Davis Energy Conservation Report.* Davis, CA, 1970.

DeGraaf, Richard M., and Witman, Grethin M. *Trees, Shrubs, and Vines for Attracting Birds.* Amherst, MA: University of Massachusetts Press, 1979.

Detwyler, Thomas R. "Modern Man and Environment." In Detwyler, Thomas R., ed., *Man's Impact on Environment.* New York: McGraw-Hill Inc., 1971.

Detwyler, Thomas R., and Marcus, Melvin G. *Urbanization and Environment.* Belmont, CA: Duxbury Press, 1972.

Dobrovolny, Ernest, and Schmoll, Henry R. "Geology as Applied to Urban Planning: An Example from the Greater Anchorage Area Borough, Alaska." In Frederick Betz, Jr., ed., *Environmental Geology.* Stroudsburg, PA: Hutchinson and Ross, 1975.

Dubos, Rene. "Man and His Environment: Scope, Impact, and Nature." In Detwyler, Thomas R., ed., *Man's Impact on Environment.* New York: Mc-Graw-Hill Inc., 1971.

Environmental Quality. The Eighth Annual Report of the Council on Environmental Quality. Washington, D.C.: U.S. Government Printing Office, 1977.

Environmental Quality. The Tenth Annual Report of the Council on Environmental Quality. Washington, D.C.: U.S. Government Printing Office, 1979.

Environmental Quality. The Eleventh Annual Report of the Council on Environmental Quality. Washington, D.C.: US Government Printing Office, 1980.

Everett, Michael D. "Roadside Air Pollution Hazards in Recreational Land Use Planning." *Journal of the American Institute of Planners* 40, no. 2, March (1974): 83–89.

Federer, C. A. "Effects of Trees in Modifying Urban Microclimates." In *Trees and Forests in an Urbanizing Environment.* Amherst, MA: University of Massachusetts, Cooperative Extension Service, Planning and Resource Development Series, no. 17 (1971): 23–28.

Fleming, Robert W.; Varnes, David J.; and Schuster, Robert L. "Landslide Hazards and Their Reduction." In *United States Geological Survey Yearbook.* Washington, D.C.: U.S. Geological Survey, 1978.

Gilbert, O. L. "Plant Communities in an Urban Environment." *Landscape Research* 6, no. 3, Winter (1981): 5–7.

Godin, Gaeton; Wright, Geoff; and Shephard, Roy J. "Urban Exposure to Carbon Monoxide." *Archives of Environmental Health.* 25, no. 2 (1972): 305–313.

Greenberg, James. *Energy Efficiency and Design.* Washington, D.C.: National League of Cities, 1981.

Guy, Harold P. "Sediment Problems in Urban Areas." In Donald R. Coates, ed., *Environmental Geomorphology and Landscape Conservation.* Vol. 11: Urban Areas. Stroudsburg, PA: Hutchinson and Ross, 1976.

Hamilton, Judith L., and Willard G. Owens. "Effects of Urbanization on Ground-Water Lands." In Utgard, R. O. *et al.,* eds., *Geology in the Urban Environment.* Minneapolis, MN: Burgess, 1978.

Heidorn, K. C. "A Chronology of Important Events in the History of Air Pollution Meteorology to 1970." *Bulletin of the American Meteorological Society* 59, no. 12, December (1978): 1589–1597.

Herrington, Lee P. "Urban Vegetation and Microclimate." In *Proceedings of the National Urban Forestry Conference.* Syracuse, NY: State University of New York, College of Environmental Science and Forestry Publication, 1978.

Holden, Constance. "Ian McHarg, Champion for Design with Nature." *Landscape Architecture* 67, no. 2, March/April (1977): 154–156, 180.

Howard, Walter E. "Why Wildlife in an Urban Society." In Noyes, J. H. and Progulske, D. R., eds., *Wildlife in an Urbanizing Environment*. University of Massachusetts, U.S. Department of Agriculture and County Extension Services, 1974.

Hysom, H. L., Jr. *et al*. *A Handbook for Creating an Urban Development Information System*. Fairfax County Office of Research and Statistics (Springfield, Virginia: National Technical Information Service, November 1974.) Prepared for the Department of Housing and Urban Development, NTIS no. PB–238 815.

Jaffe, Martin. "Solar Access: A Guidebook for California Communities." Sacramento, CA: California Energy Commission, 1980.

Jewell, Linda. "Construction: Planting Trees in City Soils." *Landscape Architecture* 71, no. 3 (1981): 387–389.

Juneja, Narendra. *Medford: Performance Requirements for the Maintenance of Social Values Represented by the Natural Environment of Medford Township, NJ*. Philadelphia, PA: University of Pennsylvania, Center for Ecological Research in Planning and Design, 1974.

Kaufman, Werner. "Stuttgart Cleans Its Air: Landscape Policies for Atmospheric Renewal." *Landscape Architecture,* April (1967): 176–181.

Kent, T. J. *The Urban General Plan*. San Francisco, CA: Chandler, 1964.

Landsberg, Helmut. *Physical Climatology*. Second Edition. DuBois, PA: Gray Printing Co., Inc., 1969.

Laurie, Ian. "Urban Nature: The Perspective of the Past." *Landscape Research* 6, no. 3. Winter, (1981): 1.

Leedy, D. *et al. Planning for Wildlife in Cities*. Washington, D.C.: U.S. Department of Interior, 1978.

Legget, Robert F. *Cities and Geology*. New York: McGraw-Hill Inc., 1973.

Leighton, F. B. "Landslides and Hillside Development." In Donald R. Coates, ed., *Environmental Geomorphology and Landscape Conservation*. Vol. 11: Urban Areas. Stroudsburg, PA: Hutchinson and Ross, 1976.

Leopold, Luna B. "Hydrology for Urban Planning." In Utgard, R. O. *et al.,* eds., *Geology in the Urban Environment*. Minneapolis, MN: Burgess, 1978.

Loessner, G. Arno. "An Air Quality Planning Program with Visible Results." *Practicing Planner,* March (1978): 35–38.

Lynch, Kevin. "City Design." *Urban Design International*. Vol. 1, no. 2, 1980.

Mader, George G., and Crowder, Dwight F. "An Experiment in Using Geology for City Planning: The Experience of the Small Community of Portola Valley, California." In *Environmental Planning and Geology*. Washington, D.C.: U.S. Geological Survey and U.S. Department of Housing and Urban Development, 1969: 176–189.

March, George P. *Man and Nature*. Cambridge, MA: The Belknap Press of Harvard University, 1965.

Martin, A., and Barber, F. R. "Some Measurements of Loss of Atmospheric Sulphur Dioxide Near Foliage." *Atmospheric Environment* 5 (1971): 345–352.

McHarg, Ian L. "Process, Value and Form." In Smithsonian Annual II, *The Fitness of Man's Environment*. New York: Harper Colophon Books, 1968.

McHarg, Ian L. *Design with Nature*. Garden City, NY: The American Museum of Natural History, Doubleday/Natural History Press, 1969.

Miller, G. Tyler, Jr. *Energy and Environment: The Four Energy Crises*. Belmont, CA: Wadsworth Inc., 1980.

Mudrak, Louise, and Lassoie, James. *Urban Vegetation: A Reference For New York Communities.* Ithaca, NY: Cornell University, Department of Natural Resources, Urban Vegetation Project, 1980.

National League of Cities (NLC). "City Sampler: The Greening of Dayton." *Urban Environment Design,* February (1980): 1.

Neuberger, H.; Hosler, C. L.; and Kocmond, W. C. "Vegetation As Aerosol Filter." In S. W. Tromp and W. H. Weike, eds., *Biometeorology.* New York: Pergamon, 1967.

Nichols, D. R., and Buchanan-Banks, J. M. "Seismic Hazards and Land Use Planning." In Utgard, R. O. *et al.,* eds., *Geology in the Urban Environment.* Minneapolis, MN: Burgess, 1978.

Niering, William A. "The Ecology of Wetlands in Urban Areas." In Pierre Dansereau, ed., *Challenge for Survival.* New York: Columbia University Press, 1970.

Noyes, John H., and Progulske, Donald R., eds. *Wildlife In An Urbanizing Environment.* Amherst, MA: University of Massachusetts, U.S. Department of Agriculture and County Extension Services, 1973.

Oke, T. R. "Evapotranspiration in Urban Areas and Its Implications for Urban Climate Planning." WMO-CIB International Colloquium on Building Climatology Proceedings, 1972.

Parry, G. D. R., and Brummage. "Solid Wastes," Reclamation and Management." *Landscape Research* 6, no. 3, Winter (1981): 15–18.

Patterson, James C. "Soil Compaction and Its Effects Upon Urban Vegetation." In *Better Trees For Metropolitan Landscapes* Symposium Proceedings. Upper Darby, PA: U.S. Department of Agriculture Forest Service, 1976.

Petit, C. "How Rain May Cause Smog." *San Francisco Chronicle.* 18 May 1978.

Portland, City of, Bureau of Planning. *Energy Conservation Choices for the City of Portland.* Vol. 3. Summary of Conservation Choices, Washington, D.C.: U.S. Government Printing Office, 1977.

Portland, City of. *Proposed Energy Policy for Portland.* Portland, OR: Bureau of Planning, 1978.

Ratcliffe, D. A., ed. *A Nature Conservation Review,* 2 Vols. New York: Cambridge University Press, 1977.

Raymond, G. N. "The Role of the Physical Urban Planner." In Burchell, Robert W., and Sternlieb, George, eds., *Planning Theory in the 1980's.* New Brunswick, NJ: The Center for Urban Policy Research, Rutgers University, 1978.

Reid, Samuel. "Woodland Management in the Urban Setting." *Landscape Research* 6, no. 3, Winter (1981): 22–24.

Ridgeway, James. *Energy Efficient Community Planning.* The JG Press, Inc./The Elements, 1979.

Roberts, J. J.; Croke, E. J.; and Booras, S. G. "Critical Review of the Effect of Air Pollution Control Regulations on Land Use Planning." *Journal of the Air Pollution Control Association* 25, no. 5, May (1975): 500–520.

Rowntree, Rown A., and Sanders, Ralph A. *Dayton, Ohio Climate Project: Executive Summary.* Syracuse, NY: U.S. Department of Agriculture-Forest Service, Northeastern Forest Service Experiment Station and SUNY College of Environmental Science and Forestry, n.d.

Royston, Hanamoto, Beck and Abey (RHB&A). *A Flood Control Study.* Marin County, CA: Marin, 1977.

Rublowsky, John. *Nature in the City.* New York: Basic Books, 1967.

Rydell, Peter, and Schwarz, Gretchen. "Air Pollution and Urban Form: A Review of Current Literature." *Journal of the American Institute of Planners,* March (1968): 115–120.

San Diego, City of. *San Diego County General Plan Energy Element.* San Diego, CA: City Planning Department, 1977.

Schmid, James A. *Urban Vegetation.* Chicago, IL: University of Chicago, Research Paper No. 161, 1975.

Schneider, William J., and Goddard, James E. "Extent and Development of Urban Flood Plains." In Utgard, R. O. *et al.,* eds., *Geology in the Urban Environment.* Minneapolis, MN: Burgess, 1978.

Shirvani, Hamid. "Retrieving the Environmental-Based Physical Development Plan." *UD Review* 6, no. 4, Fall (1983): 19–22.

Smith, Richard N. "Problems with Urban Wildlife." In Noyes, John H. and Progulske, Donald R., eds., *Wildlife in An Urbanizing Environment.* Amherst, MA: University of Massachusetts, U.S. Department of Agriculture and County Extension Services, 1974.

Smith, William H. "Metal Contamination of Urban Woody Plants." *Environmental Science and Technology* 7, no. 7, July (1973): 631–636.

Spirn, Anne W. "The Role of Natural Processes in the Design of Cities." *AAPSS Annuals,* no. 451, September (1980): 98–105

Teagle, W. G. "The Water's Edge." *Landscape Research* 6, no. 2, Winter (1981): 25–27.

Thomas, Harold E., and Schneider, William J. "Water as an Urban Resource and Nuisance." In Utgard, R. O. *et al.,* eds., *Geology in the Urban Environment.* Minneapolis, MN: Burgess, 1978.

U.S. Department of Interior (USDI). *Technical Note: Grass Pavement.* Washington, D.C.: Heritage Conservation and Recreation Office, 1982.

Wallace, McHarg, Roberts, and Todd (WMRT). *Woodland New Community, Phase One: Land Planning and Design Principles.* Philadelphia, PA: WMRT, 1973.

Wedding, J. B.; Lombardi, D. J.; and Cermouk, J. E. "A Wind Tunnel Study of Gaseous Pollutants in City Street Canyons." *Journal of the Air Pollution Control Association* 27, no. 6, June (1977): 557–566.

Wilson, John S.; Tabas, Philip; and Henneman, Marian. *Comprehensive Planning and the Environment: A Manual for Planners.* Cambridge, MA: Abt Books, 1979.

Wolman, Abel. "The Metabolism of Cities." *Scientific American.* March (1965): 178–190.

Design method/process

CHAPTER 5

DESIGN METHOD/process has always been a problematic and sensitive subject for designers. Many designers emphasize the art of design; that is, they seek expression of the intuitive and creative design capabilities of the individual designer. Others emphasize various systematic processes and take a philosophical approach to design. Though each perspective has merit, there is no consensus as to which is the best or most adequate procedure.

In general, the conceptual bases of design methods may be placed into six groups. While this is by no means the only possible grouping, its logic has much to offer. The six groups are the (1) internalized (Steinitz, 1979), (2) synoptic (Hudson, 1978), (3) incremental, (4) fragmental, (5) pluralistic, and (6) radical methods. This classification takes into consideration the following: First, it is assumed that all methods are rational. The models do differ significantly, however, in the degree and manner to which they use rationalized critical processes to establish their methodological approach to planning/design problems. Second, it is assumed that all the methods share areas of common concern and consequently overlap, as the following discussion will reveal.

Of the six methods, the internalized and synoptic approaches merit fullest discussion in this chapter, as they are the most common methods used by designers and planners alike. The remaining methods will be discussed at less length.

The internalized method of design

The internalized method of design is commonly described as intuitive. It may also be subjective, personal, creative, and sometimes almost irrational. Though we may be unable to determine conclusively that such a method is irrational, we also may not be able to show it to be completely rational. Therefore, it is probably most reasonable to acknowledge that there can be a certain degree of rationality associated with most internalized design methods.

The designer who uses the intuitive method first develops a design for the project in his or her mind, with the benefit and assistance of memory, training, and experience. Although at this conceptual stage, the method does not lend itself to systematic presentation on paper, on board, or with a computer, it still may proceed in a systematic fashion. The process may take place in the designer's mind and/or by sketching and resketching until the design reaches a point of maturation that satisfies the designer's desires. The internalized method is the approach professional designers most frequently use, and it has produced many positive as well as some negative results. The degree to which results are negative is less dependent, however, on the overall method than on the particular application and the individual designer. The vision and background of the designer, his or her understanding of the culture within which he or she is working, the amount of cultural baggage carried, and the level of creative ability are all important considerations in determining the degree of success or failure of the design. Hassan Fathy and Moshe Sadafi are but two of the special designers who share deep insight into the physics of design and how these relate to cultural values and human usage. The importance of the abilities and strengths of the individual designer cannot be overstated.

A recent example of an application of the internalized method is Nader Ardalan's plan for Nuran, Isfahan, Iran. Nuran, a satellite city of 100,000, was planned for the Atomic Energy Organization of Iran (fig. 5-1). The conceptual design of the city was based on the cultural and philosophic view of Iranian life as understood and defined by Ardalan:

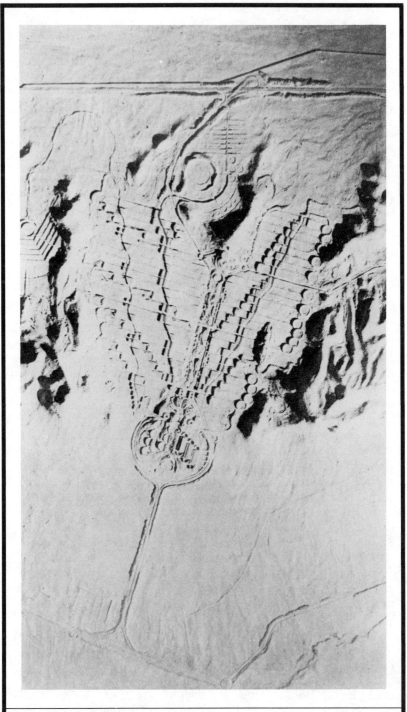

5-1: Concept plan model of City of Nuran, Isfahan, Iran, designed by Nader Ardalan (Source: Mandala International, Tehran/Boston).

Nuran accepts and extends in a new creation the timeless Iranian world view of life as a purposeful duality. A duality that seeks a balanced unity between the essential complements that govern the material world... Nuran accepts the context of its placement and locates its pivotal centers upon an axis of continuity with that of Isfahan. This spiritual axis passes approximately through the middle of the site linking a hillock area to the west with a pyramidal mountain to the east. Then polar points become the vital heads of the town. To the west and closest in proximity to Isfahan is created the "thinking or material head" of the town, while on the east and closest to the nuclear technology center is created the "imaginative or spiritual head." The latter "asks" while the former "answers." The two are united by a paradise garden wherein may be found the cultural residue of history attesting to the struggle of mankind to reach a perfect balance between the material and spiritual dimensions of existence. (Ardalan, 1978: 9)

The internalized method is currently more commonly and readily applied to developing countries than to more established Western nations. This is due to the distinctively different nature of decision-making processes in developing as opposed to established nations. Decision making is collective, pluralistic, and typically dispersed in most Western nations, when compared with the highly centralized processes in most developing lands. The role and opinion of experts in the decision-making process is held in higher esteem in developing countries than in more established ones. The fragmentation of local governments and the decision-making process in the United States often make it difficult to employ experts effectively or to apply the internalized method, at least at the urban scale. It is true that, in France and Scandinavia, where centralized government has greater control and where, because of the nature of the culture, an expert's opinion has a significant influence on the political process, the intuitive method is used to some extent. However, nowhere is the method used as frequently as in such developing countries as Saudi Arabia, Kuwait, and Iraq. The design of the University of Bagdad Campus, Iraq, prepared by the Architects Collaborative, Inc., of Cambridge, Massachusetts, is an example of a full-scale application of the process. The method facilitates a client-oriented intuitive design approach that many planners and designers have traditionally used at the city scale.

At the project level there are still a large number of planners and designers—in developing and developed countries alike—who use the internalized design method quite frequently. In fact, at this level, the method is actually used more often in Western countries, particularly in the United States. For example, Le Corbusier used this method to resolve the conflicts between "technological and spiritual points of view" (Le Corbusier, 1971: 9). "Urban Design Manhattan" was also formulated by the Regional Planning Association, using the internalized method (Okamoto and Williams, 1969). An "Access Tree," "a set of interrelated principles of functional and visual organization," was used to design a set of compatible recommendations to guide the growth of downtown Manhattan (fig. 5-2) (Okamoto and Williams, 1969: 9).

The internalized method, however, has been the focus of much criticism. Many argue, for instance, that the internalized method is inherently ill-suited for use in a pluralistic society. Many traditional planners design primarily for the needs of the middle and upper classes, and some have criticized the proponents of the internalized method for adhering to the spurious notion that a unitary public interest exists that can serve as a guide to planning and design (Appelbaum, 1978).

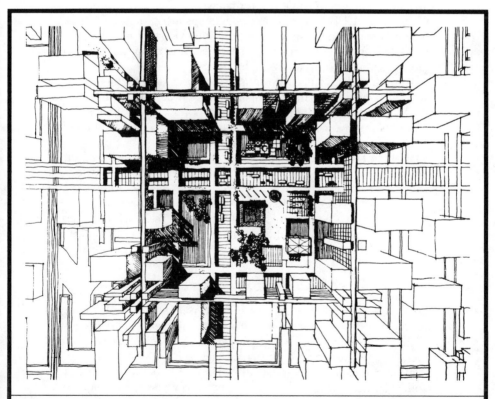

5-2: A segment of urban design for Manhattan by Okamoto and Williams (Source: Kai Okamoto and Frank E. Williams. *Urban Design Manhattan*. New York: The Viking Press, 1969).

Because it is not nearly as dependent upon explicit governmental policies or dicta, the internalized method is thought by many to be less consistent than more systematic model-based processes. As a result, local governments have sought to strengthen their grasp on future development by limiting individual design in development and have sought to implement guidelines for all forms of development within an urban setting. This, combined with man's desire to systematize growth and with a faltering economy that has restricted private growth, has limited the extensive use of the internalized approach in city design in many Western countries, particularly the United States.

The synoptic method

The synoptic method is commonly described as "rational" or "comprehensive," which is not to say that other methods are irrational. To avoid any such confusion, the term "synoptic" is more appropriate than "rational." The systematic design steps incorporated within this method typically number four (at a minimum) to six (although twelve or more steps are sometimes used), depending upon the scale, complexity, and precision sought in the design.

The intent of this decision model is to provide a methodology by which a consistent form of comparability between alternatives can be made. In reviewing the process, two important and complementary concepts are involved: value and uncertainty. For a decision model to be effective, as much ambiguity as possible must be removed by analysis and measurement of the value and the predictability of different outcomes, leaving any residual ambiguities to be acknowledged and treated as such (Boyce *et al.,* 1970). The following example of the synoptic process seeks within a reasonable number of steps to achieve this ideal and to provide a logical progression by which the alternatives reviewed can be analyzed and solutions proposed. Figure 5-3 shows the process in outline form.

STEP ONE: DATA COLLECTION

Data collection revolves around making a judgment about the environment and its natural, built, and socioeconomic components. Much of the data is statistical, dealing with quantitative spatial variations and their relationships, with each statistic tagged by subject, area, time, or some combination of these. Although there is definitely a need to collect concrete data, there is also a need to assess the quality of the existing environment. Most planners approach this step by collecting a variety of socioeconomic data in a variety of forms and using various methodologies (statistical information, geographic surveys, aerial photos, and so on). When they come to review the built environment,

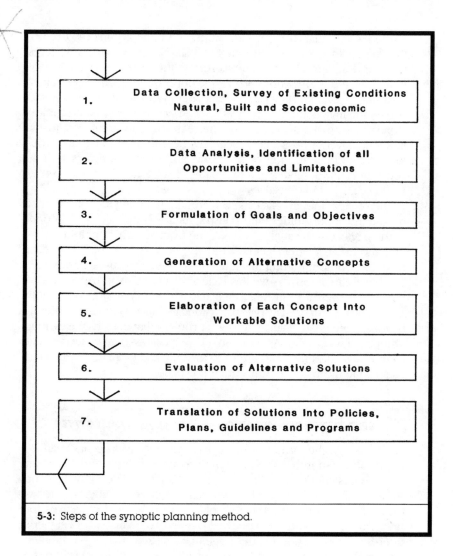

1.	Data Collection, Survey of Existing Conditions Natural, Built and Socioeconomic
2.	Data Analysis, Identification of all Opportunities and Limitations
3.	Formulation of Goals and Objectives
4.	Generation of Alternative Concepts
5.	Elaboration of Each Concept Into Workable Solutions
6.	Evaluation of Alternative Solutions
7.	Translation of Solutions Into Policies, Plans, Guidelines and Programs

5-3: Steps of the synoptic planning method.

however, they tend to focus only on its infrastructure and other quantifiable aspects, leaving out important segments that lie within the overall environment. Some designers of suburban development have taken the natural environment into consideration, but rarely has this been true of urban designers.

STEP TWO: DATA ANALYSIS

Data analysis can be regarded as the first or preliminary step in converting information into design alternatives. The analysis can incorporate a variety of techniques, each of which promotes understanding of the basic spatial variations, qualities, and relationships captured in the data or inventory process (Roberts, 1974). Data analysis requires that the designer take the time to review the materials and information collected and identify problems, opportunities, and constraints. This step is an important one, as it is often necessary to stimulate and stretch the imagination, improve the perspective, and obtain technical expertise in order to clarify, define, expand, and argue the major issues involved. The process facilitates definition of the exact problems faced, identification of problems and opportunities as well as constraints and limitations, and, finally, clear delineation and formulation of goals and objectives.

Quite often, though, data analysis and the resulting identification of problems, opportunities, and constraints are combined in step one, to the neglect of the analysis phase. The trouble with combining steps one and two is that designers sometimes assemble an elaborate data inventory without putting in sufficient time on an analysis of the data. Technical limitations, as well as lack of planners' expertise, may also mean that even a quite elaborate data inventory is not thoroughly analyzed (Lee, 1973). Despite provisions for data collection and evaluations, inadequate data analysis is a problem that plagues the various synoptic approaches. As Stretton (1978) points out, ensuring that diverse analytical methods are used to study and evaluate inventoried data is one means of circumventing this problem.

STEP THREE: FORMULATION OF GOALS AND OBJECTIVES

Traditionally, the formulation of goals and objectives occurs near the end of the comprehensive planning process. *Theoretically,* however, it is the designer's first task; or, to put it slightly differently, it is the step that leads us into design, wherein we have to differentiate between facts and values. The formulation of goals and objectives for urban design should be based on facts rather than on a designer's interests and values. It is at this stage that a citizen advisory committee or some other kind of public participation is necessary to refine the goals and objectives and structure them collectively within public conceptions (Shirvani, 1981). Involving the citizenry early in the process has been shown more efficient in generating public awareness of a project and in fostering a positive attitude toward it. When the designer presents alternative solutions to the public, the process is near, or is perceived as being near, completion. The public is uninformed about the criteria necessary to make a well-qualified judgment. Politically, early public participation can eliminate angry reactions that hinder the design's progress. Such early participation may also provide the designer with additional insights into the plan.

One of the main issues to be addressed, then, in this third step is a determination of the degree of abstraction and generality appropriate in a plan's goals and objectives. Much time, energy, and valuable resources have been wasted or lost in city master plans that propose goals and objectives stated so generally that they are almost universally accepted and are therefore without any political or legal value. Such goals may be inspiring, noncontroversial, and form the basis on which the plan is formulated, but what more do they accomplish? The goals and objectives of a design must be clear, specific, and understandable to the public at large. They should spell out the intent and purpose behind the plan, its variables, and how and to what degree the plan should be implemented and enforced. It is only in this manner that the planner/designer can explain and demonstrate the clear intent of planning and design. Unfortunately, in political environments that are so entrenched that they desire nothing more than universal goals, planning and design are of no value, and the purported policies become nothing more than paper tigers.

STEP FOUR: GENERATION OF ALTERNATIVE CONCEPTS

Generation of alternative concepts has been said to occur in two stages: (1) the identification of key organizing principles that constitute the generative idea of each scheme and (2) the definition of a more detailed set of basic attributes for each alternative as a prelude to elaboration (Boyce *et al.,* 1970). Step four is where a designer should bring his or her knowledge and previous experience into play and/or determine how others have dealt with similar issues. Each alternative derived should seek to represent a comprehensive plan for the design proposed. The various alternatives offered can include not only a variety of approaches to a certain goal but can be of value as a tool to expand on the main alternatives suggested. Alternatives, for example, can be used to challenge or confirm a recommendation, discover or verify some expected advantage inherent in one particular pattern of development, act as a means to provoke public discussion on critical issues, and/or be used to educate the public as to the values of planning per se (Boyce *et al.,* 1970).

Though the field of planning and design is relatively young, much has been written over the past two decades about the problems planners have experienced with the derivation of alternative solutions. The lessons learned from other designers and cities can offer valuable alternatives and insight into issues confronted in the situation at hand. Case studies also illustrate the effects of negative design and thereby suggest how other designers can avoid similar errors. Case studies encourage the designer to keep abreast of others' approaches and provide an opportunity to research and review proposals prior to offering them as viable alternatives. Regrettably, some designers become so involved with the "system" that they allow the method to select the substance (Stretton, 1978), thereby avoiding the necessary careful consideration of alternative concepts.

STEP FIVE: ELABORATION OF CONCEPTS

The elaboration process seeks to expand upon the previously proposed alternatives and analyze the concepts, major goals, and objectives of each. Two approaches offer varying criteria by which this step
may be approached. The first emphasizes comprehensiveness and
total consistency within the alternatives. The second emphasizes the
effect and interactions of a specific policy or program within the
larger complex of policies and plans that compose the alternatives. In
the latter approach, plan evaluation focuses on specific plan or policy
elements rather than on the entire plan. Each approach seeks to find
the concept (or concepts) that best fits the particular urban setting in
which the designer must work.

The ultimate intent of the elaboration, or plan-design step, is to
review, analyze, and criticize the available alternatives and to catego-
rize them in order of viability within the framework of the proposed
design. Following the identification and selection of the generative
concepts, this portion of the method usually constitutes a major part
of the planning process.

STEP SIX: EVALUATION OF ALTERNATIVE SOLUTIONS

Evaluation of alternative solutions is an extremely sensitive step, the
importance of which has increased over the past decade because of
the reduction of planners/designers' subjectivity in favor of increasingly objective solutions.

There are a number of interesting methods of evaluation at both
the macroscale of urban design and regional planning and the microscale of district design, neighborhood plans, and urban design
guidelines. These evaluation methods range from traditional benefit/
cost analysis to a goal-achievement matrix (Hill, 1968), from metropolitan plan-evaluation methodology (Boyce et al., 1970) and land-
suitability analysis (Hopkins, 1977) to evaluation in the planning
process (Lichfield et al., 1975). Finally, there are also various methods
of simulation for solar access, noise abatement control, and so on,
which are helpful for developing design guidelines and performance
standards.

The main problem that the urban designer faces—and to a lesser
degree, the private-sector designer also faces—at the local government level is "time/dollars," the availability of resources to undertake
an extensive evaluation process. What is really needed is a set of
performance standards with "reasoning behind them . . . laid bare, so
that they are fully open to political correction" (Lynch, 1981: 279).

Many critics have argued that actual comprehensiveness is not possible, that the methodology of this approach has been described as
being much more difficult to apply than it would appear on paper or
in thought and that the process itself is extremely time-consuming.

Modern techniques, critics argue, are only as good as the designer or programmer who implements them and can be overused or relied upon too easily and have failed in any real sense to speed up planning processes. Some critics have also suggested that the results or products of the processes are often limited in the alternatives proposed and analysis provided. A study of thirteen metropolitan planning efforts in the early 1970s indicated that, too often, plans focused almost entirely on physical development and included only a cursory examination of the potential social effects of the alternatives; that, typically, the planning horizons of the plans were of a limited time period and were marked by a tendency toward conservative assessment of the feasibility of planning options, resulting in less variation in the alternate plans than was anticipated. Also, plans tended to concentrate on a single metropolitan solution and at a single level of detail (Boyce *et al.*, 1970), and natural environment considerations tended to be overwhelmed by macrophysical, demographic, and economic calculations (Roberts, 1974). Even Boyce *et al.* (1970), in a book describing the growing sophistication of synoptic methods, reiterated the idea that alternatives proposed by such methods are both too conservative and too similar for significant differences to be obtained among alternatives. The study added that the models available were too blunt to produce differences in response to the policies involved. The Coventry–Solihull–Warwickshire study reaffirmed "that alternative plans can be so similar that individual evaluation becomes pointless" (Roberts, 1974: 55). Another widely cited concern was the failure of the method to take into account the impact of alternative plans on social and economic groups. Stretton (1978) suggested that any relation between what is modeled and what is important to the citizen can only be accidental. Finally, Michael Batty saw the planning process as essentially integrated and concluded that the method was both cumbersome and wasteful (Roberts, 1974).

Although no single process can be fully comprehensive or fully rational, the synoptic method achieves a degree of rationality, or rationalization, that may be adequate for urban design. In any case, critics of the synoptic method have not yet produced any alternative models that improve upon its shortcomings, so, for the time being, synoptic methods will continue to be used in capitalist societies that require positivist, statistically based decision-making approaches.

STEP SEVEN: TRANSLATION OF THE ALTERNATIVE SOLUTION INTO POLICIES, PLANS, GUIDELINES, AND PROGRAMS

This step involves detailed presentation and explanation of the selected alternative and formulation of policies, plans, and other planning products. It is, therefore, a wrap-up or synthesis of the entire process. Selection of particular planning products such as policies, plans, guidelines or programs depends on a particular situation or type of planning/urban design activity. By detailed development of the policies, plans, and so forth, based on the selected alternative, further implications of the solution can be explored. This, in turn, may re-quire feedback and reevaluation of the entire process.

The incremental method

The incremental method is essentially another version of the synoptic method: one goes through the entire process, developing an overall framework, and then formulates incremental plans and programs to achieve the main goals and objectives. The method is somewhat cyclical in nature, as each step builds on the last, allowing for a time lag to review, evaluate, and institute changes (if necessary) in order to reach the ultimate goals and objectives. The incremental method is a straightforward process of decision making applicable to individuals, groups, and organizations. The designer establishes a goal and then develops incremental steps to achieve it. Using this method, a number of cities presently engaged in urban design and development have worked out long-range policies and short-range plans within the framework of these policies. The concept of the California general and specific plans, based on the incremental method, depicts general community goals and objectives and sets the planning framework. The specific plan translates the general plan into a more specific one and bridges the gap between the general plan and project proposals.

The fragmental process

The fragmental process is also similar to the synoptic process except that it is incomplete. One might go through four out of the total *seven* steps suggested for the synoptic process. For example, a designer might start by gathering and analyzing data, then go on to formulate goals and objectives, and finally develop an urban design plan. In the process, the designer may have merged or even omitted essential steps used in a synoptic approach.

The fragmental process is a mixture of synoptic and intuitive methods in that it uses steps that do not necessarily follow each other logically. Consequently, it is nearly impossible to check or monitor the process. Many comprehensive land use plans and environmental impact reports of the 1960s are products of the fragmental process. Unfortunately, in the hands of some professionals, this approach becomes little more than a hodgepodge of techniques and showpieces meant to impress clients. Of course, a report that appears to show data and data analysis as part of a design makes the whole package look more impressive to an uninitiated client, even though there may be critical gaps between the data analysis and the product.

The pluralistic process

The pluralistic approach attempts to incorporate into the design process the functional/social structure of an urban area as well as the inhabitants' value systems (Appleyard, 1976). The designer who uses the pluralistic method recognizes that "simple generalizations, standard norms and deterministic approaches are not valid" (Rapoport, 1977: 359). The method attempts to avoid operating within a controlled design tradition that has in the past produced overdesigned environments (Rapoport, 1977). Instead, open-ended design, with some framework that links and relates the parts, is used to produce designs for a dynamic system (Rapoport, 1977). Vernacular situations are results of the ideal pluralistic process. In these, territorial rules are subtle, but they are willingly adhered to so that subtle design changes adapt to population changes (Rapoport, 1977). When the vernacular no longer exists or is absent, a framework is proposed to address the varied cultural and subcultural character.

Donald Appleyard's plan for the city of Ciudad Guayana, is an excellent example of the pluralistic process in urban design (1976). Appleyard was most concerned with (1) determining why residents recalled certain elements of the city and (2) identifying the significant characteristics of such elements (Appleyard 1976). Pluralistic methods recognize that the users' values and perception of the city may be very different from those of the designer. Appleyard used several surveys to gather data and analyzed the information thoroughly before proposing strategies. As his study illustrates, it is the careful attention to analysis that distinguishes the pluralistic method from other approaches, especially the synoptic method.

The way in which pluralistic methods apply to American cities *has not been quite clear.* In most cases, the methods have been employed in Third World countries. Although some planners/designers claim that they are applying pluralistic methods in the United States, they are actually using the community action approaches developed in the 1960s. That is, these designers are helping low-income groups to create a better living environment in their neighborhoods and so are confusing advocacy planning with the pluralistic method. In a sense, such designers are correct to consider their method pluralistic, since they are engaged in the design process with people; but, as pluralism has been defined by Appleyard (1976), Rapoport (1977), and others, the term does not define advocacy approaches. Advocacy designers have not really attempted to understand the culture of the people for whom they are designing. They respond to apparent needs rather than culture.

A few designers in the United States have used methods that are close to the pluralistic method..The take-apart processes used by Halprin (1974) are a good example of a method that engages people in design processes and that attempts to address material and cultural issues rather than just react to material needs.

Radical process

The radical process has its roots in Marxist theory. Although many planners consider radical approaches dated—"sixtyish"—they still have worldwide application. In fact, given the present direction of the "planned school of thought," the concept of radical process has gained validity through Marxist applications to planning theory.

The underlying concept is that, in order to understand and design for a complex urban setting, social processes must be understood first (Harvey, 1973). In the United States, the radical process arose during the civil rights and antiwar movements of the 1960s (Angotti, 1978).

In the Soviet Union, the advantage of the radical process is its ability to predetermine growth and adequately accommodate it (Bater, 1980). However, it is difficult to characterize the process there, particularly in terms of its application to "design." Although some argue that in the Western world radical methods might profitably be used to develop learning systems that increase understanding of social change (Schon, 1971), these learning systems do not define any planning/design method. There are abstract methods implicit in some of these systems, but most of these methods are purely theoretical and academic. Real applications take place only in countries with Marxist governments—the Soviet Union is a prime example. But even there, "no viable theory or set of principles has yet emerged to provide a coherent set of guidelines for the future" (Poulsen, 1980: 12). "Completed plans are not implemented because local authorities lack their own finances for capital construction, and they also lack political authority to compel industrial ministries and other agencies that do have funding resources to build in conformity with their plans" (Poulsen, 1980: 12). Although the Soviet example may not fully illustrate the radical Marxist process, it is difficult to discuss the approach effectively without reference to the Soviet system. There is, of course, a large body of planning literature in the United States that discusses planning concepts based on Marxist theory, and there is extensive criticism available that treats other planning/design methods such as the synoptic or internalized models. On the whole, however, this literature is theoretical; the various theories discussed are rarely evaluated for their potential contribution to urban design. This is particularly true of the radical Marxist process. The approach is not only very difficult to define but its advocates plainly do not consider urban design a necessary focus for planning.

References

Angotti, Thomas. "Planning the Class Struggle: Radical Planning/Theory and Practice in the Post-Banfield Period." In Goldstein, H. A., and Rosenburry, Sara A., eds. *The Structural Crisis of the 1970's and Beyond: The Need for a New Planning Theory.* Blacksburg, VA: Virginia Polytechnic Institute and State University, 1978.

Appelbaum, Richard. "Planning as Technique: Some Consequences of the National-Comprehensive Model." In Goldstein, H. A., and Rosenberry, S. A., eds. *The Structural Crisis of the 1970's and Beyond: The Need for a New Planning Theory.* Blacksburg, VA: Virginia Polytechnic Institute and State University, 1978.

Appleyard, Donald. *Planning a Pluralist City, Conflicting Realities in Ciudad Guayana.* Cambridge, MA: The MIT Press, 1976.

Ardalan, Nader. *Nuran. The City of Illumination.* Isfahan, Tehran, Iran: Mandala Collaborative, 1978.

Bater, James H. *The Soviet City.* Beverly Hills, CA: Sage Publications Inc., 1980.

Boyce, David E.; Day, Norman D.; and McDonald, Chris. *Metropolitan Plan Making.* Philadelphia, PA: Regional Science Research Institute, Monograph Series Number Four, 1970.

Goldstein, Harvey A., and Rosenberry, Sara A. *Proceedings of the Conference on Planning Theory, The Structural Crisis of the 1970's and Beyond: The Need for a New Planning Theory.* Blacksburg, VA: Virginia Polytechnic Institute and State University, 1978.

Halprin, Laurence. *Taking Part: A Workshop Approach to Collective Creativity.* Cambridge, MA: The MIT Press, 1974.

Harvey, David. *Social Justice and the City.* Baltimore, MD: Johns Hopkins Press, 1973.

Hill, Morris. "A Goal-Achievement Matrix for Evaluating Alternative Plans." *Journal of the American Institute of Planners,* January (1968): 19–29.

Hopkins, Lewis D. "Methods for Generating Land Suitability Maps: A Comprehensive Evaluation." *Journal of the American Institute of Planners,* October (1977): 386–400.

Hudson, Barclay. *Planning: Typologies, Issues and Application Context.* Los Angeles, CA: UCLA School of Architecture and Urban Planning—DP 108, 1978.

Le Corbusier. *Looking At City Planning.* New York: Grossman Publishers, 1971. English Translation (first edition), 1946.

Lee, Colin. *Models in Planning.* New York: Pergamon Press, 1973.

Lichfield, Nathaniel; Kettle, Peter; and Whitbread, Michael. *Evaluation in the Planning Process.* New York: Pergamon Press, 1975.

Lynch, Kevin. *A Theory of Good City Form.* Cambridge, MA: The MIT Press, 1981.

Okamoto, Rai Y., and Williams, Frank E. *Urban Design Manhattan*. New York: The Viking Press, 1969.

Poulsen, Thomas M. "Urban Forms and Infrastructure in the Soviet Union." In Grant, Steven A., ed., *Soviet Housing and Urban Design*. Washington, D.C.: U.S. Department of Housing and Urban Development, 1980.

Rapoport, Amos. *Human Aspects of Urban Form*. New York: Pergamon Press, 1977.

Roberts, Margaret. *An Introduction to Town Planning Techniques*. London: Hutchinson Educational Ltd., 1974.

Schon, Donald A. *Beyond the Stable State*. New York: The Norton Library, 1971.

Shirvani, Hamid. *Urban Design Review, A Guide for Planners*. Chicago, IL: The Planners Press, 1981.

Steinitz, Carl. "Defensible Processes for Regional Landscape Design." *LATIS* 2, no. 1, September 1979.

Stretton, Hugh. *Urban Planning in Rich and Poor Countries*. New York: Oxford University Press, 1978.

Design criteria

CHAPTER 6

PROFESSIONALS frequently debate design criteria: What are they? How are they constituted? Traditionally, design has been judged on the basis of aesthetic quality. More recently, efficiency and economy have been added to aesthetics as meaningful criteria. At the present time, there are three basic types of design criteria—measurable, non-measurable, and generic—with variations according to one's particuler bent.

First, technical or technologically oriented persons tend to view design as a matter of function and efficiency. They use measurable design criteria as the basis for judgments on design. A second group of designers are the artists, design and planning professionals who emphasize the art of design more than any other aspect. Their design criteria are not usually concrete or measurable but rather based on judgments by their peers. A third group emerged from planning practice and was at its peak of influence in the 1960s. Their emphasis: social justice, equality, and equity as design criteria—also, to a large extent, nonmeasurable.

Of course, a high degree of overlap exists among these three groups. Throughout the practice of urban design and planning, one can observe a range of extremes and sometimes even a balance. Seeking such a balance has always been quite acceptable to professionals. We usually wish to find a balance among measurable, nonmeasurable, and what I call generic, or given, criteria: equity, equality, and justice. To put it another way, the urban design process should incorporate both measurable and nonmeasurable criteria and work within the framework of generic criteria. In the past, the practice of urban design has focused more on nonmeasurable than measurable criteria. However, the trend is becoming more balanced, as evidenced by acceptance of the concepts of performance standards and performance zoning.

Just what should be incorporated into the design process? In this chapter, an attempt has been made to compare and synthesize the various criteria used in the theory and practice of urban design in terms of measurable and nonmeasurable criteria and to group them appropriately. The resulting list is certainly not exhaustive, and there is no claim of comprehensiveness.

Nonmeasurable criteria

The analysis that follows addresses nonmeasurable criteria by outlining and comparing the design criteria proposed by the Urban Design Plan of San Francisco (1970), Urban Systems Research and Engineering, Inc. (1977), and Lynch (1981). Traditional approaches that develop implicit design criteria are also discussed within this comparative framework.

The Urban Design Plan of San Francisco (1970) identifies ten principles, or "fundamental concepts," that underlie the methods proposed for achieving the urban design goals and objectives of San Francisco. The concepts include:

1. Amenity/comfort, the livability qualities of the urban environment and, in particular, the ways in which the city accommodates the pedestrian with street furniture, plantings, roadway design, protection from the weather, avoidance of glare, and so on (San Francisco, 1970: 3–11).

2. Visual interest, the aesthetic qualities of the environment, most particularly its architectural character and the visually pleasing detail provided especially by the built environment (3, 16).

3. Activity, a general set of criteria (or methods) stressing the

importance of movement, excitement, and the "street life" dimension of the urban environment as promoted by ground-level retailing, arcades, lobbies, and by the avoidance of blank walls and vast parking lots (3, 13, 16).

4. Clarity and convenience, achieved by strong pedestrian rights-of-way, street narrowing, as well as other characteristics that facilitate the pedestrian experience of the urban environment (4, 11).

5. Character distinctiveness underscores the importance of providing definition and identity or individuality for structures and urban spaces to set them "apart from surroundings and contribute to . . . individuality" (4).

6. Definition of space concerns the interfacing of built and open-space components of the urban fabric to achieve "clarity and ease of perception of the shape and form of exterior space" (4). By its nature, definition of space relates to three other criteria identified by the plan: views, character/distinctiveness, and access. Issues concerning these three criteria converge in the plan's discussion of visibility of open space and its role in providing contrast within the urban context as well as the critical character of built-form edges surrounding open spaces.

7. The principle of views encompasses such aesthetic issues as the value of "pleasing vistas" as well as the perceptual aspects of human orientation in the urban environment. Street layout and building placement and massing are critical components in determining the aesthetic character and visual accessibility of the community (4, 31, 37–38).

8. Variety/contrast addresses such architectural matters as building style and arrangement. "It contributes to identifiable neighborhood areas and to points of interest within the community" (4).

9. Harmony/compatibility focuses on architectural and aesthetic aspects of compatibility as well as on the relationships to topography and built form in terms of transitions, complementarity of scale, and massing (4, 24–30).

10. Scale and pattern integrates a variety of concerns surrounding the goal of achieving a "human-scaled" urban environment. Attention is given to a size, bulk, and massing of buildings as well as to the aesthetic dimensions of contextual sensitivity and the "textural effect of building scale viewed from a distance" (4, 24–27).

Another set of criteria based on visual quality has been proposed by Urban Systems Research and Engineering, Inc. (1977). USR&E contends that visual quality has not been rigorously defined and is ultimately "relative to the people who perceive it"; however, it is possible to obtain a consensus on visual problems (USR&E, 1977: 2). USR&E's visual quality criteria are grouped into eight categories:

1. Fit with setting: concerns evaluation of the harmony or compatibility of a proposed design either with its urban or residential context in terms of site location, density, color, form, and materials. Another aspect of fit is the diachronic, or cultural, component of compatibility; whether a design "conserve[s] and incorporate[s] valued buildings and artifacts and traditional paths and uses" by including "visual reminders" including "physical objects, . . . uses or activities" (21).

2. Expression of identity: the social and functional importance of the "visual expression of an identity, status, and self-image valued by users and community (22). The roles of color, building material, as well as more personalized expressions, are emphasized for making the city "visually comprehensible" (22–23).

3. Access and orientation: issues of clarity and safety in the design of "entries, paths, and important on-site destinations" (24). Design elements include the layout and illumination of public spaces as well as destination/orientation (that is, views of landmarks and large-scale elements on or near the site as well as messages conveyed by the architecture and communicated through color, signage, and so on) about where to go and what to do (25).

4. Activity support: territoriality addressed as spatially defined behavior (26). A concern that environments provide a "visible structure" of territories and/or corresponding appropriate behaviors through signs. Specific design concerns include the division, size, and location of space along with facilities to be provided in those spaces (26–27).

5. Views: encouragement of designs that reinforce or, alternatively, minimize interference with "existing valued views" and that (where possible) provide new visual access opportunities from buildings and public spaces (28–29).

6. Natural elements: provides for the preservation, incorporation, and (where possible) creation of a "significant on-site presence of nature" through sensitivity to topography, plant cover, sunlight, water, and views of the sky (30–31).

7. Visual comfort: protection of the observer from on-site as well as off-site intrusions that detract from the visually pleasurable experience of the urban environment. Hampering elements include "glare, smog, dust, confusing or attention-demanding signs or lights, views of rapidly moving traffic or other nuisances" (32).

8. Care and maintenance: refers to components of a design that promote ease of maintenance and management, particularly by user groups (34–35).

Lynch (1981: 117–118) calls for "five performance dimensions" as design criteria: "Vitality, Sense, Fit, Access and Control." In addition, he suggests two "meta-criteria," "efficiency and justice," and argues that they "are always appended to any list of good things."

1. Vitality is the most basic measure of "the degree to which the form of the settlement supports the vital functions, the biological requirements and capabilities of human beings—above all, how it protects the survival of the species" (Lynch, 1981: 118). Vitality is a universal criterion concerned with systems that contribute to sustenance, safety, and consonance, including such diverse activities and elements as croplands, soils, and sewage management. On a more direct or intimate level, vitality is a measure of the consonance with or "fit between the human requirements of internal temperature, body rhythm, sensory input, and body function" (129).

2. Sense involves consideration of the role of form and quality in shaping perceptions and identity in the environment. Sense is achieved through (a) identity, or "sense of place," created by means of special forms, events, or intense familiarity (131–132); (b) "structure," as in the sense of how things fit together or the sense of orientation that references, landmarks, gradients, time, paths, or edges provide (134–135); (c) "congruence" refers to the existence of a strong place-function association; (d) "transparency," or "immediacy," of the environmental experience; "one can directly perceive the operation of the various technical functions, activities and social and natural processes that are occurring within the settlement" (138–139).

3. Fit is concerned with the "adequacy of behavior settings," a measure of the match between "place and whole patterns of behavior" (118, 151). This is essentially a planning or process issue that is concerned with programming user groups and monitoring functions associated with particular places. Performance measures of the adaptability—that is, the "manipulability" and "resilience" or "reversibility"—of environments as well as user groups are critical aspects of fit (170–182).

4. Access addresses "the ability of persons to reach other persons, activities, resources, services, information, or places, including the quality or diversity of the elements which can be reached" (118). The key issue concerning access is "to what things is access given and to whom is it afforded" (188).

5. Control explores the user-based aspects of access. "The degree to which the use and access to spaces and activities, and their creation, repairs, modification, and management are controlled by those who use, work, and reside in them" (118).

A comparative analysis of nonmeasurable criteria

These three approaches—San Francisco UDP, USR&E, and Lynch—are quite representative of the views found within the planning/urban design profession. There are, of course, other "architectonic-urban design" schemes that also define various criteria, again with some degree of overlap. Some of these architectonic frameworks will be discussed below. The comparative analysis of these different approaches outlined below offers a new perspective on nonmeasurable criteria for urban design. Figure 6-1 demonstrates how these three

Combine all 3 ↓

CRITERIA	SAN FRANCISCO URBAN DESIGN PLAN	URBAN SYSTEMS RESEACH AND ENGINEERING, INC.	LYNCH
ACCESS	CLARITY/ CONVENIENCE	ACCESS AND ORIENTATION	ACCESS
COMPATIBILITY	HARMONY/ CAPABILITY	FIT WITH SETTING	FIT
VIEWS	SCALE & PATTERN VISUAL INTEREST	VIEWS	VIEWS
IDENTITY	CHARACTER/ DISTINCTIVENESS DEFINITION OF SPACE	EXPRESS OF IDENTITY	SENSE
SENSE	ACTIVITY	FIT WITH SETTING	SENSE
LIVABILITY	AMENITY/COMFORT SCALE & PATTERN VARIETY/CONTRAST VISUAL INTEREST	CARE & MAINTENANCE ACTIVITY SUPPORT VISUAL COMFORT NATURAL ELEMENTS	CONTROL VITALITY

6-1: A comparison table between three types of design criteria.

sets of criteria relate to each other and how a "new" set based on their commonalities can be established.

1. Access: Lynch's concept of vitality, for example, which is a measure of the environment's contribution to sustenance, safety, and consonance (1981: 118), is quite clearly·comparable to the San Francisco Urban Design Plan's assessment of livability, with its "amenity/comfort" criterion (1970: 3–11). The related concerns, safety, amenity, and convenience, are also addressed more comprehensively by the various "access" criteria proposed by each approach. Thus, the San Francisco Urban Design Plan's concern with "clarity and convenience" is paralleled in the USR&E framework by the similar set of criteria, "access and orientation" (1977: 24–25). Lynch also proposes an "access" performance criterion, with "control" as a dimension (1981: 188).

2. Compatibility: Fit with setting represents another major area of convergence among the three approaches. The USR&E and San Francisco Urban Design Plan criteria have a visual or aesthetic emphasis and focus on compatibility in terms of site location, density, color, form, materials, scale, and massing (USR&E, 1977: 21; San Francisco, 1970: 24–30). Lynch's (1981) performance criterion adds a behavioral and functional dimension to fit, considering it as a measure of behavior-place congruence.

3. Views represents another category of criterion that is clearly emphasized in all three frameworks. San Francisco Urban Design Plan's approach emphasizes the aesthetic aspect of views in its concern for the preservation of "pleasing vistas" but also notes their importance for perceptual aspects of human orientation (1970: 37–39). Its "scale and pattern" criterion is also in part a "view criterion," with its attention to the "textural effect of building scale viewed from distance" (1970: 4, 24–27). USR&E's (1977) views criterion emphasizes the visual accessibility and preservation of the important views dimension of visual management. Lynch incorporates visual concerns with the structure and legibility dimensions of his "sense" criterion, emphasizing, as did USR&E, the role of reference such as landmarks, time, paths, and edges, as well as symbolic physical features, in aiding orientation in and apprehension of the urban environment (Lynch, 1981: 134–135, 139, 141).

4. Identity: The San Francisco Urban Design Plan and USR&E have specific criteria relating to identity and distinctiveness, whereas Lynch discusses identity as a dimension of sense (San Francisco, 1970: 4; USR&E 1977: 22–23; Lynch, 1981: 131–132). All three approaches note the importance of architecture, aesthetic elements, events, and value for making the city "visually comprehensible."

5. Sense: The design criterion of sense is most thoroughly discussed by Lynch, who identifies it as one of his five key performance dimensions (1981). His explication of the sense criterion emphasizes the role of spatial form and quality along with culture in shaping

perceptions and identity in the environment. This category of criterion essentially incorporates USR&E's concern for cultural aspects of "fit with setting" as well as the San Francisco Urban Design Plan's activity criterion, which stresses the importance of movement, excitement, and street life in urban environments (USR&E, 1977: 21; San Francisco, 1970: 13–16).

6. Livability: The goal or rationale behind all urban design criteria, regardless of the form they take, is to promote the "livability" of the city. This is a crucial concept, but one that is very difficult to define. On the one hand, livability encompasses opportunities to work, to be educated, to be culturally enriched through events, places, and people. It concerns matters of tax structure, ease of access and safety, as well as the quality of retail shopping. However, as Garbrecht (1981: xi–xvi) points out, livability has a physical dimension that makes it the concern of urban design:

> Urban livability, what does it mean? Jobs, educational opportunities, quality of retail stores, taxes, and so forth. But there is also a livability of spaces, that of the interior of buildings and that of the exterior space between: the open spaces of parks, rivers, plazas, gardens around houses, playgrounds, sports fields—and streets! Cities probably were rarely neutral environments. Rather, they were more livable for this group and less so for that one. In this sense, cities today are definitely less livable than they could or should be, and while they are quite livable for the adult having a decent job, they are quite often unlivable for others like teenagers and the elderly. (Garbrecht, 1981: xi)

It is important that the concept of livability be derived from contemporary and localized interpretations. The growing emphasis on pedestrianization schemes in many cities illustrates this point quite well. In defining livability, one key design area concerns the management of people and cars, but as Garbrecht (1981: xiii) reminds us, it is folly to attempt to design and plan for street life based on images of the past and "simplified notions about social organization in space." Instead, as Appleyard (1981) has illustrated, a variety of traffic control and design mechanisms, based on careful evaluation of street types, neighborhood, and functional needs (such as safety, lighting, and parking) provides the basis for creating livable environments.

Further analytic comparison of the three approaches reveals that they are concerned wih two aspects of physical spatial form: the visual and the functional (see fig. 6-2). USR&E's criteria are explicitly visual, and those presented in the San Francisco Urban Design Plan are essentially so. In comparison, Lynch's approach is definitely functional. The distinction between visual and functional approaches is critical from several standpoints. To some extent, the distinction cap-

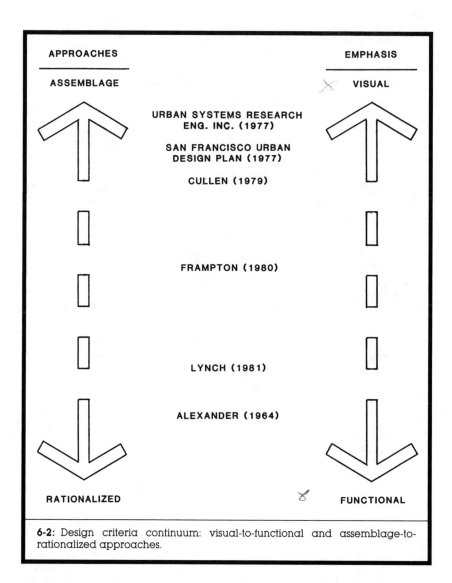

APPROACHES	EMPHASIS

ASSEMBLAGE

VISUAL

URBAN SYSTEMS RESEARCH
ENG. INC. (1977)

SAN FRANCISCO URBAN
DESIGN PLAN (1977)

CULLEN (1979)

FRAMPTON (1980)

LYNCH (1981)

ALEXANDER (1964)

RATIONALIZED

FUNCTIONAL

6-2: Design criteria continuum: visual-to-functional and assemblage-to-rationalized approaches.

tures a major trend in the field of urban design, the transition from nominalist or aesthetic approaches—"the city as an artifact"—to positivist and more fully elaborated functionalist approaches that evaluate urban environments in terms of cultural, social, and psychological dimensions as well as visual ones.

Another characteristic shared by these three representative approaches is that the criteria they delineate may be simply too general for effective communication with the general public or even other, nondesign, professionals. There are also potential validity problems

with these design-criteria frameworks; the San Francisco Urban Design Plan has already been tested but others are more theoretical.
These factors lead one to wonder whether there are, in fact, any
systematic frameworks for urban design criteria available.

However, if we compare the three approaches in terms of the
structure, internal consistency, coherency, and explicitness of the criteria they propose, a rough continuum emerges (see fig. 6-2). At one
extreme, there is the San Francisco Urban Design Plan, which proposes a set of ten "design principles" that compare "the basic measurements by which design is evaluated" (1970: Abstract). These
principles, as realized through the design examples provided, are not
prescriptive. Rather, they are a "step away" from design criteria, an
"assemblage" or checklist that, moreover, tends to conflate criteria
with physical elements. Therefore, while there is overlap with criteria
from the other two frameworks, the San Francisco UDP list contains
loosely outlined categories that interact to such an extent that priori-
ties (or any potential hierarchy of applications) are sacrificed. Instead,
all the principles appear equally important. The UDPSF framework
lacks guides or "rules of use" that would direct application in a complex planning/urban design problem.

In contrast, the USR&E scheme proposes a definite (though not
necessarily more valid) organizing principle—the visual element. It
is important to recognize that this perspective shapes the criteria
framework along prescriptive, control, and problem-based lines. In
the discussion of the analysis of visual quality, it is noted:

> The significant thing is that there is surprising consensus about
> what problems are: it is more important to eliminate them than
> it is to come up with wonderful and original solutions. The most
> useful function is to try and make excellence possible, not to try
> to create it. (USR&E, 1977: 2)

In terms of fit, for example, the authors contend: "In the end, fit
with setting is largely a matter of what communities want, or in the
negative sense, what they will tolerate" (USR&E, 1977: 20).

Another feature that characterizes USR&E's work as "semirational-
ized" is the tentative role of supporting documentation for criteria
drawn from social, cognitive, as well as psychological research. For
example, access and orientation as well as identity issues rely on these
kinds of supports (USR&E, 1977).

Lynch's approach, while sharing many substantive features with the
other frameworks, clearly demonstrates the most analytical and rationalized method discussed thus far. In the first place, there is his
continual reference to human beings as biological/cultural/psycholog-
ical beings. He insists that the analysis and evaluation of urban form
must proceed from this point. Urban form develops from his perfor-
mance-criteria framework only with reference to human ends and

needs as a raison d'être. While USR&E shares this perspective to a limited degree, in Lynch's work, we see a far more elaborated scheme of functional criteria as well as a much stronger positivist trend.

A second feature of Lynch's scheme is the critical framework he has attempted to incorporate with his metacriteria—justice and efficiency—as well as his discussion of the interaction of "good city form" performance dimensions. He considers the interdependence of performance dimensions as well as their relative value for different types of societies and cultures (Lynch, 1981).

The continuum and traditional approaches to design criteria

This continuum from "assemblage" to more fully "rationalized" design criteria (fig. 6-2) also assists us in appreciating the continuing value of traditional and ostensibly less formal approaches to urban design criteria. For example, Cullen's classic book, *Townscape,* is essentially visual in approach but at the same time must be described as semistructured. His major criteria of serial vision, place, and content provide loci of application as well as a clear rationale: the unfolding pedestrian experience. Moreover, he recognizes the inherent as well as necessary hierarchy and flexibility of urban design concepts:

> The upshot is that a town could take one of several patterns and still operate with success, equal success. Here then we discover a pliability in the scientific solution and it is precisely in the *manipulation of this pliability* that the art of relationship is made possible. As will be seen, the aim is not to dictate the shape of the town or environment, but is a modest one: simply to *manipulate within the tolerances.* (Cullen, 1961: 8)

Alexander (1964: 15) is probably one of the most outspoken proponents of functional approaches to design:

> The following argument is based on the assumption that physical clarity cannot be achieved in a form until there is first some programmatic clarity in the designer's mind and actions; and that for this to be possible, in turn, the designer must first trace his design problem to its earliest functional origins and be able to find some sort of pattern in them. I shall try to outline a general way of stating design problems which draws attention to these functional origins, and makes their pattern reasonably easy to see.

At the same time, his fully structured treatment of context is probably one of his more important critical contributions to urban design:

There are two sides to this tendency designers have to change the definition of the problem On the one hand, the impractical idealism of designers who want to redesign entire cities and whole processes of manufacture when they are asked to design simple objects is often only an attempt to loosen difficult constraints by stretching the form-context boundary.

On the other hand, this way in which the good designer keeps an eye on the possible changes at every point of the ensemble is part of his job. He is bound, if he knows what he is doing, to be sensitive to the fit at several boundaries within the ensemble at once Indeed, this ability to deal with several layers of form-context boundaries in concert is an important part of what we often refer to as the designer's sense of organization. The internal coherence of an ensemble depends on a whole net of such adaptations. In a perfectly coherent ensemble, we should expect the two halves of every possible division of the ensemble to fit one another. (Alexander, 1964: 17–18)

And, he continues:

It is true, then, that since we are ultimately interested in the ensemble as a whole, there is no good reason to divide it up just once. We ought always really to design with a number of nested, overlapped form-context boundaries in mind. Indeed, the form itself relies on its own inner organization and on the internal fitness between the pieces it is made of to control its fit as a whole to the context outside.

However, since we cannot hope to understand this highly interlaced and complex phenomenon until we understand how to achieve fit at a single arbitrarily chosen boundary, we must agree for the present to deal only with the simplest problem. Let us decide that, for the duration of any one discussion, we shall maintain the same single division of a given ensemble into form and context, even though we acknowledge that the division is probably chosen arbitrarily. And let us remember, as a corollary, that for the present, we shall be giving no deep thought to the internal organization of the form as such, but only to the simplest premise and aspect of that organization: namely, that fitness which is the residue of adaptation across the single form-context boundary we choose to examine.

The form is a part of the world over which we have control, and which we decide to shape while leaving the rest of the world as it is. The context is that part of the world which puts demands on this form; anything in the world that makes demands of the form is context. Fitness is a relation of mutual acceptability between these two. In a problem of design, we want to satisfy the mutual demands which the two make on one another. We want to put the context and the form into effortless contact or frictionless coexistence. (Alexander, 1964: 18–19)

Still another important perspective on urban design criteria comes from Frampton (1980) in his extended critique of what he terms the "mechanistic flexibility" and "reductionism" of 1960s (and, to some extent, present-day) architecture. The failure of this architecture to promote the public interest is the result of its advanced "technological design," which consists of "inaccessible images" and indeterminant solutions that undermine a sense of place and neutralize the context of indigenous cultural significance (Frampton, 1980: 285–288).

The above arguments are certainly valid as far as architecture and "urban physical structure" are concerned. Questions arise, however, about the applicability of these criteria within the context of complex urban problems and how these criteria can be translated into any sort of specific guidelines and/or control mechanisms.

Measurable criteria

Measurable criteria are those that can be measured quantitatively. Some examples are the natural factors discussed in chapter four: urban climate, solar energy, urban geology, urban hydrology, and so on. Others deal with the actual measurement of physical form: height and bulk, floor-area ratio, setback, coverage, and so on. Various standards can be used for measurement; here, the measurable criteria are divided into two groups: (1) environmental–natural criteria and (2) building form, massing, and intensity. The first group has been generally discussed in chapter two; in specific terms, the measurement of environmental-natural factors is beyond the scope of a planner/ urban designer unless he or she develops special expertise. Planners/ urban designers are always advised to consult the experts on environmental/natural factors. As mentioned in chapter four, a planner/urban designer must be aware of such factors and should know enough to be able to communicate with the environmental expert about his or her design concept and plan.

The second group, building form, massing, and intensity, which concentrates on the measurement of three-dimensional urban form, is indeed within the scope of the planner/urban designer's expertise.

There are generally two types of measurement: (1) conventional and (2) innovative. Conventional measurement includes floor-area ratio (FAR), sky-exposure plane, and density. Floor-area ratio is "the total floor area on a zoning lot, divided by the lot area of that zoning lot" (DeChiara and Koppelman, 1982: 594) (fig. 6-3). Sky-exposure plane is "an imaginary inclined plane beginning above the street line at a set height and rising over a zoning lot at a ratio of vertical distance to horizontal distance" (DeChiara and Koppelman, 1982: 595) (fig. 6-4). Density is, of course, the number of persons or units of space per

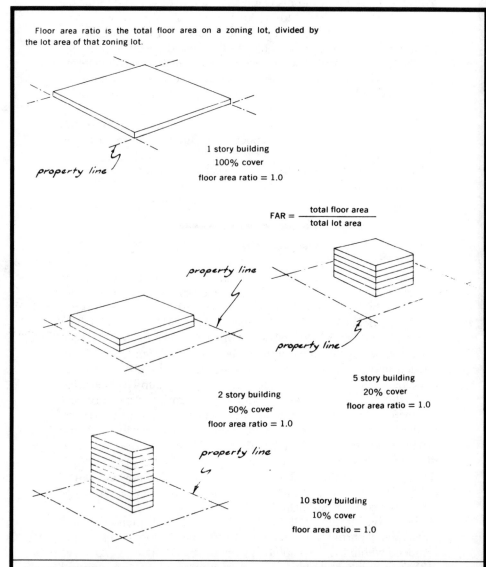

Floor area ratio is the total floor area on a zoning lot, divided by the lot area of that zoning lot.

property line

1 story building
100% cover
floor area ratio = 1.0

$$FAR = \frac{\text{total floor area}}{\text{total lot area}}$$

property line

property line

5 story building
20% cover
floor area ratio = 1.0

2 story building
50% cover
floor area ratio = 1.0

property line

property line

10 story building
10% cover
floor area ratio = 1.0

6-3: Illustration of floor area ratio (FAR) (Source: Joseph DeChiara and Lee Koppelman. *Urban Planning and Design Criteria.* New York: Van Nostrand Reinhold Company Inc., 1975).

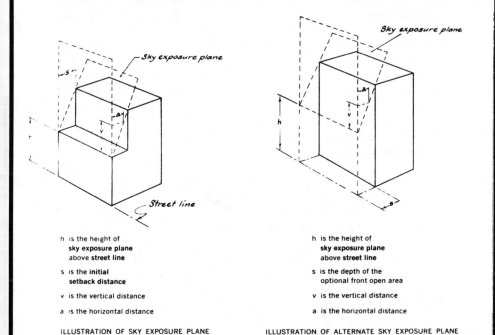

h is the height of sky exposure plane above **street line**	h is the height of sky exposure plane above **street line**
s is the initial setback distance	s is the depth of the optional front open area
v is the vertical distance	v is the vertical distance
a is the horizontal distance	a is the horizontal distance

| ILLUSTRATION OF SKY EXPOSURE PLANE | ILLUSTRATION OF ALTERNATE SKY EXPOSURE PLANE |
| Sky Exposure Plane = $\dfrac{\text{Vertical Distance}}{\text{Horizontal Distance}}$ | On narrow streets, the slope will be less than on wide streets. The height (h) should relate to the general scale of the neighboring structures. |

6-4: Illustrative analysis of sky exposure plane (Source: Joseph DeChiara and Lee Koppelman. *Urban Planning and Design Criteria.* New York: Van Nostrand Reinhold Company Inc., 1975).

two-dimensional unit plane (for example, six dwelling units per acre). These measurements are well-known tools, which planners and designers have used for many years. However, they are not as effective for urban design as are some innovative methods developed as early as ten years ago and some more recent efforts.

In the early 1960s, one of the most far-reaching sets of standards for ensuring design quality through land use controls was developed by the Urban Land Institute in cooperation with the Federal Housing Authority (Hanke, 1969). The land-use-intensity (LUI) system is a numerical scale designed to measure intensities of land use in residential developments. It assesses the relationship of building to land (and the open spaces that remain), which the LUI system interprets as the relation of floor area (rather than density, which is a poor indicator of numbers of people) to land area. From this ratio it derives the amount of space that should be allotted to garages, streets, and so on, and, most importantly, to open space—especially "livability space."

LUI does not derive a simple percentage of open space, but, rather, provides site-based criteria for determining the kinds of open space that should be available: open space, parking, and recreation space (fig. 6-5).

The LUI system is incorporated into the design process in the following manner: once a proper density for a given site has been determined (a specific number of living units to the acre), the planner/designer needs only to plot a vertical line on the LUI graph to define "workable relationships" of land and floor area as well as open, livability, and recreation space (Hanke, 1969: 8).

Another example of an innovative measurement method, developed for New York City, integrates floor-area allowances, setback, height, bulk, and site-coverage controls with land use and other urban design proposals (such as pedestrian ways, preservation of views, and coordination with transportation system facilities). The proposed method is well illustrated by proposals for the sixty Wall Street sites in lower Manhattan (New York, 1976). Anticipated expansion of a major office building on the sixtieth block of Wall Street led to a number of urban design alternatives that demonstrated how site coverages, FAR, height, and setback could be manipulated with substantially different results and benefits. Whereas existing zoning for the site constrained building location to the site's back or center, the new measurement system enabled the city to coordinate a number of urban design proposals that include through-block pedestrian access to subway and retailing and service activities (fig. 6-6).

Another recent example of measurable criteria is the one developed by the City of Seattle, Washington. "Floor area districts" have been established based on such special land use and transportation conditions as retailing, residential, light manufacturing, commercial-office, and so on that exist in various districts (Seattle, 1982). Seattle's method provides floor-area allowances by establishing a base and maximum floor area ratio (FAR) for each district; but only relative magnitude rather than specific floor-area allowances are indicated for each permitted use (fig. 6-7).

Seattle uses maximum building-height controls in conjunction with FAR and land use to reflect and manage the intensity of development within districts (Seattle, 1982). The height standard, though, introduces a dimension of scale control that simultaneously relates to existing physical context, including the natural topography of downtown, existing development in and around the downtown district (historic character, and so on), and coordination with transportation capacity, "as well as other determinants of building density for the different parks and downtown" (Seattle, 1982: 37). Height limits, then, are still designed to be coordinated with FAR allowances and setback criteria (for both street and upper levels) to define general building envelopes and to reflect the intensity and scale of development within

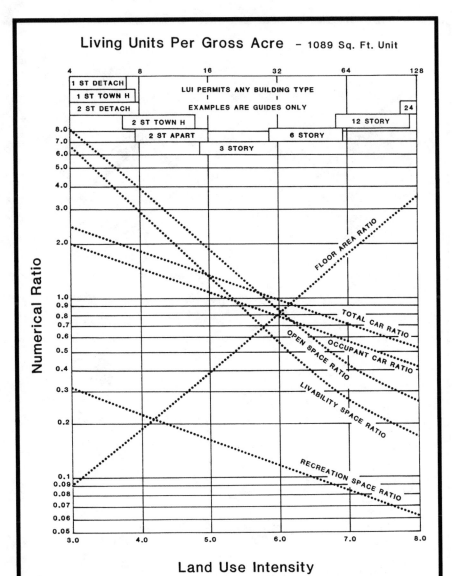

6-5: Land use intensity chart developed by Byran R. Hanke (Source: Byran R. Hanke. "Land Use Intensity, A New Approach to Land Control," *Urban Land,* Urban Land Institute, 1969).

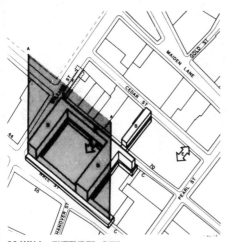

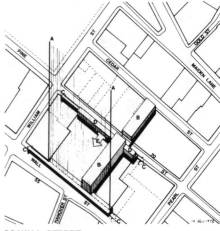

60 WALL – EXTENDED SITE

PROPOSED URBAN DESIGN CRITERIA

A Build to lot line, without setback, along Wall Street.
B Covered pedestrian spaces, providing through block cir-
   culation and access to the subway.
C Future connections to the Second Avenue subway.
D Arcade along Pine Street.
E Access to truck loading area,, either from Pine Street
   or Cedar Street.
F Future connection to Chase Manhattan Plaza.

OFFICE OF LOWER MANHATTAN DEVELOPMENT, OFFICE OF THE MAYOR, CITY OF NEW YORK

60 WALL STREET

PROPOSED URBAN DESIGN CRITERIA

A Build to lot line, without setback, along Wall Street.
B Through-block covered pedestrian space, at both street and
   subway level.
C Passages to subway stations.
D Arcade along Pine Street.
E Access to truck loading area (and parking) from Pine Street.

OFFICE OF LOWER MANHATTAN DEVELOPMENT, OFFICE OF THE MAYOR, CITY OF NEW YORK

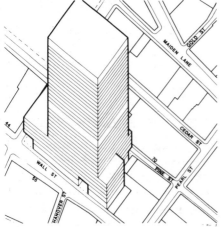

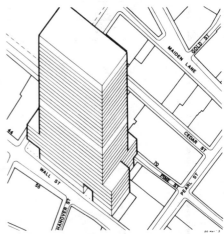

60 WALL – EXTENDED SITE

55% TOWER – 100% BASE – STAGED CONSTRUCTION

In this location the 55% tower could be built before demolish-
ing the two buildings adjacent to William Street; however, the
spatial definition of Wall Street is relatively weak and the
light and air to Pine Street very restricted. Tower floors
would be approximately 220 ft. by 170 ft.

60 WALL – EXTENDED SITE

55% TOWER ON WALL ST. – 100% BASE – COVERED PEDESTRIAN SPACES

This alternative assumes that the extensive covered pedestrian
spaces would justify both a 55% tower and an FAR of 18.0 and
that, for light, air, and definition of urban spaces, the
tower should be located along Wall Street. The setback along
William Street weakens the definition of Wall Street but increases the access of 44 Wall to light and produces a relatively
regular tower floor (270 ft. by 138 ft.).

6-6: An example of urban design criteria developed for the 60 Wall Street site in New York
City by the Office of Lower Manhattan Development (Source: City of New York).

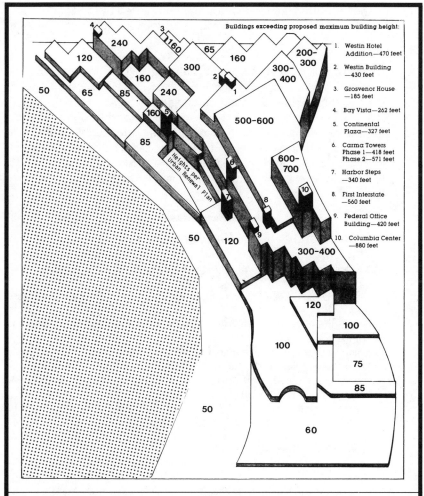

6-7: Seattle's floor area district identifying maximum building height (Source: City of Seattle, WA).

each district as well as transitions between them. Therefore, it is important to note that each of these features is subordinate to the floor-area allowances as designated by the downtown land use plan:

> Areas governed by different building heights would be coordinated as closely as possible with the boundaries of floor area districts to reinforce the relationships between height and density. Coordination with the floor area districts will also insure

that opportunities for development supported by the floor area allowances are not foreclosed by restrictions on height. (Seattle, 1982: 37)

Within the plan, then, maximum building heights are "tentative" to facilitate fit with proposed densities, setbacks, and proposed heights that together define permitted building envelopes.

The approaches outlined above are examples of flexible and effective urban design methods incorporating measurable criteria. It should be emphasized here that such criteria and measurement mechanisms have to be consistent with established qualitative criteria in order to be effective parts of an urban design process.

References

Alexander, Christopher. *Notes on the Synthesis of Form.* Cambridge, MA: Harvard University Press, 1964.

Appleyard, Donald. *Livable Streets.* Berkeley, CA: University of California Press, 1981.

Cullen, Gordon. *The Concise Townscape.* New York: Van Nostrand Reinhold Company Inc., 1961.

DeChiara, Joseph, and Koppelman, Lee. *Urban Planning and Design Criteria.* Third Edition. New York: Van Nostrand Reinhold Company Inc., 1982.

Frampton, Kenneth. *Modern Architecture, A Critical History.* New York: Oxford University Press, 1980.

Garbrecht, Dietrich. Forward to "Creating Livable Cities." Norman Pressman, Guest Ed., *Contact* 13, no. 2/3 (1981): xi–xvi.

Hanke, Byran R. "Land Use Intensity, A New Approach to Land Use Controls." *Urban Land* 28, no., 10 (1969): 3–11.

Lynch, Kevin. *A Theory of Good City Form.* Cambridge, MA: The MIT Press, 1981.

New York, City of. *Water Street Access and Development.* New York: Office of Lower Manhattan Development, 1976.

San Francisco, City of. *Urban Design Principles for San Francisco.* Preliminary Report No. 5. Springfield, VA: National Technical Information Service, 1970.

Seattle, City of. *1982 Downtown Alternative Plan.* Seattle, WA: Executive Department, 1982.

Urban Systems Research and Engineering (USR&E). *Environmental Assessment of Visual Quality—Draft.* Cambridge, MA: USRE, Inc., 1977.

Products

CHAPTER 7

DESIGNING an object such as a chair or a table can lead directly to a "product," in this case, a manufactured or built chair or table. The concerns of the designer are varied—comfort and other behavioral factors as well as aesthetics and economics. The designer identifies all the factors involved, designs his or her product, and sees it through the production process. However, consider the situation shown in figure 7-1. The design process becomes more difficult as a designer undertakes an increasingly complex project. Designing a room involves more factors than designing an object, and designing a house increases the external ramifications even if the internal, or specific-client, factors are ignored. The designer probably still has but one client and one program, but an increase in the external factors is obvious because of the impact of that particular house on neighboring houses and on the site. Perhaps the house blocks the sun from its

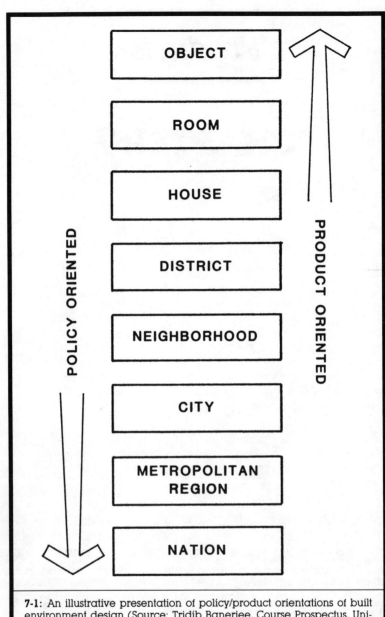

7-1: An illustrative presentation of policy/product orientations of built environment design (Source: Tridib Banerjee, Course Prospectus, University of Southern California, 1980).

neighbors, or perhaps its siting may cause surface water runoff across adjacent properties. In such circumstances, contextual and fitness factors come into play. Zoning regulations and building codes are a response to these matters. Yet, the architect who designs a house is given a framework: his or her task is to take this design framework and, after considering all other factors, to design the house.

As figure 7-1 shows, the design of a neighborhood, district or city becomes more process-oriented within a framework where a designer can design more specific and individual user products. Here the individual user as well as the public at large are the clients of design and should benefit from it. Proceeding a step further, state and federal policies on urban and regional development are pure policy framework.

With this background in mind, note in figure 7-1 that urban design deals with a neighborhood and/or city. This does not mean, of course, that the design of a region cannot be the province of urban designers. Rather, we wish only to indicate that the scale from neighborhood to city has been traditionally—and is presently—the focus of urban design. But, regardless of scale, urban design has two types of output: process-oriented and project-oriented. Developing an urban mall in the downtown is an example of a project-oriented product. On the other hand, developing design guidelines for downtown developments is a process-oriented product, as in an urban design plan for an entire city. "The location of planning within the organization's decision-making process tends to define the planning process" and, subsequently, the output (Munson, 1974: i). The essential point here is that a realistic urban design process can include both types of products.

One of the major problems of the traditional practice of urban design has been its orientation toward project versus the combination of process and project. So-called "one-shot/one-sheet planning" was also the project approach to urban design that envisioned the whole city as a project and developed beautiful futuristic designs on paper —something like designing a house or a building without much consideration of all necessary factors.

The main issue to emphasize here is that we should deal with "physical development" regardless of the type of products and scale. As Raymond (1978) put it, the formulation and articulation of the physical development plan is the central focus of planning. Lynch (1980: 48) elaborates:

> This is a return to that old-fashioned field of physical city (or land use) planning; but it is simultaneously more focused and yet also more amply connected to other concerns, and given a sharp sense of humanistic purpose.

Perfecting earlier methods is supported by Hudson (1978: 8): "Planning evolves through the continual application of old methods to new problems, and discovery of new methods to deal with old problems." Others support the validity and the usefulness of the physical plan and stress the importance of such environmental issues as natural resource conservation. (See Burchell and Steinlieb, 1978—especially McHarg, Hoppenfield, Krumholz, Cogger, Linner).

The basis for such arguments is not only that urban physical development planning is still a vital function, but also that the results of a well-organized plan, which combines quantity and quality, are evident. A prime example is the Urban Design Plan of San Francisco, which in "essence seeks to define physical quality stated in terms of human need" (Jacobs, 1971: 27). More than a decade after its adoption, one can observe the positive results: buildings stairstep down to the waterfront, and view corridors are intact; historic buildings have been preserved, and open space is protected; and the quality of neighborhood life has been improved.

In recent years, however, cities have become aware of the fact that the "plan" is not the only "product" of design. Indeed, other products are needed for successful urban design. Cities now realize that there are several *frameworks that they can use* to control physical development of the city and at the same time create a high-quality sensory environment.

The products of urban design can be classified into four major groups: policies, plans, guidelines, and programs.

Policies

Design policies are indirect design methods that include regulatory means of implementation or investment programs and other means of "causing direct designs to be implemented." To put it another way, urban design policies are primarily a framework for the overall design process. Sometimes planners and designers can get involved directly in planning and design without structured or overall urban design policies. Framework is a response to the socioeconomic setting, an inclusive umbrella under which planning and design can take place. Strategies—how to make an urban design on paper work in reality—can also be a part of framework, and they should identify and demonstrate all the advantages the urban design may bring to an area and explain these advantages to the public.

Urban design policies are thus a framework for action. They are not generalized goals and objectives; but neither are they specific implementation strategies—even though some cities have recently referred to more specific design proposals or guidelines as "design policies."

It is very important to remember that such a framework should be flexible enough to allow specific design to take place within it. Yet, one should not get lost in policymaking. In truth, the word *policy* does not have a good reputation among designers since in most instances the policymaker is not a designer, nor has he or she consulted a designer. Therefore, the resultant "policies" are often unimaginative and uninteresting and could not produce a high quality urban environment. The planning practice of the mid sixties and early seventies illustrates this.

Very few cities have produced a realistic set of urban design policies. However, many realize their value and are beginning to structure a planning process within which such policies can result. A prime example is Seattle. Its Office of Policy and Evaluation has produced a *Background Report of the Downtown Land Use and Transportation* (1981), which addresses policy issues relating to land use and urban design, housing and residential service, transportation, natural environment, utilities, and land use regulation by first generating extensive background studies and analysis. Another interesting aspect of Seattle's policies is that land use and urban design are considered as a single set of issues. In addition, this policy document has established the framework within which the Downtown Alternative Plan (1982) has been developed.

Plan

A plan is the most essential of all the products of urban design. Whether urban design is product- or process-oriented, the necessity of producing a plan is quite evident. As discussed above, it should be developed within the framework of a set of policies. This is a key issue that has not been given much attention in the past. Either there has been a plan without an understanding of the realities of the setting for which the design plan is proposed, or there have been too many policies and no plan. The urban design plan is a three-dimensional depiction of urban design policies.

The traditional approach to urban physical planning has been controlling change by establishing a set of harmonious relationships in the urban area. Two planning products dominate—the master, or development, plan, which is concerned with the physical environment; and the comprehensive plan, which describes general community policies.

This "end-state" planning style was in peak use during the 1950s and 1960s, and many plans were developed in this manner. While some communities produced comprehensive plans of some validity and benefit to their citizens, other localities simply went through the motions of planning in order to receive federal funds. According to Beal and Hollander (1979: 160), some of the hundreds of plans produced in the 1960s can be described as "mechanical and unimaginative." By the 1960s, it was becoming "apparent that the static, goal-oriented master plan approach was not working." It is largely true that the end-state linear planning method has been rejected by professionals because it "refer[s] only to completed form" without taking into "account the process by which the form is achieved" (Lynch, 1981: 280). Such a form-making direction "ignores the reality of continuous change, in which no form is a permanent feature. . . . Process is the key" (Lynch, 1981: 280).

It is self-evident that a plan can be made within certain limits of generality and detail and then reviewed and updated from time to time. As Kent noted (1964), this procedure is still valid, and Raymond (1978: 4) agrees: "There is a great deal to be gained from trying to follow an overall plan even if it has to be changed frequently in response to changed objectives brought on by unforeseen circumstances." A valid physical plan, then, can be expressed as a general framework within which incremental changes are made, implemented, and their implications and side effects realized. This is in close agreement with the assertion that planning "will serve no useful purpose unless it leads to an action" (USHEW, 1967: 1).

There is no doubt that physical plans have had many problems, mostly centered around the very important relationship between the plan itself and the intended *modus operandi*—the institutional processes through which the plan is implemented. This relationship may be evident, but it is often neglected. It is clear that we need a plan that focuses on the physical development of the city. There are many environmental demands and constraints to which a physical plan should be responsive, and most planners have become aware of the realities and practical implications of planning practice. The emphasis on both process and plan attempts to bridge the gap that usually exists between the plan and its implementation.

> The urban design plan was prepared with the intention that its policies would be carried out. It included a list of measures to be taken to implement the policies, and one preliminary report was devoted entirely to implementation. Throughout the study period, two questions were asked over and over again: "How would you carry it out?" and "How realistic is the proposal in terms of its being implemented?" This does not mean that no proposal could or should be made without a surefire way of carrying it out. It does mean thinking continually about means of achieving desired ends (Jacobs, 1978: 219).

Guidelines

Developing urban design policies and an urban design plan is not enough to address the "specific" elements of urban physical form. The lessons learned from the Urban Design Plan of San Francisco clearly demonstrate this point.

Although San Francisco's plan was unique and has been largely successful in its application, it has been weakened by a lack of specific design guidelines. Planners working in the city realized this deficiency and have translated the urban design plan into specific design guidelines to ensure quality at the microscale. As a result, *Guiding Downtown Development* (1982) was produced. It is clearly a model example for comprehensive urban design. It is comprehensive since it does not merely go through a few physical items; rather, it is divided into seven sections with an extensive set of appendixes to explain the guidelines further. These sections include "Building Size," "Design and Appearance," "Retail Services," "Recreation and Open Space,"

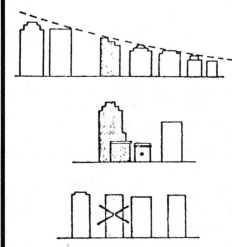

The overall form of the building is appropriate to the context, working with nearby buildings to produce a graceful, coherent city form.

The project relates harmoniously to nearby structures of historic and/or architectural merit and, if necessary, provides transitionally scaled sub-elements to minimize extreme differences in scale.

The increased height does not result in a project similar in height to nearby buildings, nor does it contribute to the impression of benching.

The increased height does not result in shading of outdoor recreational space or sitting and sunning areas that are accessible by the public.

7-2: Examples of San Francisco design guidelines for downtown development (Source: City of San Francisco, CA).

7-3: New York's Fifth Avenue streetline.

"Transportation and Circulation," "Housing," and "Preservation of Significant Buildings and Industry." Supplemental graphics (although of poor quality) further explain the text (fig. 7-2).

Design guidelines do not necessarily result in more control or restriction. What they do is develop a design framework at the district, street, or even project/parcel scale. Design guidelines also may present alternative forms or approaches for a specific design element such as a plaza, housing, landscaping, and so on. Essentially, guidelines are intended to ensure built-form quality. In fact, urban design in New York City grew out of the Special Zoning District concept, which established specific design guidelines in response to the specific problems and opportunities of a particular district. For example, consider Lower Manhattan Special Zoning District's pedestrian design and planning guidelines or Fifth Avenue Special Zoning District's preservation of retailing at the ground level of buildings and street wall (keeping the street line) (fig. 7-3).

It is obvious that a city is pieced together from many parts at different times, with each part having a different physical character and function. An urban design plan can deal with design issues in terms of the relationship among these parts. Design guidelines then will focus on specific districts or areas of a city, districts of specific character and in need of specific treatment: a historic preservation district, a commercial district, a district with a mix of uses but exhibiting specific physical character or function, and so on.

Design Guidelines for Downtown Long Beach (1980) is an example of guidelines developed for a specific area, in this case, the downtown. These guidelines delineate the various design issues involved in the public's enjoyment of the physical environment. In a very organized way, they cover land use along pedestrian routes, parking and access to property, building appearance and configuration, landscape, hardscape, and signs. They also include two further sets of specific guidelines relative to a mall development zone and an avenue of a specific character and function in the downtown. Application of these guidelines in practice has been successful and is helping Long Beach to revitalize its downtown (fig. 7-4).

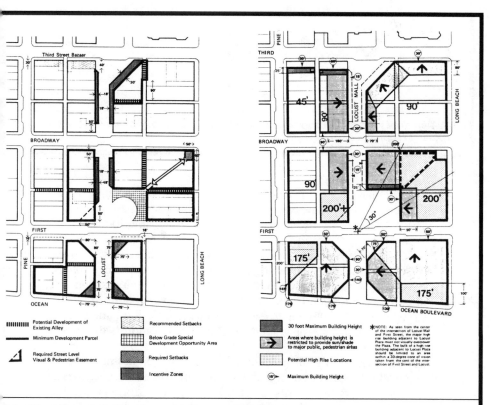

7-4: City of Long Beach design guidelines graphically presenting guidelines' application to a mall development (Source: City of Long Beach, CA).

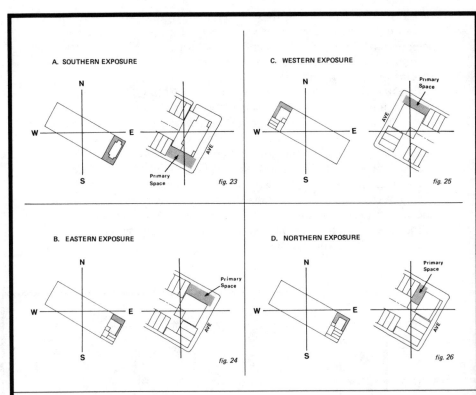

A. SOUTHERN EXPOSURE

N

W — E

S

Primary Space

fig. 23

C. WESTERN EXPOSURE

N

W — E

S

Primary Space

fig. 25

B. EASTERN EXPOSURE

N

W — E

S

Primary Space

fig. 24

D. NORTHERN EXPOSURE

N

W — E

S

Primary Space

fig. 26

7-5: New York's Plazas for People design guidelines graphically presenting various solar exposures (Source: City of New York).

A city may choose design guidelines focusing on specific physical elements that could be designed and built in various parts of the city. The guidelines may even identify criteria for suitable location. New York City's study report, "Plazas for People, Streetscape and Residential Plazas" (1976) is an example of design guidelines that "instruct" the developers and their architects about making plazas better. It also introduces a variety of guidelines on streetscape, emphasizing "the importance of pedestrian experiences and perceptions from the street" (fig. 7-5). Of course, each city must decide the particular organization and style of guidelines that will accomplish the design goals of that city.

The nature of the design guidelines, a major issue, has recently received more attention. One determines the nature of guidelines by first deciding whether they are prescriptive or performance guidelines. Prescriptive guidelines attempt to establish the limit or framework within which individual designers must work, as in FAR requirements. For example: "The allowed FAR in the downtown is

12"—meaning that the floor area of a proposed building may not be more than twelve times the area of its site. Performance guidelines provide the designer with various measures and criteria as well as methods of calculation, while leaving concept development up to the designer. Instead of saying, "FAR = 12 is the limit," performatory guidelines might specify the amount of sunlight required in the open space and surrounding area, capacity of infrastructure to handle the additional load by the building, required landscaping and vegetations, and so on.

The advantage of performance guidelines is that they apply standard measurements to all the sites but do not demand standard forms that may or may not be appropriate to all the sites. Therefore, the physical form can vary depending on the site location. Moreover,

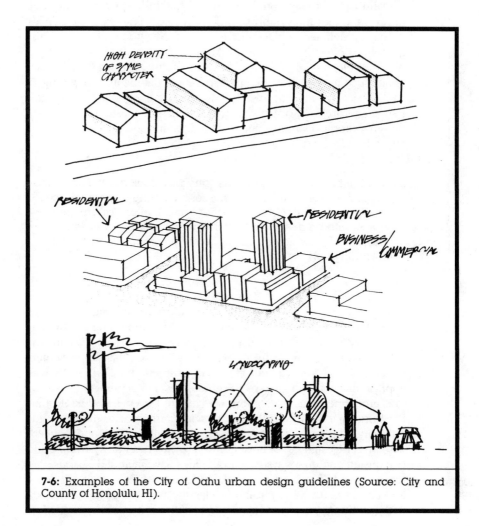

7-6: Examples of the City of Oahu urban design guidelines (Source: City and County of Honolulu, HI).

performance guidelines are more flexible than prescriptive techniques and leave creativity and innovation in the hands of the designer and planner.

Regardless of the scope and type of issues covered, urban design guidelines should include the following sections: (1) purpose and objectives of the guidelines, (2) classification of major and minor issues to be covered, (3) applicability, and (4) examples illustrating some applications. Each of these four areas is important, although some cities have put together elaborate design guidelines that emphasize some but not all of the sections. The result is usually confusion on the part of developers and their architects. For example, many guideline systems do not discuss applicability; if they do, the criteria, conditions, and so on, are not fully explained or illustrated.

Oahu Urban Design Study, prepared by Phillips, Brandt, and Reddick for the City and County of Honolulu (n.d.), is an example of poor design guidelines. Applicability is not referred to at all, nor are the guidelines effectively organized. Moreover, discussion of specific issues and elements is sacrificed in favor of emphasis on broad policy issues such as "urban form, open space, circulation and view" (fig. 7-6). By contrast, Pittsburgh's (1978) design guidelines cover specific issues and are well-organized with emphasis on establishing urban design criteria. Planning and Urban Design Criteria for the Grant Street East Development, for example, states:

> Any tall building should be designed to block as little sunlight as possible from public open spaces, including any new spaces created as part of Grant Street East and Mellon Square. Buildings should be designed in such a way that view corridors into and out of downtown are maintained through the site (Pittsburgh 1978: 2).

Pittsburgh's guidelines do not, however, include any graphics to show what these statements mean. Furthermore, although the guidelines are focused and specific, they are at the same time too flexible and thus can be interpreted in many ways. Downtown Washington, D.C.'s Streetscape Guidelines represent somewhat of an improvement over Pittsburgh's document (D.C. Government 1982). It starts with applicability and then groups the guidelines into general and specific. The guidelines are much more specific and even less flexible than Pittsburgh's, but they still lack sufficient graphics to illustrate the guidelines. Dallas Arts District Design Guidelines (1982) and Denver's 16th Street Design Guidelines (1980) are two examples of very effective design guidelines systems. Both cities have included various photographs and illustrations to explain the text, which is well-organized and covers issues of applicability, classification of design guidelines, and definitions of terms (figs. 7-7, 7-8). Thus it is clear from these

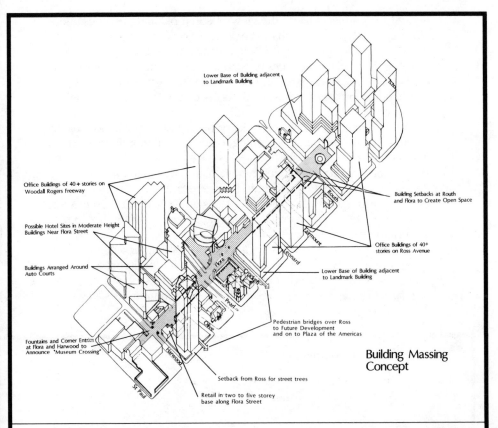

Lower Base of Building adjacent
to Landmark Building

Office Buildings of 40+ stories on
Woodall Rogers Freeway

Building Setbacks at Routh
and Flora to Create Open Space

Possible Hotel Sites in Moderate Height
Buildings Near Flora Street

Office Buildings of 40+
stories on Ross Avenue

Buildings Arranged Around
Auto Courts

Lower Base of Building adjacent
to Landmark Building

Pedestrian bridges over Ross
to Future Development
and on to Plaza of the Americas

Fountains and Corner Entries
at Flora and Harwood to
Announce "Museum Crossing"

**Building Massing
Concept**

Setback from Ross for street trees

Retail in two to five storey
base along Flora Street

7-7: Massing design concept developed for Dallas Arts District by Sasaki Associates, Inc. (Source: Sasaki Associates, Watertown, MA).

examples that graphics and actual photographs should always be included within the guidelines.

Programs

It is not always clear what designers mean when they talk about a *design program*. Different professionals use this term in different ways to describe different aspects of planning and design. A design program usually refers to an implementation process or sometimes, to the overall design process. I use the term to refer to those aspects of planning and design that maintain and preserve the existing environment as well as the environments that will be created. Planning and design do not end with the completion of the construction phase, though this appears to be the view of some planners and designers. We need only look at urban renewal projects in many parts of the United States for proof of the lack of design programs. Some of these projects have been well designed but after five to ten years of use they have developed into slum areas that are worse than what they replaced—primarily because maintenance and supervision programs have been lacking.

This aspect of design—the preservation of new as well as existing environments—is finally beginning to get the attention it deserves. In the past, most planners and designers have focused solely on making new creations; they have neglected to plan for care and maintenance, falsely assuming that these would be taken care of by the city and the user. Consideration of this aspect of design early in the design stage is quite crucial, since many care and maintenance factors should be a part of the basic design.

Community associations are a very positive approach to design programming. Members of a community (or their representatives) meet regularly to develop policies and to organize various programs for care, maintenance, and preservation of the community's assets and

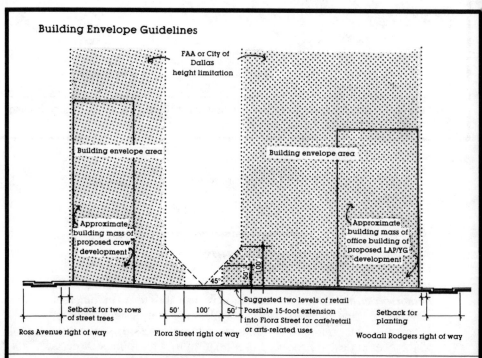

Building Envelope Guidelines

FAA or City of Dallas height limitation

Building envelope area

Building envelope area

Approximate building mass of proposed crow development

Approximate building mass of office building of proposed LAP/YG development

45°

Setback for two rows of street trees

50' 100' 50' Suggested two levels of retail
Possible 15-foot extension into Flora Street for cafe/retail or arts-related uses

Setback for planting

Ross Avenue right of way

Flora Street right of way

Woodall Rodgers right of way

7-8: Building envelope guidelines developed for Dallas Arts Districts by Sasaki Associates (Source: Sasaki Associates, Watertown, MA).

character. In California, some developers of planned communities hire planning and design specialists to develop a whole program for this purpose—before construction is completed. Associations have usually formed in high and middle income communities, particularly in condominium and co-op developments. There has been some question, however, as to whether they are really community associations or exclusionary tools to keep the so-called undesirables out of the community. In addition, associations are usually found in new communities but rarely in existing built environments. At the other end of the social spectrum, community action groups in some low-income neighborhoods have formed another type of association that has relied on residents rather than outside financial sources for labor, materials, contributions, and the like.

The issue of maintenance is not new. The local government has traditionally had this responsibility through the taxes they received. Most local governments, however, prioritize their tasks and maintenance is often at the bottom of the list. Furthermore, even if a local government maintains public space perfectly, it needs cooperation and input from the public. After all, it is the public who is using it. Clearly, the maintenance issue is more complicated than one thinks —especially in areas where residents do not own their own homes or in areas of cities that are not occupied by luxury shops and stores. Cities should develop, therefore, urban design programming that handles maintenance issues through cooperative effort, such as neighborhood associations, street associations, and so on. Planned communities in the south and west have had two decades of experience in associations and one can use many of the already available models.

References

Beal, F., and Hollander, E. "City Development Plans." In So., F.S., *et al.*, ed. *The Practice of Local Government Planning*. Washington, D.C.: International City Managers Association, 1979.

Burchell, Robert W., and Sternlieb, George. *Planning Theory in the 1980's*. New Brunswick, N J: Center for Urban Policy Research, 1978.

D.C. Government. *Recommendations for the Downtown Plan*. Mayor's Downtown Committee Summary Report. Washington, D.C.: Government of District of Columbia, 1982.

Dallas, City of. *Dallas Arts District*. Watertown, MA: Sasaki Associates, 1982.

Denver, City of. *16th Street Design Guidelines*. Denver, CO: Denver Planning Office, 1980.

Honolulu, City and County of. *Oahu Urban Design Study, Phase A*. Honolulu, HI: Phillips Brandt Reddick, Inc., n.d.

Hudson, Barclay M. *Planning: Typologies, Issues, and Application Contexts*. Los Angeles, CA: UCLA School of Architecture and Urban Planning, DP 108, 1978.

Jacobs, Allan. "San Franciscans Seek to Save Their City." *AIA Journal* 56, no. 5, 1971.

Jacobs, Allan. *Making City Planning Work.* Chicago, IL: ASPO Press, 1978.

Kent, T.J., Jr. *The Urban General Plan.* San Francisco, CA: Chandler Publishing, 1964.

Long Beach Redevelopment Agency. *Design Guidelines for Downtown Long Beach.* Long Beach, CA: The Arroyo Group, 1980.

Lynch, Kevin. "City Design." *Urban Design International* 1, no. 2, 1980.

Lynch, Kevin. *A Theory of Good City Form.* Cambridge, MA: The MIT Press, 1981.

Munson, Michael J. *Planning: Process and Product.* Princeton, N J: Princeton University School of Architecture and Urban Planning, Working Paper No. 5, 1974.

New York, City of. *Plazas for People, Streetscape and Residential Plazas.* New York, Department of City Planning, 1976.

Pittsburgh, City of. *Planning and Urban Design Criteria for the Grant Street East Development.* Pittsburgh, PA: Department of City Planning, 1978.

Raymond, George M. "The Role of the Physical Urban Planner." In Robert W. Burchell and George Sternlieb, eds., *Planning Theory in the 1980's.* New Brunswick, N J: Center for Urban Policy Research, 1978.

San Francisco, City of. *Guiding Downtown Development.* San Francisco, CA: Department of City Planning, 1982.

Seattle, City of. *Background Report of the Downtown Land Use and Transportation.* Seattle, WA: Office of Policy and Evaluation, 1981.

Seattle, City of. *Downtown Alternative Plan.* Seattle, WA: Executive Department, Land Use and Transportation Project, 1982.

U.S. Department of Health, Education and Welfare. *Environmental Health.* Washington, D.C.: U.S. HEW Public Health Service, 1967.

Implementation: administrative mechanisms

CHAPTER 8

DISTINGUISHED urban designer Edmund Bacon was a pioneer in the development of urban design as a part of the local government function. In the late 1960s, Allan Jacobs, Jonathan Barnett, Jacqueline Robertson, and others in the Urban Design Group of New York City's Planning Department added their own particular orientations and further legitimized the practice of urban design. They used many different approaches and models to process urban design and pass it through the bureaucratic and political morass that engulfs the city—with varying degrees of success. Their story and achievements are chronicled elsewhere and need only to be mentioned here as a reminder of early administrative efforts.

Since the late 1960s, other cities and towns have also managed to incorporate urban design functions into their local governments. Interest in urban design is increasing as the realization grows that it can lead to successful economic development for a community by providing a quality living environment for the city's residents. The federal government has also been sympathetic to these issues and has been supporting urban design since 1969, first "through the Urban Environmental Design Program as a part of the National Environmental Policy Act of 1969, and then through the Housing and Urban Policy Act of 1974" (Shirvani, 1982: 17). HUD support is continuing through Community Development Block Grants and their authorizations for design expenditure.

The institutionalization of urban design, through its incorporation into the city's administrative framework, remains a key to the success of urban design. It is clear that the critical issue of urban design is "how to administer it" (Shirvani, 1981). In the past two decades many American cities have commissioned fancy, even grandiose, designs and plans but very few of these have ever been implemented—even though they actually may have been quite rational and well thought-out. What has stood in the way of implementation? Lack of an administrative framework and specific implementation strategies are typical problems.

In this and the following two chapters, several approaches to the implementation of urban design are examined, and the likelihood of their success or failure and their applicability to different city environments are discussed. For purposes of this analysis, the implementation of urban design is divided into three major topics: administrative, legal, and financial.

First, a definition of implementation must be established. To some planners, implementation means the detailed and specific proposals resulting from goals and objectives of urban design. In this volume, I have assumed that such proposals are a part of the design process and products. Thus, here implementation clearly refers to building the actual physical product that results from the urban design process.

Organization of the administrative framework

The administrative framework required for the implementation of urban design has two parts: (1) the organization within which the design function is administered and (2) the techniques cities use to implement design.

Cities presently are organizing their administration of urban design according to the following orientations: city hall; third sector; and a combination of the two. All three types of organization must work cooperatively with the private sector in order to ensure success.

City hall-oriented models are of three types: ad hoc, dispersed, and centralized (Lu, 1976). The ad hoc model is problem-focused and temporary; it may be a design committee or outside group that helps the city for a certain period of time and works on a specific project or problem (Lu, 1976). The AIA Regional Urban Design Group has served in this capacity (Lu, 1976). Healdsburg, California, is a recent example of a community assisted by the AIA Regional/Urban Design Assistance Team (R/UDAT). Within this process, a team of professionals and experts come to an area, study it, and make design recommendations in a charette. Public officials and citizens are usually involved in this process (fig. 8-1). Louisville, Kentucky, also used AIA, R/UDAT for assistance with its downtown design (fig. 8-2). Another application of the ad hoc approach is in Special District Zoning in New York City. Here, "minimal amount of municipal involvement," provides "regulations for a special district range from simple change in use regulation to the development of incentives to developers" (Davis and Weston, 1975: 3). Small communities that cannot afford a permanent urban design group may be persuaded to use this model. The results will vary; in some circumstances, a longer term model may be necessary.

HOW TO GET FROM HERE TO THERE

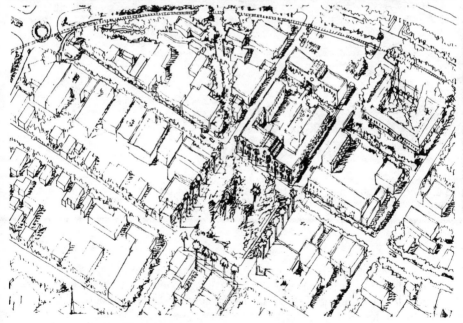

8-1: Design concept developed by AIA regional urban design assistance team for Healdsburg, CA (Source: City of Healdsburg, CA).

8-2: Urban design concepts and pedestrian connection developed by AIA regional/urban design assistance team for Louisville, KY (Source: City of Louisville, KY).

Use of the dispersed approach simply means that responsibility for urban design is shared by several city agencies (Lu, 1976). The redevelopment agency, planning department, and transportation department, for example, may all handle urban design matters; each agency deals with the particular design issues that may fall within its general responsibilities. Missing may be an overall policy and commitment to urban design, resulting in an unevenness in achieving urban design goals. New York City, Seattle, Portland (Oregon), Los Angeles, San

Diego, Baltimore, and St. Paul have tried this approach. Although this model also has its disadvantages, it should not be discarded. As a matter of fact, both the ad hoc and dispersed models are in frequent use; they enable a city to move toward and participate in urban design before making a commitment to a centralized urban design agency.

The centralized model is the most efficient and administratively productive of the city hall-oriented models. In this case, the urban design function is under the control and supervision of a single office. Many cities use the centralized model, including: San Francisco, Washington, D.C., Dallas, Irvine, Minneapolis, Atlanta, and Milwaukee.

A new group, the third sector, (Robertson and Euston, 1981) has become influential in the urban design efforts of many cities and small communities. Third sector groups are nonprofit, quasi-public organizations that perform design services or act as go-betweens and catalysts. They may even act as developers, and always strive for good urban design. They have been successful in getting things done and in improving city environmental quality and they are playing increasingly important roles in local design efforts. A significant majority of third sector organizations are involved in planning and urban design. They provide services and try to influence decisions and make things happen in a "better way." They are also involved in the development process and investment packaging and try to preserve, reuse, develop or redevelop various neighborhoods of the city.

Third sector groups are an underused source of human and financial resources and they are a feasible alternative to city agencies for promoting needed urban design and community development. For example, San Francisco Planning and Urban Research Association (SPUR), a nonprofit citizen's organization, attempts to help the public understand the advantages of sound urban design, stimulates planning and rehabilitation, and works as a catalyst in new development proposals (Robertson and Euston, 1981). Another similar group is the Community Design Center of Atlanta, Inc., which provides urban design and planning assistance to the community's neighborhoods and works with residents and financial institutions in developing comprehensive revitalization programs (Robertson and Euston, 1981). The Neighborhood Design Center of the Baltimore/D.C. area is a nonprofit organization composed of planners and designers who provide architectural and urban design services and assistance to communities evaluating development proposals for their neighborhoods (Robertson and Euston, 1981). Unfortunately, many communities—including public and private groups and citizens—are not aware of this sector and the advantages of using their talents.

Some cities may have no urban design body at all and instead may ask for recommendations from a third sector group. This is more common among smaller towns but a large city neighborhood or district that has somehow been ignored by city agencies may seek guidance and funds from the third sector. In Syracuse, New York, the

Metropolitan Development Agency, a private nonprofit organization composed of seventy-five chief executive officials, addresses problems relating to the central business district. They created a downtown committee that was able to pass legislation for a downtown special assessment district in which every property is equally assessed based on square footage. The third sector already has proven itself to be a very effective tool in solving urban design problems when federal and municipal funds are in short supply.

City hall and the third sector may find it advantageous to cooperate in urban design efforts. In Denver, Colorado, a nonprofit group provided urban design services in a high growth area. The Denver Partnership, "a nonprofit, private organization of business, civic, educational, and community groups" studied the Denver 16th Street Zoning Project and made recommendations to the city council for the project (Fleissig, 1982a: 23). A city that has a complexity of problems may need counsel on urban design from the third sector as well as from city hall. In Ohio, such a task force made up of Cincinnati's city agencies and the University of Cincinnati planned "the revitalization of a 117-acre inner-city slum known as Queensgate II" (Miller and Jenkins, 1982: 15). In these situations, the third sector can focus on a specific area, problem, or project and take the load off the city's urban design bodies. The necessity for specialized effort in urban design is another common reason for cooperation. Finally, the strongest justification of all may be the cutbacks in federal assistance and local finance. The applicability of each of these models depends on the socioeconomic and political environment of the city that is considering urban design action. Indeed, a city should tailor a model that best fits and is most practical in its unique environment.

Regardless of which model a city selects to administer urban design, cooperation with the private sector is always critical to the success of urban design efforts. In fact, present budgetary problems and economic decline are beginning to prompt many local governments to accept the reality that public money is not sufficient for all the things they want to do. For building and rebuilding the city, private money must be sought. Cooperation and communication between the city and the private sector save time and hassles for both parties and bring other mutual advantages as well. Such a partnership usually results in a better product for the public in a shorter time span. It would be an overstatement, however, to suggest that the key to success in urban design is a public/private partnership, no matter which administrative model is selected or in use. Of course, the most efficient urban design administrative model is one that is highly centralized (and possesses a specific urban design agency) and maintains district communication and coordination with the private sector. Quality urban design "can take place only if the actors [private citizens, corporations and city governments] work together in a truly collaborative process" (Fleissig, 1982b: 12).

These last statements logically lead us into a broader discussion of recommended techniques for implementing urban design.

Techniques for implementing urban design

We can identify four prerequisites to successful urban design, assuming that a city already has been able to establish an urban design group. This urban design group (1) must establish a direct communication link to the chief executive of the city, be it the city council, city manager or mayor; (2) should be given a certain level of discretion, limited in varying ways, dependent on many factors, and specific to the particular city; at the very least, the reviewers should have a chance to review proposed design and to respond directly to the chief executive; (3) must develop a strong rapport with business and public interest groups and with other departments of the city; (4) should have an adequate budget, a competent staff, and the ability to engage outside consultants when required (Lu, 1976).

The HUD publication, *Lessons from Local Experience* (1981), suggests that success in urban design "often hinges on several detailed arrangements" and that the organization of the design function "may not be the crucial factor" (UEDAR , 1981: 26). Important ingredients include (1) a "political constituency that supports the ... group doing urban environmental design"; (2) a "match between what elected officials consider to be the most pressing environmental issues and the agenda of designers"; (3) "durability of organizational arrangements" (a long-term project requires a long-term commitment by a management team; the design committee or third sector groups already discussed might fulfill this role); and (4) "the ability to attract and maintain highly skilled staff" (UEDAR, 1981: 26). As in the first list above, *Lessons* mentions "formal and informal linkages between decision-makers and designer" as essential to effective urban design and to the gaining of sufficient funds for the agency (UEDAR, 1981: 26).

Euston (1976: 49) has indicated that successful urban design results from overcoming "the familiar intramural habits of mind and prerogative that tend to rigidify [sic] public decision-making." He further states that "consensus building, option identifying, commitment seeking ... must characterize the behavior and procedure adopted by local government" (Euston, 1976: 49).

The ground rules for successful urban design processes are a well-established planning program, a clear statement of purpose, a procedural description (design manuals, logical steps, and so on), a well-developed financial program, citizen participation, and lobbying (Shirvani, 1981: 191-198).

Lessons, based on the experiences of fifteen cities, provides "keys to effective urban design" and observes:

> Designers—even those who have been most successful in seeing their proposals accomplished—seem to have great difficulty explaining what is required to mount an effective urban environmental design program. Maybe they are too close to their work, or perhaps very little can be generalized from one situation to another, as most designers believe. Yet, in the 15 cities studied, a number of themes do reappear. These do not apply globally, nor are they panaceas guaranteeing success. Rather, they are practical guides, sometimes rules of thumb, that may help identify why a city's efforts seem to be at a standstill and where it might look for a new injection of energy (UEDAR, 1981: 53).

Indeed, urban designers may become discouraged because a program seems to be stalled or even completely rejected by the mayor, council, and the public. Take heart:

> ... urban environment design is seldom a linear process, beginning with a widely accepted view of an environmental problem and ending with a modified city environment. More usually, it involves experimentation and trial, several successive approximations of the "right" action. It is best thought about as a learning process, where the course is adjusted based on reactions to each step along the way (UEDAR, 1981: 53).

HUD's "practical guides" are well worth noting. They are the result of the researchers asking themselves: " 'Why did something occur here and not elsewhere?' By generalizing, many of the answers may seem self-evident, but if they are, many places have yet to discover them ... The calculations of experienced individuals who know how to weigh the odds ... may help ensure the odds favoring success" (UEDAR, 1981: 54).

The unique aspects of the city both suggest special techniques for ensuring the success of urban design efforts and, as environmental factors, limit the models and techniques that can be chosen for application.

References

Davis, Robert E., and Weston, Jon, eds. *The Special District Zoning Concept in New York City*. New York: New School of Social Research, Center for New York City Affairs, 1975. .

Euston, Jr., Andrew F. "Municipal Urban Environmental Design." In Weiming Lu, Principal Investigator, *Urban Design Role in Local Government*. Report of a Conference in Dallas, TX, Washington, D.C.: The National Science Foundation, 1976.

Fleissig, Will. "16th Street Zoning Project: Lessons From Denver on Establishing Policy." *Urban Design International* 4, no. 1, Fall (1982a): 22–23.

Fleissing, Will. "How Partnerships Encourage Revitalization." *Urban Design International* 4, no. 1, Fall (1982b): 12–13.

Lu, Weiming. *Urban Design Role in Local Government*. Report of a Conference in Dallas, TX, Washington, D.C.: The National Science Foundation, 1976.

Miller, Zane, and Jenkins, Thomas, eds. *The Planning Partnership: Participant's Views of Urban Renewal*. Beverly Hills, CA: Sage Publications, 1982.

Robertson, Jack, and Euston, Andrew. "The Third Sector In Urban Development." Washington, D.C.: A CDBG/UED Study, 1981.

Shirvani, Hamid. *Urban Design Review, A Guide for Planners*. Chicago, IL: The Planners Press, 1981.

Shirvani, Hamid. "An Urban Design Prospect." *UD Review* 5, no. 3, December (1982): 17–20.

Urban Environmental Design Administration Research (UEDAR). *Lessons from Local Experience*. Washington, D.C.: U.S. Department of Housing and Urban Development, Office of Policy Development and Research, 1981.

Implementation: legal mechanisms

CHAPTER 9

EXPRESSING the same philosophy as private enterprise, cities have in the past and present tended to favor "passive and indirect" regulation of urban development (Pratter and Conway, 1982: 11). A city might have zoning in place and might provide services to encourage development, but, too often, the resulting development (and redevelopment) proceeded largely unchallenged and unchecked:

> The gentle web of zoning controls restrained only the most flagrant abuses of the land. But environmental losses mounted and the economic crunch began. Urban development on the fringe or in built-up areas resembled a free-for-all, and development in the inner cities resembled a tug-of-war, often played with an unraveling economic rope (Pratter and Conway, 1982: 11).

167

In addition, "varying judicial attitudes have had such an enormous influence on state legal systems that there are now fifty individual state systems of land use law with little in common" (Dimento, 1982: 92).

With the advent of increased urban planning, cities have realized the value and usefulness of strengthened and expanded zoning regulations as an implementation tool for planning and control of private development. The growing citizen concern about the environment and ambience of cities has also promoted the use of tougher zoning and other legal mechanisms that put planning and urban design on a firm footing and show developers that the city is serious about controlling development.

As a result of this change in attitude, new approaches have expanded the basic concepts of zoning: incentive zoning, performance zoning, and special districts. A number of supplementary regulatory controls have also developed, including transfer of development rights, sign ordinances, interim ordinances, antidemolition ordinances, historic district ordinances, mandated environmental impact reports, and design review. In 1983, I conducted a survey of twenty cities across the country in order to acquire firsthand information about these ten commonly used controls. A list of cities and the particular techniques each used is presented in figure 9-1. Each city was asked if it uses each of the ten techniques. For each mechanism the city had in place, further response was requested with regard to how the mechanism was used and its advantages and disadvantages. Finally, the cities were queried as to the circumstances under which they would recommend use of each mechanism. Based on the survey findings, this chapter will discuss each of the above techniques and conclude with an analysis of the issues involved in their selection and application.

Incentive zoning

American cities have found incentive zoning to be a most desirable technique for controlling development. "Many people consider this technique to be *the* zoning control for urban design, believing it channels the benefits of development to the improvement of the public environment" (Cook, 1981: 8). Basically, incentive zoning invokes a conditional exchange between the city and the developer. The city permits the developer to build a larger building in exchange for some public amenity, such as a plaza or open space, wider sidewalks, or retailing at the ground level. The developer earns certain development bonuses, such as additional square footage, for certain provisions—up to a maximum specified in the ordinances. Cities have learned, however, that the end result of incentive zoning can be

	Incentive zoning	Performance zoning	Special districts	TDR (Transfer of Development Rights)	Sign ordinance	Interim ordinance	Antidemolition ordinance	Historic districts	Mandated EIR (Environmental Impact Reports)	Design review
Albuquerque, NM			■		■			■		
Atlanta, GA			■	■	■			■		■
Bellevue, WA	■	■	■	■	■				■	■
Birmingham, AL			■		■		■	■		■
Buffalo, NY			■		■		■	■	■	■
Columbus, OH			■		■			■		
Dallas, TX	■		■	■	■	■	■	■	■	■
Denver, CO				■	■		■	■		■
El Paso, TX			■		■			■		
Forth Worth, TX					■			■		
Honolulu, HI			■		■	■		■	■	■
Long Beach, CA	■	■			■			■	■	■
Memphis, TN	■	■	■		■					
Milwaukee, WI	■		■				■	■		
Oakland, CA	■	■	■				■	■	■	■
Oklahoma City, OK		■	■		■	■	■	■		■
Omaha, NB			■		■		■	■		
Phoenix, AZ	■	■	■	■	■				■	■
San Antonio, TX		■	■			■	■	■	■	
San Diego, CA	■		■	■	■	■	■	■	■	■

Implementation techniques — Selected cities

9-1: A matrix presenting the use of various implementation mechanisms by twenty surveyed cities.

negative as well as positive. Critics claim that the developers receive greater benefits than the public. Value given should be equal to value received, but there are instances when the cost to the public is much higher than what it receives.

San Francisco and New York City were the first cities to use this technique. New York City's Incentive Zoning Ordinances of 1961 were a major attempt at urban improvement, based at least in part on urban design considerations. Although the ordinances have introduced valuable open space plazas into the city (a very popular move with developers), the zoning incentive idea was not quite successful. It created towers standing in seemingly random open spaces and has interrupted shopping frontage; sometimes it has ignored considerations of sunlight and the presence of adjacent buildings and nearby plazas. In both San Francisco and New York, "overbuilding is perceived as a problem. . . . Not only are larger buildings created, but the cumulative effect of the additional floor space may cause overloading of the urban infrastructure" (Cook, 1981: 8). Likewise, public amenities may be placed on a site with little concern for how they will serve the public.

In Dallas, where incentive zoning is used in the central business district (CBD), a formula that allows additional FAR (up to 4 to 1) for comparable open space at the base of buildings (on the same block) has generated similar problems where rigid interpretation by developers has resulted in cold open space. In Milwaukee, weak market demand is indeed a limiting factor for incentive zoning, but the city has also found that insufficient bonus ratios may prevent the mechanism from working. Similarly, Phoenix has found that underlying zoning requirements such as setbacks and lot coverage requirements may prohibit full utilization of density incentives.

Another problem associated with the incentive mechanism emerges in the administrative process. In Oakland, California, for example, the planning commissioner reviews staff work on appeal; not surprisingly, depending on the composition of the commission rules may be abused and privileges may be given to applicants who do not deserve them. Oakland's experience, in short, is that flexible zoning rules are obviously desirable to achieve urban design goals but they can be misapplied in the political process. A similar situation exists in San Diego. The time involved in the review, as well as disagreements or interpretation arguments that may arise, also pose problems in administering incentive zoning. In fact, the planning department in Bellevue, Washington, cautions that the mechanism should be used only if an agency has a staff that includes architects/ landscape architects with development experience.

An interesting aspect of incentive zoning is its increasing usefulness in achieving expanded urban design goals such as residential development or neighborhood amenities and transitions between land uses within the CBD. In Phoenix, high-rise incentive districts allow greater building heights and density in the downtown, but the mechanism is also used to promote infill residential development. A similar method has been used in Memphis. Long Beach, California, also emphasizes residential development by granting bonus units for land assembly (15,000 square feet or more) in exchange for site and neighborhood amenities. San Diego has used the mechanism in conjunction with planned unit developments. In Oakland, California, the mechanism has been used to coordinate land use relationships.

The advantages of incentive zoning depend on the area of application or urban design goals, as well as the economic climate in which they are administered. The guidelines from some cities where incentive zoning is being used target specifically their area of application. Examples include Phoenix, which limits incentive zoning to districts where a perceived need for development exists, residential and/or commercial; Long Beach, which recommends it for older, established cities, especially in or near downtowns; and Dallas, where incentive zoning is applied in denser areas where open space is lacking and land is expensive.

Other recommendations from cities point to the importance of well-defined criteria and review processes (San Diego), as well as an administration that has development experience (Bellevue). The design or organization of the incentive zoning mechanism itself is also important. Oakland recommends that the mechanism be used when there is good likelihood that it would be used, and used correctly. If the incentives being offered, for example, are not sufficiently financially attractive to the developer, there is no point in even providing them. Potential overbuilding or "overintensification," such as is the case in Milwaukee, is another problem associated with incentive zoning programs. Dallas's experience is that in dense areas incentive zoning policies should be coupled with transportation planning to relieve potential congestion.

The keys to successful incentive zoning are identification of specific design features and justification of their public need and use. Incentive zoning is more appropriate in cities with moderate to high market pressures that indicate high interest in development. In fact, the anticipation of profit in a strong market makes consenting to specifications to gain additional FAR (or other concessions) very appealing. Developers also appreciate the possibility of being able to negotiate changes in specifications. Incentive zoning rewards developers who provide amenities in a positive manner, rather than proceeding negatively by penalizing them for not providing amenities.

Performance zoning

Performance zoning is designed to set standards for measurable physical conditions: sunlight, noise, vibration, infrastructure capacity, and so on. This is one of the most progressive approaches to design control of the quantitative aspects of development. At the same time, it is a significant environmental planning tool. The concept was developed during the early 1970s by the Bucks County, Pennsylvania planning commission to permit flexible standards for residential zoning while protecting natural features on a site-by-site basis (Frank 1982: 21; Kendig 1980). Performance zoning standards can limit subjective opinions during the planning and design process and reduce the length of the entire process. A relatively simple calculation determines compliance with the standards because objective limits are set. In addition, model ordinances are available so that "planners need only study their own local environmental conditions to discover which concepts are directly transferable and which need modification" (Kendig, 1980: vii).

Increased sophistication in measurement devices and techniques will permit greater precision in standards. For example, New York City is considering the addition of the Waldrum diagram to their performance standards. It allows investigators to determine the effect of a new structure on the natural street lighting before a permit to build is granted (Cook 1981: 9). In the case of smaller cities, administration becomes more important. In Bay City, Oregon, the town was divided into three intensity zones where performance zoning was administered by the planning commission through a one-step permit process (Pease and Morgan, 1980). Improved development occurs with performance zoning and more and more cities are using this technique.

The various ways in which performance zoning is being used is impressive. In Largo, Florida, the ordinances have been modified "to deal with a subtropical environment and city, rather than suburban, problems" (Kendig, 1982: 24). Lake County, Illinois has also directed its performance controls toward existing rather than developing or expanding districts (Kendig, 1982). Phoenix and Oklahoma City have used performance zoning mechanisms in industrial parks and single user employment districts (Phoenix) to establish standards relating to noise, odors, dust, waste materials, outside storage, and the like. Long Beach has established planned development districts with special performance and design standards developed for its coastal zone. San Antonio has used performance standards to increase flexibility within its residential district and to promote mixed use within the district by allowing for certain commercial uses. Finally, Oakland has focused on properties, rezoning them through contracts between the property owner and the city to control future uses and introduce design controls such as landscaping, setbacks, and sign control. Still, as Kendig states, relatively few communities have incorporated performance zoning techniques into their planning mechanisms. One reason may be that "performance zoning represents a truly major change, and the average citizen usually opposes a change in land use, whether the projected change takes the form of a landfill or a simple reduction in lot size," which can mean controversy and disputes that planning agencies are likely to want to avoid (Kendig, 1982: 24). Furthermore, communities rarely undertake major overhauls in their ordinances (Kendig, 1982).

Other problems stem from the continuing administrative tasks surrounding performance zoning. The system can be difficult to set up initially and then to maintain and monitor over time. Staff time, their sophistication, and the difficulties of enforcement are some of the problems cited by cities using performance zoning. Examples of cities experiencing such difficulties are Phoenix, Long Beach, and San Antonio. On the development side, some of the drawbacks or limitations of a performance zoning mechanism are increased costs to the developers (Long Beach) and the need for education of the development community (San Antonio).

Special districts

Special districts are "overlay districts, superimposed on one or more existing zoning districts for the purpose of protecting or enhancing the special qualities of the area" (Cook, 1981: 8). As the name implies, special districts have some unique qualities or characteristics that need protection or enhancement or both. New York City has made use of this procedure thirty-eight times to protect the quality of areas such as Little Italy, the theater district, Fifth Avenue retailing, and the Greenwich Village district.

Because of the likelihood of legal challenges to design standards in a special district, they "must be based on a documented set of physical criteria" (UEDAR 1981: 97). In New York City's Fifth Avenue Special District, for example, the developer must build on the propertly line of Fifth Avenue and up to a height of three stories; must provide retail uses at the ground level along Fifth Avenue; must have an FAR of not less than 1.00, and so on. (Shirvani, 1981a). Note that these are very specific and specialized requirements especially tailored to the Fifth Avenue Special District. In a special district of a different nature, it might be wise to specify facade details,color, and texture for uniformity of appearance and style—whatever is deemed necessary to develop and/or redevelop within the confines of that particular special district. For excample, special districts in Hawaii are tailored to "specifically address the entire range of factors which affect the form and character of a community" (Hawaii, 1975: 80). In Portland, Oregon, the South Waterfront special district is created "to strengthen the downtown and to reestablish its relationship to the Willamette River" (Portland, n.d.)

Implementation of design control is often achieved by the building permit procedure (Cook, 1981). Review early in the permit process by the city agency responsible for urban design will quickly reveal whether a project is likely to require special adjustments in the overall requirements. Such a review can save time later in the process for both the developer and the city agency. Historic districts are often appropriate special districts.

A commonly noted advantage to the special district mechanism, then, is that it can be tailored to fit the needs of specific districts, providing flexibility to control special aspects of uses while retaining the overall zoning classification system (San Antonio). Along with the need for documented design criteria, a special district approach also requires detailed delineation of district boundaries in order to avoid any question of whether or not a parcel is in the overlay district. The district delineation may be based on intrinsic physical features that are characteristic or unique to the area and are stipulated in the design criteria, as in historic neighborhoods or in special land use or development districts such as in Memphis, Birmingham, and San Diego.

In summary, many cities have found the special district mechanism useful where there are clear-cut targeted or planned development-district goals for an area. The issue of controlled development and design and use compatibilities make the special district approach a viable alternative where existing control mechanisms are too flexible, outdated, and not focused on main development issues.

Transfer of development rights

Transfer of development rights (TDR) is an innovative and adaptable design control mechanism that some cities are finding most useful. It enables a city to gain desired development with preservation of the special features it values in return for certain concessions and relaxations of regulations. Transfer also enables developers who agree to use fewer development rights on one site to transfer these "leftover" rights to another site they wish to develop. This second site may or may not have to be adjacent to the first site; some cities require adjacency whereas others allow transfer within the same district.

The very features of this technique that make it appealing to both the developer and the city have led to criticisms by both sides as well as the public. Developers may find, for example, that the rights they transfer may not prove beneficial on the second site. Changed market conditions at the time of development may make the second site less desirable than orginally perceived. The devloper must also decide whether it is economically beneficial to stay within limited parameters on one site to gain benefits elsewhere. In Dallas, for example, the FAR is so high (20 to 1) that there is little market for the extra rights.

The primary use of this mechanism has been to take economic pressures off historic properties, land markets, and the like, such as in Dallas, San Diego, and Denver; and for open space preservation (San Diego). An interesting trend that has developed regarding TDRs is indicated by communities that are either investigating or currently have TDRs but do not use them. Oklahoma City is currently exploring the concept for use in floodplain areas. Albuquerque has been considering using transfer or purchase of development rights for open space and agricultural land preservation. Phoenix has also studied the mechanism and at this time is anticipating its use. On the other hand, Bellevue already allows TDRs by code but has not yet used them. Atlanta has also made only infrequent use of the mechanism.

Based on these studies and first cut attempts, some cities have identified a number of potential problems with TDRs. Among these are administration and record-keeping difficulties (San Diego, Long Beach, Phoenix); the difficulty of designating receiving areas (San Diego); and the need to establish meaningful—and marketable—development rights (Dallas). The newness of the mechanisms, as well as the fact that there has been no definite resolution regarding the legality of the process by the courts, has prevented it from being readily accepted by the public (Phoenix). Finally, there is the problem that after excess development rights have been sold or transferred, landmark structure may be in jeopardy (Denver).

Some of these shortcomings appear, however, to have been dealt with successfully in Montgomery County, Maryland, where TDRs are being used for farmland preservation in the face of residential development pressures (Coleman and Perrine, 1982). The community's profile is probably most relevant here:

> TDR is not for the community where simpler zoning approaches will work to save farmland. It probably has the most potential in urbanizing areas like Montgomery County, where a comprehensive planning and zoning program is in place and where the housing market is strong enough to encourage transfers (Coleman and Perrine, 1982: 17).

Another important feature of Montgomery County's use of TDRs is its expansion of incentives offered to developers. Higher densities are used but in addition, one of the most effective lures is the extension of services (see also Medford Township, New Jersey). Still another key element already indicated is their comprehensive plan, which has designated some 14,000 acres of farmland as a "rural density transfer zone" where only one lot per twenty-five acres is eligible for development but where one development right may be sold for every five acres of farmland for use outside the zone. Receiving areas are monitored to ensure that TDR densities are compatible with existing residential densities and housing types and that they do not "outstrip the carrying capacity of public services" (Coleman and Perrine, 1982: 17).

In using TDRs, all the benefits need to be specifically spelled out in order for a developer to accept them. Still, the "what-have-you-done-for-me-lately?" syndrome often affects TDR negotiations. The city and the public quickly forget all the good things (amenities, historic preservation, and the like) a developer has provided on the restricted site and views the second site's increased density, FAR, and height as excessive. It is important for both the city and the developer to have common goals to ensure the success of this design control mechanism—and all other mechanisms, for that matter. Allowing all interested groups to participate in setting the requirements and providing a forum so that all have an opportunity to develop an understanding of each other's problems, interests, and goals are forward-looking steps.

Sign ordinance

Building signs and billboards have always been important areas of concern in urban design. Over the years, various legal cases have delineated the destruction of property and the visual discomfort that billboards cause. The response to this problem has been sign ordinances and they have proven to be an excellent tool for the establishing of harmony, visual comfort, and protection of landscape and urbanscape. Cities that have these ordinances usually establish as strict controls as possible, specifying size, measurements, and even style for various uses and activities. While many cities are just starting to work on this issue and are moving slowly toward greater control, others have already pioneered far-reaching sign ordinances.

Dallas, for example, has adopted one of the most comprehensive sign ordinances in the United States. Passed in 1973, its ordinance requires that all signs have a permit, including those in place before 1973. Property owners with existing signs were given ten years to comply with the ordinance and to receive the required permit. The fact that half of the signs in the city are not yet licensed, and that there is still disagreement and opposition from businessmen and the sign industry, should not diminish our admiration for the accomplishments of this ordinance. To establish any sign controls in a city requires a long battle.

The usual problem in meeting the established specifications—and this was true in Dallas, as well—is with the existing buildings and signs and not the new ones. In fact, "the attempted elimination of nonconforming uses . . . has been one of the most persistent problems in zoning" (Riegler, 1982: 65). It often takes a lot of time, energy, and money to change exisiting conditions. The stricter the sign ordinance, the greater the opposition and the longer the delay in complying. On the other hand, if the sign ordinance is too lenient, the desired improvement in visual quality is not met. In Portland, Oregon, unique sign districts were created to enhance the character of each district. Demonstrating that sign ordinances need not be restrictive, the Portland ordinance "provides opportunities for . . . large, bright and flamboyant signs which exhibit exceptional graphic design and sign craftsmanship and which enhance the . . . environment" and also provides for unique sign sites (Portland, 1982: 1).

A good many cities—Phoenix, Albuquerque, and Oakland, for example—have developed sign ordinances as part of their zoning districts. This and other relatively comprehensive approaches have the advantage of establishing design control on a city-wide basis. Phoenix, too, views such ordinances as key elements in urban design, stating that without exception, any urban design strategy should include a comprehensive sign and advertising design and display control mechanism.

This strong endorsement underscores another critical feature involved in administering or enforcing sign ordinances—namely, that the community that establishes the ordinances must be very clear about the design characteristics it wants as stated by Phoenix, Oakland, Columbus. There are pitfalls, however, even when this is achieved. Dallas, for instance, has found that it is difficult to address the issue of ugly, ill designed or distasteful signs and that, as a result, sign/graphic creativity may be sacrificed. Another related problem cited by Oakland is inflexibility and the possibility that not all circumstances have been considered.

The importance of a consistent enforcement program to detect and bring into compliance signs created outside the mechanism process and the estimable administrative battles surrounding use of signage ordinances have been found by most of the cities using this mechanism. In some cities, sign ordinances are more appropriate for suburban communities than fully developed urban areas (for example, Long Beach). On the other hand, as is the case in Dallas, sign ordinances can have metropolitan area application. It appears that there are three critical features for developing a sign code in any community:

1. Establish sufficient agreement and commitment to a design theme or at least clearly articulated design criteria.
2. Develop an efficient review process that incorporates provisions (funds and long-term commitments) for monitoring and enforcement of the signage and ordinances.

3. Generate as much informed support as possible from responsible and involved members of the community, such as AIA, merchants, and the planning commission.

Joint city/business cooperation in setting this design control may be helpful in gaining compliance. It may be necessary to move slowly to guarantee business and public support. Good public relations may speed the process.   ·

Interim ordinances

Interim ordinances provide for a moratorium in a specific urban area, thus subjecting development there to a case-by-case evaluation and review. Examples are Cincinnati and Dallas, which have both adopted interim ordinances to control development and signs. It seems that many communities have used interim devices of one sort or another to manage development pressures. Other specific applications of interim ordinances include limits on billboards (San Antonio); prevention of sign construction, new construction, and demolition in potential historic districts (Dallas); limits on new construction in specific neighborhoods where the zoning is changing (Dallas); and temporary general controls on development (San Diego, Oklahoma City).

An interim ordinance can buy time for a planning staff and community but because of this, the mechanism appears to have a built-in vulnerability to legal challenge. San Diego cautions, for instance, that if time for interim controls is too long, it creates hardship on property owners if banks will not make loans due to the unclear future. San Antonio has found that interim ordinances tend to be tricky, causing constitutional and discrimination questions to arise. This is likely to be true where the ordinances are enacted as a stalling mechanism or roadblock rather than to reserve a legitimate period of time for planning studies and the like. In Oklahoma City, for example, moratoriums have been declared to halt construction of apartments because of sewer and drainage concerns, when the real issue is density; the aim is force the developer to give up and leave. Cases such as this, obviously, are symptoms of other planning strategy problems and should not be associated too closely with interim ordinances. Moreover, although there are mixed feelings about the positive effects of enacting interim ordinances, it is evident that the time frame for such ordinances is crucial. Typically, long-term ordinances are more helpful because they allow enough time for the results of controls to be seen. In fact, the greatest advantage of this procedure is its resemblance to a testing and evaluation process: adopt an interim ordinance, see if it works, then make it permanent.

Antidemolition ordinances

After urban renewal and its massive-scale approach to redevelopment in the 1950s and 1960s, many American cities found themselves burdened with a lot of "super-holes" (Pratter and Conway, 1982: 24), vast numbers of surface parking areas and empty and undeveloped lots. Antidemolition ordinances put an end to further demolition of buildings unless they are empty and a threat to public safety. Destruction of historic buildings that may be valuable and possible to repair is also prevented. Antidemolition ordinances are most often used in conjunction with preservation districts and activities (Oklahoma City, Buffalo, Milwaukee, Omaha, Dallas, Oakland, San Diego, Birmingham, Denver, San Antonio). Some communities have also used the mechanism for neighborhood and low-income residential protection (San Antonio, Oakland, San Diego, Denver). In all cases, however, it is a temporary measure that provides necessary time for negotiation and bargaining.

Since developers use demolition to clear lots that then can be combined for speculative development, antidemolition ordinances control this process as well. An antidemolition ordinance accompanied by a mandatory review process gives additional controls to a city. Case-by-case review of each project requiring demolition can determine the appropriateness of waiving the ordinance under propitious conditions.

The interim or temporary character of the antidemolition ordinance also makes it subject to a variety of problems and shortcomings as an implementation tool. Dallas noted that in the case of historic properties, for example, use of the mechanism can result in confusion in the community about how much can be done to save historic properties. By the same token, San Antonio found that the process can block the financing of good development, especially since preservationists do not always agree on the merits of a building versus the value of development. San Antonio is attempting to overcome this shortcoming with a task force that is evaluating all the buildings in its downtown, thus developing an agreed upon list of structures with historical significance. Finally, the temporary character of the strategy can aggravate conflicts within a community's planning/urban design administration. In Oakland, it has been noted that interdepartmental conflicts can arise when the building and safety department, for example, wants to demolish a poorly maintained building or public hazard while the planning department advocates saving it.

Historic districts

Both federal and state registration (in some states) are avilable for historically significant structures and sites, and this is an effective means of protecting them from demolition or destruction. In addition, many cities have been expanding the registration process by designating entire districts as historic and adopting a set of ordinances and guidelines to control renovation and redevelopment. The guidelines often include height and bulk control for development of vacant lots within the district, as well as specific architectural design guidelines for both old and new buildings. A design review is usually required as part of the building or renovation process. Design review can provide the flexibility required for such sensitive development.

There are many well known and respected examples of historic preservation. Old Town Alexandria, Virginia, has successfully restored old buildings, maintaining the original use of some; concurrently, that city's ordinances allowed demolition of some structures to build a new hotel that blends in with the remaining older buildings. Imaginative ideas for attracting businesses to the area by making the second and third floors of restored buildings available for offices and shops has made the project viable. Much has also been written about Williamsburg, Virginia. The area attracts thousands of visitors every year; yet this project, in which millions of dollars have been invested, has had one out-of-character residence along its historic streets as a reminder to all designers of the difficulty of assuring 100 percent compliance with ordinances and regulations.

Hundreds of American cities and towns have used historic preservation ordinances to salvage locally significant buildings and sites. There are side effects, however, to preservation programs. Individual property owners, for example, may seek registration because it provides certain tax advantages such as tax abatements only to later discover that they have been priced out of the market. The link some cities may see between historic districts and economic investment may, therefore, be challenged. As Thoresen (1981:46) notes:

> It could be argued that the economic investment would have occurred even without historic districts because of the discounted value of the property and because such economic investment is occurring in areas where there are no districts. . . . The lack of agreement on function focuses on whether or not historic districting is primarily an economic investment tool or a preservation/design tool.

Certainly, various funding mechanisms can assist in stimulating renovation of historic structures and neighborhoods, which may also fit into some other revitalization program such as revolving funds, such as TDR's and antidemolition ordinances. Essentially, however, historic districts and related preservation techniques are primarily design control measures and therein is where their problems and potentials lie.

In Albuquerque, establishing historic and special districts has been found effective and useful in maintaining an identifiable character but a number of potential problems associated with defining special character and interpreting guidelines have arisen. Many cities have experienced similar problems with the extensive, expensive, and politically volatile administrative issues occurring during the designation and design review process (Buffalo, Columbus, Dallas, Fort Worth). Problems surrounding design quality and the fair and uniform application of standards represent other problematic areas in historic district administration. In his study of design review commissions, Thoresen found that the "single most difficult issue facing design commissioners is the paradoxical consequences of their design decision-making" (1981: 46). Capriciousness of administration, where matters of taste rather than law prevail, has been identified in many cities, such as Buffalo, San Antonio, and Columbus.

Another particularly interesting trend in the design review process for historic districts is their tendency to be conservative rather than creative. Thoresen (1981) suggests that the design review process itself follows a narrow, precedent-based approach. A side effect of this characteristic of the design review process is that it contributes to the often highly restrictive character of many historic or preservation district approaches—a feature that has frustrated developers and property owners in many cities and has often weakened support for the overall approach (Oklahoma City, San Antonio, Buffalo, Columbus, Fort Worth, Omaha, Birmingham).

<hr>

Mandated environmental impact report

Though legislation has been in place for many years, sometimes it is still a rude awakening for a developer to discover that the National Enviromental Policy Act and some state and local environmental laws and ordinances require an assessment of the environmental impact of a project before a permit can be issued. In the face of the nationwide emphasis on environmental quality that grew out of the 1970s, and the politically volatile nature of these issues, some community planning agencies have ambivalent attitudes toward impact assessments. Environmental impact assessments are required on all federally funded projects and the connection between funding requirements and the impact report is quite clear. However, within the local impact assessment requirements the question of what constitutes a significant project is, of course, an important issue that may often be problematic and difficult for many community planning agencies to determine—even when considerable amounts of information may be available to them. The question of enforcement raises still another set of issues. In any case, it is clear that many cities are dissatisfied with mandated environmental impact procedures and the potential problems with this mechanism (Oakland, Long Beach, San Diego, Bellevue). Once again, the debate centers around what constitutes a major versus a minor project in terms of its likely environmental impact.

Design review, the essential element

During the discussion of most of these techniques, I frequently have indicated the need for design review, primarily because there is always a need for further explanation of guidelines and regulations regardless of their detail. In addition, the flexibility that is required for designing a piece of built environment is an integral part of the interactive process of negotiation that characterizes effective design review. Guidelines cannot provide a response to every special or unusual proposal. Design review provides the opportunity for such proposals to receive proper scrutiny. In this way, such projects can conform to specific guidelines within the specified framework of goals and objectives of the city's urban design policies.

Design review processes are incorporated into planning/urban design efforts in a variety of ways. Some cities, such as Oakland, Albuquerque, and San Antonio, require review for special zones (special districts, special use zones, overlay zones, historic and cultural districts, and so on). Other cities, including Long Beach, Denver, Dallas, and Omaha, also review planned unit developments (residential, commercial, office), subdivisions, parking lots, bonus (incentive) projects, as well as projects over a given size. Buffalo conducts design reviews of new construction in which city funds are a major component. Also, there are some cities, such as Oklahoma City, which have design review "on the books" but do not use the process.

There is a strong consensus regarding the advantages of design review. Frequently cited benefits include promoting better quality design; increasing potential for project acceptance (Denver), and promoting compatibility of design and use (Phoenix, San Diego, Bellevue, Dallas, Buffalo). There are, however, a number of shared concerns about the potential (or ongoing) problems of design review processes. The considerable staff time required and the consequent costs to developers are two of the frequently cited drawbacks (San Diego, Long Beach, Bellevue, Dallas, Denver). The need for a qualified staff is another important criterion for successful design review as has been found in cities such as Omaha, Oklahoma City, and Bellevue. Staff preparedness is, in turn, related to two additional issues: the necessity for established criteria and clear-cut administrative procedures. A successful design review model is dependent upon at least eighteen environmental factors, starting from political and financial support to qualifications of review members to size of city bureaucracy (Shirvani, 1981a; Shirvani, 1981b). Therefore, a city interested in the design review mechanism should identify a realistic model of administering such a process based on the environmental factors particular to it.

References

Coleman, Lyn, and Perrine, Phillip E. "Homegrown TDR." *Planning* 48, no. 1, January (1982): 15–17.

Cook, Robert. Innovative Zoning Tools for Downtown, Washington, D.C.: The National League of Cities, Technical Bulletin, 1981.

Dimento, Joseph F. "The Consistency Doctrine Continuing Controversy. In Fredric A. Strom, ed., *1982 Zoning and Planning Law Handbook*. New York: Clark Boardman Company, Ltd., 1982.

Frank, Michael J. "Performance Zoning" *Planning* 48, no. 11, December (1982): 21–23.

Hawaii, State of. *Urban Design Primer: Hawaii*. Honolulu, HI: Department of Planning and Economic Development, 1975.

Kendig, Lane. *Performance Zoning*. Chicago, IL: The Planners Press, 1980.

Kendig, Lane. "The Bucks County Technique Is Slowly Catching On." *Planning* 48, no. 11, December, 1982.

Pease, James R., and Morgan, Michael. "Performance Zoning Comes to Oregon." *Planning,* August (1980): 22–24.

Phoenix, City of. Phoenix Planning Issues, *Profile of the Special Conservation District,* 1982.

Portland, City of. "Staff Report and Recommendations to the Design Committee." PC File D27-80, Pacific Square/Daon, Portland, OR: Bureau of Planning, 1980.

Portland, City of. *Ordinance No. 153246.* Portland, OR: Bureau of Planning, 1982.

Portland, City of. *South Waterfront Project Special District Design Guidelines.* Portland, OR: Bureau of Planning. n.d.

Pratter, S. Jerome, and Conway, William. *Dollars from Design.* Washington, D.C.: The National League of Cities, Technical Bulletin, 1982.

Riegler, Eugene W. "Amortization of Nonconforming Uses." In Fredric A. Strom, ed., *1982 Zoning and Planning Law Handbook.* New York: Clark Boardman Company, Ltd., 1982.

Shirvani, Hamid. *Urban Design Review, A Guide for Planners.* Chicago: The Planners Press, 1981a.

Shirvani, Hamid. "Urban Design Through Review Process." *Environmental Comment,* August (1981b): 4–10.

Thoresen, A. Robert. "Historic Districts Aren't Obsolete, But . . ." *Historic Preservation* 33, no. 4, July/August (1981): 46–47.

Urban Environmental Design Administration Research (UEDAR). *Lessons from Local Experience.* Washington, D.C.: U.S. Department of Housing and Urban Development, Office of Policy Development Research, 1981.

Implementation: financial mechanisms

CHAPTER 10

IN PREVIOUS chapters, frequent reference has been made to the present state of economic decline in cities and to the problems they are having with financing urban development and redevelopment. Where can cities find the necessary funding to improve their environments? There is still some federal and state funding but these sources are not always enough. This chapter assumes that a city has explored the federal and state funding possibilities and still needs other sources for financing projects. I will discuss the usual, the newer, and the alternative mechanisms for financing; the concluding section will describe the challenges of public/private partnerships for co-development and will give an example of innovative financing.

Marketing the city

A city that is in financial difficulties because of economic conditions or problems in its basic industries, such as steel, automobiles, and housing will first have to convince itself that it can attract new businesses and industries and encourage capital investment in the downtown. Will it be possible to enlist the support of downtown merchants and businesses who are hurting already? Will they support a special tax assessment, for example, to finance a parking garage so that the public will find improved downtown shopping convenient again? How can a city gain sustained support from the public for the proposed economic growth? The following list briefly suggests some preliminary steps that can be taken:

1. Form a community-wide private/public committee to pursue these economic development efforts.
2. Make use of the local media to thoroughly publicize the committee's actions, report progress, and explain what economic development will do for the city.
3. Involve the general public by keeping them informed and by scheduling meetings where their suggestions can be heard and their questions answered.
4. Relate an economic development program to local needs. Economic growth can mean creation of jobs or community development or downtown rejuvenation—whatever the city needs.
5. Set realistic goals that can be met by general support (Greenwell, 1981).

Can a city start and follow through on such an ambitious program on its own or must an expert—a public relations firm or a consultant—be hired? The answer to this question is dependent on whether the city's Chamber of Commerce, for example, can help with manpower, money, ideas. Can a local industry lend its support—psychological and/or monetary—and perhaps provide the services of some appropriate personnel? Certainly, a city's planning and design staff can contribute, or start the process, but an economic development program will require the backing of city government. It will take the work of many people with a vision of the city that can rise above its present difficulties, "a shared vision of what the city ought to be" (Beals, 1981: preface). Pratter and Conway (1981: 10) remind us:

Private enterprise cannot fill the gap left by withdrawn federal funds. But ... the efficiency and clarity of local development processes can pave the way for more private investment in areas that had been passed by lenders and developers for years and still produce a significant public return. For any city to realize fiscal and physical improvements from private investment, a change in local governmental attitudes toward development is often needed. What government can do . . . is to clarify issues and procedures, making it relatively easy for business to do business with government.

A dollar spent on streamlining the development process, said developer Scott Tooms, "will return better developments at lower total cost than a dollar subsidy." His examples: "The cost of one day's delay on a $30 million project is about $8,000." Faced as they are with deal-breaking interest rates, he added, "no one knows the time value of money better these days than the real estate development community."

We have established that a city has to have confidence in its future and that it can encourage private investment by creating a planning process that is easy for the developer to follow and also contains the environmental safeguards that are important to the city and its residents. The stage is set to consider the financial mechanisms that can sweeten the pot, attracting the megadollars necessary for urban development and redevelopment projects that will turn a city's future around.

Basic financial mechanisms

At the beginning of this discussion, the complexity of financing urban development and redevelopment should be emphasized. One should be aware at the outset that the options for financing are limited by the nature of a state's enabling laws. Undoubtedly, a city contemplating such projects will find that it must use a number of the mechanisms that follow. It will take experience, vision, and knowledge of finance and urban design to decide which are the most promising procedures, and this is but the beginning of the many consequential decisions that will have to be made. Important, then, is the caliber of the leader of a project and the staff, for they set the tone that says to all involved that the city is committed to building a better place for us to live and work.

USING THE TAX STRUCTURE

The property tax. American cities have traditionally used property taxes to finance the services they render for their citizens. In recent years, however, increases in the property tax have become less acceptable to homeowners. They feel burdened by property taxes, local income taxes (sometimes on the state level as well), and often sales taxes. Cities have sought to broaden their tax base, adding commercial, service, and industrial properties to the tax rolls. In some cities, this has resulted in more expense for the city than income generated. The number of taxes levied by some states, municipalities, and school districts has risen to the point that they are sometimes called "nusiance taxes."

With the tax structure already pushed to the brink, cities have to look elsewhere for financing urban improvements, which will themselves increase tax revenues. Yet, "however much tax revenues may be needed right now, government must be concerned about and aware of the long-term social, economic, and environmental consequences of physical change. In other words, government must anticipate" (Pratter and Conway, 1982: 11).

Cities, therefore, must be prepared to bend the tax structure to encourage development. Three popular methods are tax abatement, tax increment financing, and special assessments. The latter two are tied to the issuance of bonds and will be discussed later in this chapter.

Tax abatement. Those of us concerned about urban design probably would agree that the chief advantage of tax abatement is its usual requirement that plans for a project must be approved before the developer gains abatement of property taxes on the project. What it accomplishes for the devloper is reduction in the cost of doing business (Hager and Pratter, 1981). One cannot guess the factor that tips the cards a developer is holding in favor of pursuing a particular project.

Many cities are fairly well convinced that they may have to make concessions of one kind or another to get a developer to move on a project they see as important to the future of their cities. Tax abatement may be one of the city's options and may take one of several different forms. Sometimes, the assessor carries a property on the tax rolls at its predevelopment value. Alternatively, the city may grant a percentage reduction in taxes. In a third option, the city and the developer agree in advance on gradually increasing taxes. Texas law enables cities to use partial or full tax abatement to aid developers who are renovating historic structures if they "prove the abatement is necessary to keep a project financially sound" (UEDAR, 1981: 106).

Tax abatement strategies do have their drawbacks, however; because they are achieved by a selective process, those not receiving such savings may be resentful. The other taxpayers may be paying increased taxes to support the new infrastructure required by the development that gains abatement. If the city opens the door to abatement, it may regret all the applications it receives (Hager and Pratter, 1981).

Lyons and Mahan (1981) have suggested that the costs and benefits of downtown commercial revitalization that has been subsidized by tax incentives have not been fully analyzed by communities that undertook them. They argue that the public role (as far as tax financing or abatements are concerned) in revitalization efforts is based on two assumptions: first, that commercial development would not take place without tax incentives and secondly, that ". . . it is not really important to evaluate proposed uses of tax incentives because they involve only the foregoing of revenue which was not being collected anyway" (Lyons and Mahan, 1981: 22). The authors point out that while tax incentive programs appear to have been a stimulus to revitalization in many cities, it is equally important to consider national trends in supply and demand. The value of tax incentives is undercut, they argue, in several ways. Since state and local taxes represent only 2 percent to 5 percent of an average firm's operating costs, location decisions do not hinge on the availability of incentives. Then again, businesses take deductions for property taxes on their federal tax returns:

> As a consequence, when local governments forego one dollar of property tax revenue, developers retain only about 60 cents. . . . Hence, even if tax abatements did make a difference, they are remarkably inefficient as subsidy mechanisms. (Lyons and Mahan, 1981: 23)

Four key points underscore the authors' critique of tax incentive techniques:

1. They prevent return/replacement of property lost to the tax rolls (due to fire, abandonment, demolition), thereby cutting into the revenue available to a community through its property tax.
2. They shift "the burden of providing public services from new commercial taxpayers to property owners who do not qualify for tax incentives . . . [as a result] they are only encouraged to relocate out of the city or not improve their property."
3. Incentives affect future revenues of schools, the park district, and so on, as well as the city.
4. Finally, tax incentives tend to "proliferate" with potentially disastrous results for the city as a whole (Lyons and Mahan, 1981: 23–25).

BOND ISSUANCE

General obligation bonds.   General obligation bonds might be described as a conventional type of bond. They are backed by the full faith and credit of the city. The difficulties with this method of financing are well known:

- The interest these bonds bear and their acceptability to investors are dependent on a Standard and Poor (or other) rating. A city that is financially unstable cannot gain a favorable rating and attract investors.
- The voters generally have to approve the decision to issue bonds. This may be problematical when the citizens are asked to support school revenue bonds, bonds to replace or repair sewer systems, and so on. They may be less likely to favor bonds that finance city improvements—a somewhat nebulous prospect to many. The message to those in charge—those who should have a clear image of the city that can be—is: tell your story well. In Baltimore, voters have approved bond issues for the improvements to Charles Street and the Inner Harbor eleven times during several different city administrations and over a period of some twenty years (Pratter and Conway, 1982: 23).

General obligation bonds have financed city projects of all types as government interests and involvement have increased. Massachusetts, for example, has used bonds to acquire surplus federal and state property such as military bases, school buildings, as well as "blighted open, decadent or substandard" land in general (Bacow, 1981: 41–46). The purchase and subsequent planning, development, and project implementation is administered by the Massachusetts Government Land Bank, an agency responsible for acquiring property, taking such mortgages, and funding planning studies. Projects developed under the auspices of this agency include Boston's inner harbor redevelopment, a historic building acquisition for conversion into a hotel-inn in Newburyport, and a comprehensive canal development project in Cambridge that includes retail and office development.

Bonds have also been a critical element in the development of the Dallas Arts District. A $27 million bond issue approved in 1979 permitted the city to assist with construction of a fine arts museum and to purchase land and underwrite construction costs for a symphony hall in this sixty-acre site at the north end of downtown (Geotsch and Haderlein, 1983: 10–14).

Revenue or industrial revenue bonds. These bonds are not dependent on the city's credit rating, but they are tax-free and available, or mandated in most states. The critical factor is the credit rating of the business or industry seeking to have the bonds issued in their name by the city. The revenue to be generated by the project is pledged to paying off the bonds; therefore, the project has to be viable to gain buyers for the bonds. Because this bond program is inexpensive to administer, has below market rates, and is easy to combine with other sources of capital, it has become a popular method of financing the enhancement of city environments.

Tax increment financing. In this case, the city issues bonds in its own name, anticipating the increased tax revenues from improved properties that will allow it to pay off the bonds. Developers like tax increment financing because it decreases front-end costs. The city delivers "a complete land package," often with utilities and sidewalks installed, a cleared site, a larger parcel (put together by the city), "land write-downs", and amenities and improvements in place (Stout and Vitt 1982). (In a land write-down the city or redevelopment authority acquires an expensive parcel of prime downtown land at, for example, fifty-five dollars per square foot, including costs of purchase and clearing. Developers say they cannot afford to pay more than forty dollars per square foot. Therefore, the city authority sells the land to the chosen developers for thirty-seven dollars per square foot. Future tax dollars will be allocated to repay this subsidization as well as other costs absorbed by the city [Stout and Vitt, 1982: 16]).

The usual process involves the following: a redevelopment authority prepares a plan for a specified area, including a justification for the special inducements and reasons why developers have problems building without them. In contrast to procedures with industrial revenue bonds, state laws may well prescribe public hearings to gain citizen reaction to the proposed development. One of the chief advantages of tax increment financing is that it cannot be criticized for offering special tax advantages to developers. While inducements are given to developers, all citizens, businesses, and industries pay the same taxes. Tax equality is a sensitive issue. Additionally, city-wide taxes are not increased to finance these favors, and start-up times probably will be reduced. Also note that bonds issued for this purpose fall outside constitutional or local charter limits on the indebtedness a city may incur.

Of concern to urban designers is the likelihood that a project will have to have quite a high density in order to be economically feasible (Hager and Pratter, 1981). Another issue is that if a city uses a great deal of tax increment financing to fund new development, those increased tax revenues will not be available for other city expenses. The city may well be forced to find additional sources of revenue (UEDAR, 1981).

Since 1975, Wisconsin has been using "one of the most liberal tax increment financing laws in the country" to rehabilitate blighted or declining areas and promote industrial growth (Huddleston, 1981: 14). Wisconsin follows only California (which allows counties as well as municipalities to establish districts) and Minnesota (where local agencies and industrial development corporations can establish districts) in its use of this financing mechanism. The basic process for establishing the tax districts in Wisconsin consists of three steps. First, detailed plans are drawn up of public improvements; estimates of improvement costs as well as anticipated revenues are also prepared as well as additional planning related information, such as land use maps. Once the plans have been accepted by public resolutions, district boundaries are determined and, like the plan, subject to public mandate.

The schedule for predevelopment expenditures such as land lots write-downs, provision of public utilities, and land purchases allows for up to five years with an additional fifteen years to recoup development costs involved in financing the district. Development expenditures have typically been met through municipal general funds, revenue bonds, and general obligation debts. Development costs have been recovered through "yearly payments of tax increments funneled through other local governments" such as the county, special and school districts, and the like (Huddleston, 1981: 15). The tax increments themselves are generated by applying "the total property tax rate to the growth of property value" that occurs within the district (Huddleston, 1981: 15).

Three cities in Wisconsin—LaCrosse, Milwaukee, and Fond du Lac —have used tax increment financing to redevelop parts of their downtowns. In the first two communities, the city contributed public improvements including parking, pedestrian walkways, and a convention center. In both cases, private development was attracted, and a major hotel complex and offices were built. Substantial increases in property value were realized in each city in the period from 1978–1980 (Huddleston, 1981).

Fond du Lac has financed its public improvements for its downtown with $9 million in short-term bond anticipation notes. It is the first Wisconsin city to use specific tax increment financing bonds (TIF) for a redevelopment district—a process that only became possible in 1980. The mechanism has enabled the city to keep a local industry downtown with a land write-down that enabled the company to build a 72,000-square-foot building in the district. The city has since built a city-county building on the edge of the downtown, constructed a parking garage, and made pedestrian improvements at the downtown. At present, inflation has increased construction costs and halted some of the planned public improvements in an otherwise encouraging effort (Purcell, 1981).

Maryland's use of TIF has been somewhat different that in most states where the mechanism has focused on redeveloping blighted or underutilized areas. In Prince George's County, Maryland, an expanding suburban area of Washington, D.C. , a TIF program has been used to "finance public improvements that encourage commercial and industrial development within urbanized areas that are relatively strong" (Schwanke, 1983: 3). Two additional features of Maryland's program are worth noting. First, because TIFs are not counted among county revenues from property taxes and therefore are not "capped," they provide a new source of revenue. Moreover, funds raised by TIF are no longer used only to pay off bonds—an amendment that allows any new development, whether or not financed through public investment, to use TIF funds to finance future capital improvements (Schwanke, 1983: 3).

The benefit of Maryland's TIF program is essentially that it has enabled counties to proceed with public improvements without drawing funds from county tax budgets. From an urban design standpoint, however, it is too early to judge the effectiveness of Maryland's approach. The weak link, as Schwanke (1981: 7) has pointed out, seems to be the role of TIFs in a county's planning/urban design goals:

> The crucial factor which has not been squarely confronted in many localities, is the necessity of formally tying the TIF districts and their capital improvements programs to the overall planning process. If these elements are not carefully coordinated, property owners and developers may rightly make accusations that they have been treated unfairly by a haphazard system of public improvements.

Schwanke points out that policies are also needed that stipulate what developers are required to provide by way of public improvements that are comparable to practices outside of TIF districts. In addition, he recommends the need for guidelines "to ensure that small developers can also benefit from the program" (Schwanke, 1983: 7). As the Wisconsin and Maryland experiences show, tax increment financing is flexible enough to meet development activities and planning goals essential for the district.

Special assessments. If a city is running short of ways to finance improvements, it may want to investigate whether its state laws permit establishment of special assessment districts. The rationale behind the mechanism is that those property owners who benefit specially from a proposed improvement pay for it through increased taxes— special assessments—to finance the bonds that finance the project. Depending on state law, bonds may or may not be subject to municipal debt limits.

The difficulty is, of course, that it may be nearly impossible to prove that the benefit accrues to the specified property owners and is not a public benefit for which all should pay. In addition, there is the question of how costs are apportioned within a special assessment area. Equally? By taking into consideration how far a particular property is from an improvement? Differently for different types of property? Who benefits most and pays most?

LOAN MECHANISMS

Following are common loans that cities make available for civic improvements. More complicated and alternative financing methods will be discussed in the next section.

Equity participation loans let the city participate in a citizen's efforts to become a homeowner. A typical candidate for this type of loan is a person who may have difficulty in raising funds for a down payment while being able to afford monthly payments (UEDAR, 1981).

Similar are *loan guarantee/subordinate financing* for developers. With these loans, developers gain a longer pay-back period or interest rate reduction, or both. Funding sources include "Community and Development Block Grant (CDBG), Urban Development Action Grant (UDAG) funds, city reveues, foundations, tax increment financing (where the law allows), and UDAG repayments in cities that are receiving income from UDAGs" (Stout and Vitt, 1982: 20). A deferred payment mortgage permits a developer to pay no principal or interest for a specified period (with interest rate specified, as well). At the end of the period, the loan increases to a higher amount to reflect the payments and interest missed, and the interest rate at this time might be higher.

Muncipal loans for rehabilitation, which are financed by bond issues, can make a difference in a city's ability to rehabilitate a fairly large urban area. Such loans can supplement other financing, as well as federal funds. An advantage is that interest is charged at a rate lower than from other funders.

A variation in the usual requirements for loans is the deverloper's "buying-down" the interest rate by making a prepayment "roughly proportionate to the present value of the expected loss of interest over the term of the loan" (from a banker, for example), (Stout and Vitt, 1982: 20). The city might or might not be the seller of the loan and might grant money to the developer to cover the prepayment (Stout and Vitt, 1982).

Revolving Loan Funds enable a city to lend money for various aspects of urban improvements. A local historic preservation society can buy and suitably renovate a property with such a loan. When the society sells the property, it has achieved historic preservation and money from the repaid loan is back in city coffers and ready for reloaning (UEDAR, 1981).

Methods of alternative financing

Hard times have inspired cities (and the states that have to legislate for city action to occur) to be more innovative in arranging financing for urban enhancements. The following section outlines several alternative methods.

AIDS TO LENDERS

A principal stumbling block in getting banks and savings and loan institutions to lend enough money to finance an entire project is their mortgage policies. They traditionally see the appraised value of an inner-city property as its value in the undeveloped state. This makes a large loan impossible and encourages investors to buy such property for resale—without improvements, of course. The remedy is *inner-city value estimation models* that allow appraisals "beyond comparable sales prices, which take account of a range of factors related to the future potential of an area" (UEDAR, 1981: 105).

Another aid is the *community investment fund program*, which authorizes the twelve regional Federal Home Loan banks to make money available to local savings and loans at lower rates than otherwise available (UEDAR, 1981). The federal government established the Community Investment Funds in June, 1978 with an initial $10 billion (UEDAR, 1981). This takes some of the burden to fund projects (like rehabilitation) off the city's back and encourages: "development interest in the inner city, but with an emphasis on small-scale, community-focused projects." "This reinforces neighborhoods in a way that past public programs often have not been able to" (UEDAR, 1981: 107–108). The neighborhood reinvestment corporations that work with neighborhood housing services (locally controlled nonprofit organizations) are a prime example of this program at work. Its activities include management of revolving loan funds that are made available to neighborhood homeowners unable to qualify for market rate home improvement loans, rehabilitation and financial counseling, housing code inspections, and public improvements. Another key element of this community investment program is that it represents a partnership of community residents (who also serve on neighborhood housing service boards), lenders, and community government officials. The apartment Improvement Program (AIP) in Yonkers and Mount Vernon, New York; Hartford, Connecticut; Los Angeles; and Washington, D.C. are examples of this program at work (Whiteside, 1981). These projects have improved the marketability of deteriorating apartment buildings and have increased the stability and attractiveness of neighborhoods.

In Oakland, California, infill housing has been designed, built, and financed (for the most part, conventionally) through Neighborhood Housing Service (NHS) efforts. City-owned vacant lots in NHS neighborhoods there are allowing new housing to be built in central city areas and are offering "substantial benefits to an overall revitalization effort" (Whiteside, 1981: 71). Another aspect of the program is commercial reinvestment in neighborhoods. In Portland, Oregon and Baltimore, NHS efforts have worked with merchant's associations on physical improvements and marketing and programming techniques to strengthen commercial resources with neighborhoods (Whiteside, 1981).

OTHER INNOVATIVE TECHNIQUES

Urban homesteading helps enterprising citizens buy a run-down property from the city for as little as one dollar. They invest "sweat quality" and building materials in the property, agreeing to rehabilitate it within a specified time when it becomes their property free and clear. The city may have acquired these dilapidated dwellings by eminent domain or by tax default. It also may be possible for these prospective homeowners to get aid from the city in the form of rehabilitation loans.

If a city is flexible, it might be willing to work out an arrangement with a developer who plans a project near a proposed city project so that both would save money. This is the *shared land costs* technique. For example, both parties may need to acquire land and then the nearby sites will need preparation. Cooperation will reduce costs for both, especially if the city already owns some prime land for development or acquires it through eminent domain.

As a further inducement to private development, some cities fund *land buy-back* programs that guarantee that developers can opt out of a project within a given period—and not lose the money they invested in the land. Typically, developers receive from the city a sum equal to the purchase price or not exceeding a certain price per square foot. On the surface, this sounds like an investor's bonanza, but there are also considerable advantages for the city.

Assume that a city has a critical need for housing. The buy-back ordinance can be written so as to give particular benefits to developers of housing of a type the city wishes to encourage. The developers draw up plans and make a private land purchase. If the plans are approved, the city enters into a land buy-back agreement. This is a much simpler process for the city—no city land purchases, no eminent domain proceedings, and no housing authority.

A final suggestion for alternative financing may put the amenities a city wants to provide for its citizens within reach. The city or a non-profit group provides on-the-job training in rehabilitation of housing (or other structures) by contracting with construction firms (or a labor union) to supervise and train the unemployed who get the jobs they need. In return, the city gains newly restored neighborhoods. Opportunities for training are most important to unemployed workers whose old jobs will never be available again. At the present time, Comprehensive Employment Training Act (CETA) funds are available for this type of program, as well as the other funding sources already mentioned.

Job targeting can be an important facet of any development effort, particularly if a community stipulates employment opportunities in exchange for the loans and tax breaks it offers to developers. CETA and the Emerging Jobs Bill (April 1983) provide services that enable cities to make a definite link between economic development efforts and creating private sector jobs for local residents. Pittsburgh, for example, is using $1 million of its $7.1 million CDBG to pay "half the salaries of some 200 people who will take new jobs ... with private companies or nonprofit corporations" (Peters, 1983: 26). The effort is intended to get people into the private sector in permanent jobs. Portland, Oregon requires hiring agreements from developers as a condition of public development assistance through a HUD-funded targeted jobs demonstration program (TJDP) (Peters, 1983: 27–28). Portland's experience has shown that an economic-development–job-targeting plan demands a coordinated, ongoing, and strong administrative commitment on the city's part. Baltimore's Harborplace development partnerships with Rouse Company also tied the city's land deed to a permanent jobs agreement. New York's South Street Seaport, also developed by city assistance and Rouse Company, has arrived at a similar agreement (Peters, 1983).

Public/private partnerships for codevelopment

The previous discussion of financial mechanisms may well have raised a number of questions. It is quite clear that a mere listing of the various means of financing is not enough to make a sound decision on which to choose. It also takes more than merely saying, "We want a better city, and we will use x method of financing to achieve it." Inevitably, cities need to do more than make their regulations manageable. As such, the term "codevelopment" (as used in this section) implies much more than mere cooperation between government, developers, and business. Codevelopment entails participation by (1) "an entrepreneurial city government or its development entity" (for simplicity, "the public partner"), (2) "a resourceful developer or development team" ("the private partner"), and (3) "local business leadership" ("the collective business community") (Witherspoon, 1982: 1).

Witherspoon (1982: 5–6) stresses the importance of the predevelopment phase of a project ("feasibility and planning"), and this, of course, is also the essential phase for meeting the concerns of the urban designer. After this preliminary and often lengthy stage, the process moves into development ("construction and leasing") and, finally, to post-development ("operation"). Codevelopment demands total involvement by the three participants, an involvement that goes far beyond any cooperation that may already exist in a community.

Stout and Vitt (1982: 1–8) have established some "prerequisites" for municipalities that must "work with the private sector as partners in codevelopment." These include understanding "the real estate process and its politics" and conveying "a readiness to act and follow through." They further outline how cities may acquire land, take advantage of underused land (railroad property, surplus school and city property), and offer incentives when developers do not have enough funds or have capital costs that are too high (Stout and Vitt, 1982). Absolutely essential are the services of an extremely competent planning and design staff whose senior staff members will perform leadership roles in codevelopment.

Witherspoon's definition of codevelopment (1982: 7) may well cause these professionals to wonder (and worry) if such a venture is possible in their city: "Codevelopment involves the joint, sustained efforts of business and government, with the partners sharing more equally in the risks and benefits." He explains that "a city, its private business leadership, and one or more developers (who may be public or private) [will be partners in] formal or informal relationships [to] deal with broad community problems" (Witherspoon, 1982: 7–8). While this total commitment to community may not be necessary in every instance, valuable lessons can be carried from codevelopment to smaller projects and other cooperative endeavors a city may undertake to improve its environment (Witherspoon, 1982). This new cooperation for codevelopment requires "public/private leveraging" so that smaller amounts of public funds will bring forth larger private investments, "deal-making between business and government and much earlier involvement of the private sector" than we usually have seen or might expect, and expenditure of public funds and gaining of income, so there must be accountability, "consideration of *public objections*" as well as private goals (Witherspoon, 1982: 8–9).

The predevelopment stage deserves special attention. Here, the waters are being tested constantly so that the feasibility of the venture can be judged and rejudged before any of the three partners is totally committed. The closer a venture is to commitment, the more stringent the testing and the larger the financial expense involved for all. A city that wants to gain the confidence of and a commitment from developers and the business community must assume some of the financial risks and basic costs the others are unwilling to assume early in the proceedings. Some financing methods that accomplish this have already been mentioned. Developers and the business community are concerned most about financial return, whereas the city's concerns are livability and a wise expenditure of limited public funds. At this stage, the city may find it necessary to spend money for public relations (as previously mentioned) to help the developer acquire tenants. A developer may desire at least tentative bookings before making final commitment. Market research conducted by the planning staff can be of assistance here.

Codevelopment came of age in the 1970s. Government now sees itself more as an investor than a grantor in its efforts to achieve

economic development. Its strategy now is to invest its public resources where private investment is likely to occur. What usually is
needed is improvement of the economic base. The three partners
must constantly search for better ways of doing business together.
Developers often become involved earlier in the process—negotiating, lending their expertise to aid and influence the nature of the
venture, and committing some funds. (Some federally funded programs require "firm upfront investment" prior to the granting of
federal funds.) Financing of joint ventures has become increasingly
complex, requiring "flexibility and quicker response by both public
and private partners" (Witherspoon, 1982: 44). There may be easier
mixing of funds from both. On the part of the public partner, this is a
good reason to make certain that the public will benefit, to assume a
role in project management, and to be flexible enough to be responsible for some improvements that are usually the province of private
investors (Witherspoon, 1982: 43–44).

> Diminution of federal funds means that there must be: public
> risk-taking and investment . . . where (1) sufficient private capi-
> tal is not available on reasonable terms, (2) important advan-
> tage to codevelopment cannot be achieved through indirect
> means, and (3) benefits from the project are reasonably ex-
> pected to exceed costs. . . . (It is further) indicated by the exis-
> tence of certain special circumstances: Fragmented land
> ownership, . . . complex requirements for physical design and
> construction, (and) transit service (and others) to convention
> centers . . . where public and private components interconnect
> (Witherspoon, 1982: 44–45).

A city's ability to form effective partnerships with the private sector
is shaped by its economic situation, its administrative structure, and
its urban design goals (Shirvani, 1982). In addition, there are certain
ways in which cities normally do things (planning, development, and
so on) that may well preclude their acting as good faith partners with
the private sector. As Heckman (1983: 21) points out:

> Private-sector partnerships usually have clearly defined and
> measurable objectives. Their support organizations are accus-
> tomed to complicated negotiations. If the partners have
> worked together before, they may leave some of the project
> details open for resolution during implementation, but gen-
> erally such ambiguity is avoided.

In contrast, local governments are rarely organized or equipped to
make and carry out initiatives and the necessary authority is typically
dispersed among various agencies and/or elected officials. Secondly,

a locality's ability to come up with a negotiating plan or reasonable timetable requires experienced professional staff:

> A skillful negotiating plan creates deadlines for the opposition, anticipates deadlines placed on the opposition by others, and provides for contingencies on both sides. A poor plan is one that creates unrealistic deadlines that developers can't possibly meet (Heckman, 1982: 12).

Finally, lack of expertise—particularly in real estate deals and finance —can be a stumbling block (Heckman, 1983: 12).

Although cities differ in the kinds of resources (economic, administrative, and so on) they have when they establish public-private partnerships, some clear approaches can be identified based on the kinds of organizations they set up to manage economic and urban development. One approach is to set up a separate nonprofit corporation, such as Philadelphia's Industrial Development Corporation (PIDC) (Adell, 1983). Some of the advantages Philadelphia sees in the model include: (1) flexibility and effectiveness, (2) freedom from restraint, and (3) protection of the city from financial risk (Adell, 1983: 18). The nonprofit organization also derives considerable power from its association with the city, including its zoning and taxing powers and its right of eminent domain (Adell, 1983).

St. Paul has taken a different approach by keeping its economic development planning within the local government. Bureaucracy and public disclosure requirements are, St. Paul admits, decided drawbacks that can delay the development process, but they argue that in this, their situation differs very little from corporations and nonprofit development agencies: "They, too, are accountable to boards and community groups" (Bellus, 1983: 16). Recent changes in St. Paul's development procedures—including its rights to obtain options in property without a public hearing—have further increased that city's effectiveness in dealing with developers (Bellus, 1983).

Once a city begins to explore partnership models that fit its economic needs, administrative structure, and urban design goals, it should not overlook the potential role of private funders such as corporations and foundations. Although Buchman (1982: 40) points out that "almost no one funds urban design *per se* ... a few private foundations are forging innovative approaches to community development without realizing that they are backers of urban design projects." One of the reasons that private funders are not directly involved in urban acitivities is that they "believe they lack expertise to make discriminating judgements about valid nonprofit urban activities" (Bachman, 1982: 40). Bachman suggests, however, that these funds are potentially available to urban designers who understand the patterns and goals of corporate giving.

There are a few cases where private funding organizations have made very clear commitments to urban design. The Dayton-Hudson Foundation in Minneapolis; the Mott Foundation in Flint, Michigan; and Piton Foundation in Denver have all been involved in community development projects ranging from neighborhood studies and reinvestment programs to downtown revitalization (McNamara and Hummel, 1982; Bachman, 1982). At the federal level substantital changes have also been made in a number of federal funding programs, most notably the Community Development Block Grant Program (CDBG). Key changes include greater control by the cities over CDBG funds that enable them to leverage private sector resources (Stokuis, 1982).

References

Adell, Patricia. "Philadelphia: We Set Up a Separate Corporation," *Planning* 49, no. 9, October (1983): 18–19.

Bachman, Geraldine. "Philanthropic Backing for Urban Development." *Urban Design International* 4, no. 1, Fall (1982): 40–41.

Bacow, Adele Fleet. "The Massachusetts Government Land Bank: Aid for Community Economic Development." *Planning 1981: Proceedings of the National Planning Conference.* Chicago, IL: The American Planning Association, 1981.

Beals, Alan. Preface to Connie Hager and Pratter, S. Jerome, *Financial Incentives For Design.* Washington, D.C.: National League of Cities Technical Bulletin, 1981.

Bellus, James J. "St Paul: We Kept It In City Government." *Planning* 49, no. 9, October (1983): 16–17.

Goetsch, Robert, and Haderlein, Mary. "Art for Downtown's Sake." *Planning* 49, no. 7, July/August (1983): 10–14.

Greenwell, Richard L. *Using Design to Market Your City's Image for Economic Development.* Washington, D.C.: National League of Cities Technical Bulletin, 1981.

Hager, Connie, and Pratter, S. Jerome. *Financial Incentives for Better Design.* Washington, D.C.: National League of Cities Technical Bulletin, 1981.

Heckman, Bruce W. "Learning to Be A Partner." *Planning* 49, no. 9, October (1983): 21–24.

Huddleston, Jack R. "Tax Increment Financing in Wisconsin." *Planning* 47, no. 11, November (1981): 14–17.

Huddleston, Jack R. "A Comparison of State Tax Increment Financing Laws," *State Government* 5, no. 1 (1982): 29–33.

Lyons, Arthur, and Mahan, Toni Hartrich. "Tax Incentives for Commercial Development: Should Planners Be Concerned?" In *Planning 1981: Proceedings of the National Planning Conference.* Chicago, IL: The American Planning Association, 1981.

McNamara, John, and Hummel, Joan. "Dayton Hudson Foundation: Corporate Partners Help Whittier Work." *Urban Design International* 4, no. 1, Fall (1982): 42–46.

Peters, James. "Job Targeting: What Planners Can Do." *Planning* 49, no. 9, October (1983): 26–29.

Pratter, S. Jerome, and Conway, William. *Dollars from Design.* Washington, D.C.: National League of Cities Technical Bulletin, 1981.

Purcell, Edward J."Fond Du Lac Tried It and Liked It." *Planning* 47, no. 11, November (1981): 16.

Schwanke, Dean. "Putting Tax Increment Financing to Work in Prince George's County." *Urban Land* 42, no. 5, May (1983): 2–7.

Shirvani, Hamid. "An Urban Design Prospect." *UD REVIEW* 5, no. 3 (1982): 17–20.

Stout, Gary E., and Vitt, Joseph E. *Public Incentives and Financing Techniques for Codevelopment.* Monograph in the Development Component Series. Washington, D.C.: The Urban Land Institute, 1982.

Stokuis, Jack. "Giving Private America A Chance." *Urban Design International* 4, no. 1, Fall (1982): 38–40.

Trimble, Gerald M., and Rogel, Stuart L. "Horton Plaza—Codevelopment Rebuilds Downtown Excitement." *Urban Land* 42, no. 7, July (1983): 15–19.

Urban Environmental Design Administration Research (UEDAR). *Lessons from Local Experience.* Washington, D.C.: U.S. Department of Housing and Urban Development, Office of Policy Development and Research, 1981.

Whiteside, William A. "Neighborhood Reinvestment Corporation." *Federal Home Loan Bank Board Journal* 14, no. 4, April (1981): 69–72.

Witherspoon, Robert. *Codevelopment: City Rebuilding by Business and Government.* Washington , D.C.: The Urban Land Institute, 1982.

Urban design prospects

CHAPTER 11

CHAPTERS 2 through 10 covered the state-of-the-art of urban design and its components. Turning now to future directions, there appear to be several potential avenues for growth, improvement, and development in the field. Overall, it is obvious that the field is expanding, gaining wider recognition, and gradually becoming part of local government agendas. This recognition and growth of the urban design field is taking place in small towns and suburban communities, as well as in urban areas. There are, however, several aspects of this expanding influence of urban design that may not be completely advantageous or supportive of the field's generic goals—namely, its concerns with the overall improvement of environmental quality and livability and its strong commitment to the public at large.

First, there is the development/entrepreneurial emphasis of much planning and urban design practice, which in many cities has become an integral function of local government. This urban design approach retains its focus on traditional, large-scale architectural projects and tax generation and only secondarily attends to issues such as public amenities or promoting the city as a place to work and live. Despite its drawbacks, however, this private sector approach is appropriate in many settings—in particular in the declining cities of the northeast. Moreover, there are several ways in which private approaches can be developed into defensible and viable urban design strategies that can be improved through increased emphasis on public amenities and through the development of an overall design guideline/framework that coordinates development that occurs in different areas of an urban environment. In other words, a physical design plan structured in terms of three-dimensional guidelines is essential if urban design is to play an effective role in private development approaches.

Another prevailing urban design approach that many cities are beginning to take is actually a version of the architecturally based private strategies just discussed. Typically this approach is adopted by cities experiencing development pressures and as such is subject to a number of problems and constraints that have been identified throughout this book. Individual building designs—their scale and architectural style—provide the reference or starting point for this approach. Essentially, most of the buildings in an area are architecturally designed and then the design is made compatible with a city's development controls, regulations, and guidelines for that area, and perhaps its future expansion. Here again the approach is quite fragmented and ad hoc. Although the environmental quality of the areas where the approach is applied may be improved, incompatibilities with surrounding areas may become quite pronounced, creating conditions that lead to gentrification and other similar negative impacts.

A third approach to urban design that many cities continue to use emphasizes historic preservation strategies and techniques. Larger cities often find that preservation techniques are appropriate for districts as well as individual structures, whereas smaller towns are concentrating on "main street" to preserve and revitalize their downtown cores. There are many advantages to historic preservation; it enables communities to save and reuse valuable historic structures and thereby helps to enhance the quality of the built environment. However, historic preservation alone results at best in piecemeal improvements unless it is incorporated into an urban design framework plan.

A key problem shared by the above three approaches is that they are all stopgap measures in that they are rarely part of an overall plan or urban design framework. When applied in older cities with ailing infrastructures, such short-range and fragmentary solutions can actually compound problems in a very short time. Other characteristics shared by the three approaches are their emphases on subjective design criteria and the entrepreneurial aspects of the development process to the neglect of human and natural environment dimensions

—shortcomings that have been explored in previous chapters of this book. Chapter 3 noted that the planner/designer does not yet have the kinds of tools and methods necessary to reliably translate social-science findings into plans or designs. The natural environment dimension, on the other hand, is comparatively well developed—an enormous body of research in this area (both theoretical and applied) is now available that can be incorporated directly into the planning/urban design process. Where expertise is lacking, consultants on every aspect of the urban environment can be used, provided that city governments begin to maintain the kinds of natural-physical inventory base that is needed for a well-developed planning/urban design framework.

With this in mind, two critical avenues for improvement of such approaches—and subsequently urban design processes—can be identified. The first involves development of a set of criteria, measures or tools that will enable practicing planners and designers to incorporate human dimensions into actual physical planning/design tasks. A second area for improvement is in the field of urban environmental planning. More comprehensive methods and approaches to the use of natural environment-physical standards in the development process and also in the ways in which natural factors and elements are incorporated into actual physical plans, designs, and planning processes are needed. One of the strongest prospects for planning/urban design is an environmentally based approach to urban design planning that can help to enhance urban environmental quality.

For some time now, segments of the planning community have contended that their cities lack the financial resources necessary to undertake urban design activities. This argument no longer holds true. As this book has demonstrated, there are a number of implementation mechanisms—legal, administrative, as well as financial—that individually or in combination can be used by many different types of cities to further their urban design goals. Public/private partnerships offer another extremely promising resource to communities that need to improve their negotiations and working relationships with the private sector.

There is another aspect to the question of why some planning agencies and administrations are reluctant to embrace an urban design framework. A physical design framework does not mean a traditional comprehensive plan. Rather, the phrase implies a real three-dimensional physical guide that forms part of a city's development policies. The precise character and components of such a guide were discussed in chapters 2, 5 and 7. Briefly, it should be hierarchical and simultaneously generate various planning products. That is, cities require urban design processes that incorporate design policies, plans, programs, and guidelines. The term "require" as it is used above underscores several assumptions as well as clear assertions presented throughout this book with regard to the role of urban design processes in modern city planning. First and foremost the approach adopted here implies that all cities are engaged in urban design in one form or another. Their involvement may be active, productive, and explicit or it may take place by default, but the essential fact is that all cities shape and influence the development that takes place (or fails to occur) in them. This is obviously true in cities where planning agencies lack trained designers or are hostile to the prospect of urban design. Thus, even in cities where the planning processes do not produce or generate a blueprint for design, the planning professionals in place are inevitably engaged in indirect design simply because their policies explicitly and/or implicitly affect the physical character and quality of their urban environment.

The above assertion is not merely academic; on the contrary, it is pivotal in terms of a city's efforts to market itself. Presently, in some cities where development pressures are high, building and development seem to require little encouragement. Do these cities need urban design and environmental policies or is it simply an interesting (but unnecessary) luxury—better left to architects? We heartily reject this possibility: we can look at the artifacts of planless urban renewal programs and formalist postmodern urban design efforts in cities throughout the country to understand why this laissez-faire approach is unacceptable and frequently diastrous.

There is another aspect to this issue as well, namely, the public service role of the city and its environs. City administrations can never absolve themselves of this responsibility—even when they manage to bring some advantages to their communities. So what, then, does marketing the city involve? Many factors certainly, but the starting point for every city has got to be finding ways to improve itself through appropriate urban design mechanisms that are, in turn, vehicles that work in conjunction with marketing methods. In sum, effective marketing of a city requires recognition and institutionalization of urban design mechanisms within local government—not as beautification schemes or efforts but as an essential part of community service.

Index

Access criteria, 125, 127
Acid rain, 90, 92
Activity patterns
  hubs of larger cities, 38
  spatial segregation of, 58
  systems of, urban, 60
Activity support, 23, 37–40
  coordinating patterns of, 38
  indoor-outdoor integration, 39
Administrative Procedures Act (1946),
  54
Advertising, outdoor, 40
Advocacy planning, 51–53
  advisor role of planner in, 54
  typical clients of, 53
AIA Regional/Urban Design Assistance
  Team, 159
Air and climate quality, 73–75
Air pollution
  monitoring and preventing, 74
  urban vegetation stressed by, 91
Alaska, earthquake in, 84
Alburquerque, NM; historic districts in,
  181
Alternative concepts, 113–16
  generating, 113
  evaluation of, 114
  policy translation of, 115
Amenities, coordinating, 36
Anonymity, tempering through design,
  58
Antidemolition ordinances, 179
Antiwar movements, 118
Appleyard, Donald, 117

Architects Collaborative, Inc.
  (Cambridge, MA), 108
Architecture, emotional reactions to, 61
Ardalan, Nader, 106
Arroyo Group (Santa Monica), 18
Associations, community, 154
Atlanta, GA, 161
Atomic Energy Organization of Iran, 106
Austin, TX, 69
Automobile, influencing urban design,
  23–24

Bacon, Edmund, 157
Baltimore, MD, 161
Barnett, Jonathan, 157
Barrington, RI, 87
Bay City, OR, 172
Bellevue, WA, 170
Billboards, 40, 176
Bogs, destruction and abuse of, 90
Bonaventure Hotel (LA), 37
Bonds, financing development with
  general obligation, 189–90
    revenue, 190
    tax increment, 191–93
Boston, MA, sign regulations in, 42
Boulder, CO, 81
Boundaries, cognitive and social
  functions of, 59
Bucks County, PA, 172
Building
  bulk, 13
  form and massing 11–23
  relationship of land to, 135

Charlotte, NC
  sign design guidelines of, 42
  urban design study of, 33
Chicago World's Exposition of 1898, 3
Cincinnati, OH, 162
  sign regulations, 43
Citizen participatory planning, 51–54
City
  anonymity in, tempered through
    good design, 58
  development in, controlling, 144
  ordering principle, 58
  physical aspects of planning, 57
  place identity role in, 57
  structure of, and effects on
    environmental cognition, 59
  unique spatial character, 58
Ciudad Guayana, 117
Civil rights movements, 118
Climate and air quality, 73, 133
Codes, energy planning, 80
Codevelopment, 197, 198
Cognitive maps, 60
Cognitive process in planning, 57–58
Coherence, 60
Communities, planned, 155
Community action approaches, 117
Community and Development Block
  Grants, 194
Community associations, 154
Community Design Center of Atlanta,
  161
Community Development Block Grants
  (HUD), 158
Community orientation of urban design,
  4
Compatibility criteria, 127
Comprehensive planning, 70, 145, 147
  early public participation in, 112
  goal formulation, 112
Concepts, design, 113–14
Congestion, 32
Conservation. See also Preservation
  code revisions relating to, 77
  energy, economic incentives, 77
  urban design orientation to, 4
Coverage, building, 11
Crime control, urban design aspect of,
  59
Cultural pluralism, factoring into design,
  56
Culture, social data relating to, 55

Dallas Arts District Design Guidelines,
  152
Dallas, TX, 161
  incentive zoning uses in, 170
  open space plan, 28–29
  sign ordinances in, 176

transferring development rights in,
  175
Davis, CA, 76, 77
Dayton, OH
  energy planning in, 78
  grass pavement, 96
  greening of, 73
  temperature impact, efforts to
    reduce, 75
Dayton-Hudson Foundation, 201
Decentralization, Toronto, 27
Density, urban, 84, 134
Denver Partnership, The, 162
Denver, CO, 162
  16th Street Design Guidelines, 152
Design. See also Urban design
  conceptual bases of, 105, 113–14
  context, structured treatment of,
    131
  control implementation, 174
  criteria
    measurable, 121, 133–40
    nonmeasurable, 122–31
    traditional approaches to, 131
  energy-efficient, 82
  evaluation of, 62
  form concept, 132
  frameworks, 18
  guidelines. See Guidelines, design
    and planning
  methods, urban, 105 ff
  plans, 145
  policies, 144–45
  products, 141
  programs, 153
  review process, 182–83
  social data in, current role and use
    of, 61–62
  social scientists role in process of,
    62
Designers
  behaviorally oriented, 60
  language differences between
    clients and, 61
Developing countries
  design methods in, 108
  esteem of experts in, 108
Development(s)
  city, controlling, 144
  financing, 187–97
  historic place, 44
  inward-looking projects, 37
  moratoriums on, 178
  plans focused on, 115
  regional, federal policies on, 143
  regulating, 167
  rights transfers, 174
  urban, financing, 185
Development orientation of urban
  design, 4

Development planning, 145
Development rights, transfer of, 174
Diversity
    as design issue, 59
    factoring into design, 56
Domestic oil production, 76

Earthquakes, 84
Ecological modeling, 71
Ecology, open space as issue in design, 29
Efficiency, design, 121
Energy
    audits, 77, 82
    crisis, 76
    planning
        development bonus, 81
        incentive strategies, 81
        performance standards, 80
        regulatory strategies, 78
        tax incentives, 82
        technical information
            dissemination, 82
        techniques, 78
    policy, 76
    solar, 76–82, 133
Energy-efficient design, 82
Environment
    citizen concern about, 168
    comprehensive analysis of, 82
    designing, 6, 69–72
    hydrology resources in planning, 90
    monitoring air pollution, 74
    natural
        preservation of, 8
        relationships with built, 72
    open space planning, 28
    parking effects on, 24
    physical, design relating to, 57
    planning issues of, difficult to
        identify, 70
    urban, 71, 86
Environmental blight, 86
Environmental cognition, city structure
    and its effects on, 59
Environmental impact reports, 181–82
Environmental legibility, 60
Environmental planning
    performance zoning used in, 172
    urban design process issues in, 71–72
Environmental Protection Agency, 71, 94
Equity, as design criteria, 122
Erosion, soil, 91
Evergreen trees, 94
External form and image (of design), 6

Facilitation approach to planning,
    techniques of, 51

Fairfax County, VA, 71
Fathy, Hassan, 106
Fault hazards, 84
Federal Housing Authority, 135
Federal Policies, 143
Fifth Avenue Special Zoning District
    (New York City), 37, 148, 173
Financing, development, 187–97
Fitness, design, 125, 130–32
Flood disposal systems, 90
Flood plain management, 84–85
Floor area districts (Seattle), 8
Fond du Lac, WI, 192
Forests, urban, 95
Form and massing, building, 11–23, 132
Fragmental design process, mixture of
    synoptic and intuitive, 116–17
France, urban planning methods in, 108
Freedom of Information Act (1966), 54
French Geological Institute, 83
Fresno, CA, Fulton Mall, 39

Geddes, Sir Patrick, 3
Geology, urban, 83–85, 133
Georgetown, DC, 44
Ghiradelli Square (San Francisco),
    preservation
    benefitting, 44–45
Glasgow, Scotland, 95
Grass pavement, 95
Greenwich, CT, 87
Groundwater, urbanization effects on, 87
Guidelines, design and planning
    alternative solution, 115, 147
    developing framework of, 148
    general, 59, 144
    scope of, 152
Gutman, Robert, 50

Hartford, CT, 35, 76
Healdsburg, CA, 159
Height control, building, 11, 136
Historic districts, 180–81
    administration of, 181
    antidemolition ordinances and, 179
    needs and problems, 46
    preservation and, 204
    redevelopment, 44
Homesteading, urban, 196
Honolulu, HI, 152
Housing and Urban Policy Act of 1974, 158
Houston-Galveston Area Council's
    Environmental Decision
    Assistance System, 71
        Community Development Block
            Grants, 158
        design guides, 163, 164
Hydrology, urban, 85–90, 133

Identity, role of, in city planning, 57, 128
Incentive zoning, 168–71
    advantages of, 171
    promotes infill residential
        development, 171
    successful techniques of, 171
Incremental design methods, 105, 116
Indigenous vegetation, 96
Industrialism, pluralistic planning
    initiated by, 51
Internalized design methods, 105–9
    applied to developing countries,
      108
    criticism of, 109
    intuitive, 106
Internal pattern and image (of design), 6
Iraq, 108
Irvine, CA, 26, 161
Irvine Company, 26

Jacksonville, FL, 13
Jacobs, Allan, 157

Kalamazoo, MI, 39
Kent, T. J., 70
Knoxville, TN, 77
Kuwait, 108

LaCrosse, WI, 192
Lake County, IL, 172
Landfills, 85
Landscape, form and massing relating to,
    23
Landslides, 83
Land use, 8–11
    building relationship to, 135
    effected by hydrology, 85–87
    measuring, 135
    modifying existing patterns of, 8
Language, designer-client difficulties
    with, 61
Largo, FL, 172
LeCorbusier, 108
Lexington, VA, 45
Lincoln, NE, preservation guidelines in,
    45
Livability, concept of, 128
Long Beach, CA
    Design Guidelines (1980), 11, 149
    incentive zoning uses in, 171
    sign regulations, 41
Los Angeles, CA, 160
    landslide reduction plan, 84
    sediment control programs, 86
Louisville, KY, 159

Maintenance planning, 154
Maps, cognitive, 60
Marin County, CA, 89
Marshes, destruction and abuse of, 90

Marxism, radical design rooted in, 118
Massing and form, building, 11–23
Master planning, 70, 113, 145, 146
Mechanistic flexibility, 133
Medford, MA, 69
Memphis, TN, 171
Meteorological studies, 74
Methane, 85
Microclimate, influenced by building
    orientation, 73
Milwaukee, WI, 161, 170, 192
Minneapolis, MN, 161
    Nicolett Mall, 39
    sign regulations, 42
    Skyway System (pedestrian way), 31
Modeling, ecological, to monitor
    growth, 71
Montgomery County, MD, 86, 175
Monticello, AR, 87
Moscow, 83
Mott Foundation, 201

National Environmental Policy Act of
    1969, 158, 181
Neighborhood Design Center of
    Baltimore/DC, 161
New Orleans, LA, 44, 45
New York City, 160
    design guidelines, 149
    Fifth Avenue Special Zoning
      District, 37, 173
    incentive zoning of, 170
    street space balancing in
      Chinatown, 35
New York City Planning Department
    Urban Design Group, 157
New York City Special Zoning District
    concept, 148
Noise abatement, 114
Northglenn, CO, 76
Nuclear power, 76
Nuran, Iran, 106

Oahu Urban Design Study, 152
Oakland, CA
    incentive zoning uses in, 170
    infill housing finance in, 195
Oklahoma City, OK, 175
    development moratorium in, 178
    performance zoning uses in, 172
Old Town Alexandria, VA, 180
Open space, 27–31
    ecological issues of, 29
    elements of, 28
    enhanced by activity support, 38
    planning, 29
Ordinances
    antidemolition, 179
    interim, 178

sign, 176–77
zoning, 170
Orientation, urban design, 4
Ozone pollution from trees, 94

Parking, 23–27
    design approaches, 24
    environmental effects of, 24
    off-street, 39
    "package plan," 26
    urban-edge, 26
    visual impact on city form, 24
Passive solar access, 77
Pavement, grass, 95
Pedestrian plans, 128
Pedestrian systems, 31–36
    amenities within, 33–36
    movement systems, 37
    planning, balancing strategy of, 35
    reducing automobile dependency
      with, 31
    safety role in, 32
Performance zoning, 172
Philadelphia, PA
    Center City development, 21
    downtown redevelopment, 18
    Industrial Development Corp., 200
    Market East developments, 21
    sign regulations, 43
    Society Hill development, 21
Phoenix, AZ, 171
Physical development plans, 70
Pigeons, as urban wildlife, 97
Piton Foundation, 201
Pittsburgh, PA; urban development
    guidelines, 152
Planned communities, 155
Planners, behaviorally oriented, 60
Planning. See also Urban planning;
    Urban design
    Administrative Procedures Act, 54
    advocacy, distinguished from
      politically neutral, 53
    alternative concepts, generation of,
      113
    care and maintenance, 154
    concrete guidelines for, lacking, 63
    constraints of, 51
    design review process incorporated
      into, 182
    developer oriented, 70
    development bonus, rewards
      energy-efficient components,
      81
    geographical and physical aspects
      of, 57
    geological and soil data relating to,
      83
    goal formulation, 112

    human dimension, translating into,
      63–64
    land use, hydrology problems in,
      87
    limitations of, in urban design, 50
    master, 70, 113, 145, 146
    open space, 28
    participatory, mandated by
      legislation, 53–54
    performance zoning used in, 172
    pluralistic, initiated by
      industrialism, 51
    political implications of, 53, 113
    problems integrating
      environmental data into, 72
    public participatory, 53–54
    regional
      air quality management
        needed in, 75
      evaluations of, 114
    research and social data available
      for, 55
    responsibility, fragmentation of, 72
    solar energy, guidelines for, 77
    translating alternative solutions
      into, 115
    transportation, 27
    urban
      physical, problems of, 145–46
      regulating, 168
    values and, 51
    waterway, 89
Planning scale, 59
Plans, urban design. See Urban design
Pluralistic design process, 51, 56, 109,
    117–18
Policies, urban design, 115, 144
Political aspects of planning, 53, 113
Political economy, as decision
    framework in urban design, 62
Pollution
    evergreens use in removing, 94
    ground and air, 85, 91
    tree, 91
    water, 87
Population density, urban design role of,
    59
Portland, OR, 77, 160
    solar energy policy, 76
Preservation, 44–46. See also
    Conservation
    cultural benefits of, 44
    economic benefits of, 44
    guidelines for, 45
    historic
    antidemolition ordinances and,
      179
      registering significant structures,
        180
      tax incentives, 180

Preservation, historic (*cont.*)
  of natural environment, 8
  ordinances, 45
  protective policies for, 45
  tourism benefits of, 45
Products, design, 141–43
Programs, design, 144, 153
Property tax, 187
Public planning participation, 112
Public transportation, relative
  unavailability of, 24

Quality of life, in urban areas, 49
Queens, NY; Beach Twentieth Street
  revitalization, 39

Radical design methods, 105, 118
Rain, acid, 90, 92
Reductionism, 133
Regional development, federal policies
  on, 143
Regional planning
  air quality management needed in,
  75
  evaluations of, 114
Regional Planning Association, 109
Regulations, planning, 168
Robertson, Jacqueline, 157
Rochester, NY; preservation guidelines,
  45

Sadafi, Moser, 106
Safety as urban design element, 32
Salt, urban vegetation stressed by, 91
San Antonio, TX; performance zoning
  uses in, 172
San Diego, CA, 29, 31, 161
San Francisco, CA, 83, 161
San Francisco Planning and Urban
  Research Association, 161
San Francisco Urban Design Plan, 127,
  130
  Ghiradelli Square, 44
  incentive zoning uses in, 170
Santa Monica, CA; Third Street Mall
  Design, 17
Saudi Arabia, urban planning methods
  in, 108
Savannah, GA, 45
Scale as design issue, 59, 64
Scandinavia, urban planning methods in,
  108
Seattle, WA, 8, 76, 160
  design policy, 145
  floor area districts, 136
  preservation benefitting, 45
Sediment deposition, 86
Segregation patterns, racial; and
  population density, 59

Sense criteria, 127
Setbacks, building, 11
Sewer systems, 85–90
Shading, trees as, 92
Shops and restaurants, 23, 33
Signage, 40–44
  design importance, 41
  functional criteria for, 43
  semantic aspects of sign
    communication, 43
Sign districts, 177
Sign ordinances, 176–77
Sky-exposure plane, 134
Social data, 55–62
  behavioral research, 60–61
  cognitive approaches to, 57–60
  culturally related, 55–57
  relevant to design, 61–62
Social justice, as design criteria, 122
Social life, influenced by urban design,
  51, 58
Social processes, 118
Social scientists, design process role of,
  62
Soils
  controlling losses of, 84
  erosion of, 86, 91
  stability, 83
  urban, 83
*Solar Access, A Guide for California
  Communities* (1980), 78, 80
Solar access, simulating, 114
Solar energy, 76–82, 133
  commercialization projects, 82
  passive, 77
Soviet Union, 118
Sparrows, as urban wildlife, 97
Spatial boundaries, as design issues, 58–
  59
Spatial ordering, 58
Special district zoning, 173
Spreiregen, Paul, 13
Standards for Rehabilitation, Secretary of
  the Interior's, 45
Starlings as urban wildlife, 97
Storm sewer systems, 85, 87
St. Paul, MN, 161, 200
Street furniture, 36
Street-level activities, 8
Streetscape Concept (Irvine Company),
  26
Street space, balancing, 35
Studio Works (Santa Monica), 18
Stuttgart, West Germany, 73
Swamps, destruction and abuse of, 90
Synoptic design method, 105, 110–11
Syracuse, NY, 161

Tax abatement, 188–89
Taxes, property, 187

Tax incentives for conservation, 82
Third sector groups, 161–62
Topography, man-made changes to, 73
Toronto, Canada; decentralization of, 27
Tourism, preservation benefitting, 45
Traffic, circulation and management
    strategies, 26
Transportation, urban design element,
    27
Trees
    design function of, 92
    evergreen, as remover of
        pollutants, 94
    in urban landscape, 91
    ozone polluters, 94

Urban activity systems, 60
Urban animals, hazards subjected to, 97
Urban climate, 133
Urban design
    activities preservation, 44
    activity concept of, 37, 38, 122
    administration
        framework of, 158–62
        third sector groups, 161–62
    amenity/comfort concept, 36, 122
    appearance elements, 13
    automobile influencing, 24
    cities as products of nondesign, 50
    clarity and convenience concept,
        122
    climate element of, 23, 73
    comfort issues in pedestrian
        systems, 33
    comprehensive approaches to, 13,
        70
        as prerequisite for form and
            massing, 17
    conceptual basis, 18
    concrete guidelines lacking, 63
    constraints of, 51
    contextual framework, of, 5, 132
    control issue, 13, 132
    cost-benefit analysis, 114
    creative aspects of, 105
    criteria
        building form, 133
        debated by professionals, 121
        development, 204
        efficiency and economy, 121
        environment, natural, 133
        intensity, 133
        massing, 133
        measurable, 121, 133–40
        mechanistic flexibility, 133
        nonmeasurable, 122–31
        reductionism, 133
    critical issues discussions, public,
        113

    decision frameworks, political
        economy as, 62
    definition of, 5, 13
    design methods, 105 ff
    developer oriented, 70
    elements of, 6
    emergence as distinct field, 3
    energy planning in, 78
    evaluating, 62, 114
    evaluation processes, 114
    example of comprehensive, 147
    frameworks, 18
    goal formulation in, 112–13
    government function in, 204
    harmony/compatibility concept, 122
    human aspects of, 61–65
        complexity, 64
        cultural, 55
        practical, 50
        research into, 49
        translating into, 63
    implementation techniques, 163–64
    inhabitants' value system as aspect
        of, 117
    institutionalization of, 158
    limited by human dimension, 55
    monitoring growth, 71
    natural processes, role of, 98–99
    plans, problems of, 146
    principle of views, concept of, 122
    problems of integrating
        environmental data into, 72
    products of, classified, 144
    quality standards, 135
    research and social data available,
        55
    resource accessibility and, 59
    responsibility for, dispersed
        approach, 160
    review process, 182
    scale and pattern concept, 59, 122
    self-congestion, 32
    social research, incorporating into
        practice of, 60–64
    solutions evaluations, 114
    space and use interdependency, 37
    space concerns concept, 122
    traditional physical, growing
        dissatisfaction with, 70
    translation problems in, 63
    urban problems context of, 133
    urban space element of, 23
    variety/contrast concept, 122
    visual quality criteria, 122
    vitality concept, 125
    waterway planning, 89
Urban Design Group New York City
    Planning Department, 157
Urban Design Plan of San Francisco, 6,
    11, 122, 144

Urban development, financing, 185, 187–97
    community investment fund program, 195
    federal, 199
    Federal Home Loans, 195
    financing, public/private codevelopment, 197
    general obligation bonds, 189
    loan mechanisms, 193–94
    options, 187
    private sector partnerships, 199
    public/private codevelopment, 198
    regulating, 167
    revenue bonds, 190
    shared land cost technique, 196
    special assessments, 193
    tax increment financing, 191
Urban Development Action Grant program, 82, 194
Urban Development Information System (Fairfax County, VA), 71
Urban environment, 71
Urban forest, 95
Urban geology and soils, 83, 133
Urban homesteading, 196
Urban hydrology, 85, 133
Urban land, value of; as refuge for plants, 97
Urban Land Institute, 135
Urban physical planning, 145
Urban planning. See also Urban design; Planning
    as young field, 113
    design as main task, 6
    emergence as distinct field, 3
    quality of life considerations of, 49
Urban problems, 133

Urban settings, socioeconomic indicators to types of, 56
Urban social structure, 117
Urban Systems Research and Engineering, Inc., 122
Urban vegetation, 90–96
Urban wildlife, 96

Values-oriented design, 117
Vegetation
    indigenous, economy of retaining, 96
    urban, environmental stresses of, 90–91
Vieux Carre (New Orleans), 44
Views criteria, 127
Vitality, design, 125

Washington, DC, 83, 161
    Civic Design and Transportation Study, 26
    urban development guidelines, 152
Water nuisances, 86
Water pollution, 87
Water quality, 85–90
Wildlife, urban; plight of, 96–98
Woodlands, TX, 69, 87

Zoning
    development rights, transferring, 174–76
    incentive, 168–71
    performance, 172–73
    regulating, 168
    special district, 173–74
    standards of, relating to noise, 172
    traditional, 11